IMPERIALISM

and

IDEOLOGY

IMPERIALISM

and

IDEOLOGY

An Historical Perspective

John Laffey

BLACK ROSE BOOKS

Montréal/New York
London

Black Rose Books No. CC285
Hardcover ISBN: 1-55164-147-X (bound)
Paperback ISBN: 1-55164-146-1 (pbk.)

Canadian Cataloguing in Publication Data
Laffey, John
Imperialism and ideology : an historical perspective

Includes bibliographical references and index.
Hardcover ISBN: 1-55164-147-X (bound)
Paperback ISBN: 1-55164-146-1 (pbk.)

1. Imperialism--History. I. Title.

JC359.L23   1999   325'.32'09   C99-900476-X

Cover design by Associés libres, Montréal

BLACK
ROSE
BOOKS

C.P. 1258	2250 Military Road	99 Wallis Road
Succ. Place du Parc	Tonawanda, NY	London, E9 5LN
Montréal, H2W 2R3	14150	England
Canada	USA	UK

To order books in North America:
(phone) 1-800-565-9523 (fax) 1-800-221-9985
In Europe: (phone) 0181-986-4854 (fax) 0181-533-5821

Our Web Site address: http://www.web.net/blackrosebooks

A publication of the Institute of Policy Alternatives of Montréal (IPAM)
Printed in Canada

The Canada Council | Le Conseil des Arts
for the Arts | du Canada

CONTENTS

For Svetlana Bychkova

Aha! How greatly was I stirred in my mind when I turned to see Beatrice, at not being able to see, although I was near her, and in the world of bliss!

Dante, Paradiso, Canto XXV

INTRODUCTION
THE ZEITGEIST AND MYSELF

Only that historian will have the gift of fanning the spark of hope in the past who is firmly convinced that *even the dead* will not be safe from the enemy if he wins. And this enemy has not ceased to be victorious.
—Walter Benjamin

Carl E. Schorske has warned: "What the historian now must abjure, and nowhere more so than in confronting the problem of modernity, is the positing in advance of an abstract categorical denominator—what Hegel called the *Zeitgeist* and Mill 'the spirit of the age.' "[1] Historians, almost by definition, are suspicious of abstract categorical denominators, but they do not go untouched by the *Zeitgeist*. Once a fine historian of German Social Democracy, Schorske later turned his attention to Viennese culture for reasons which had much to do with changes in his own culture, essentially its abandonment of public and political concerns for private and psychological ones.[2] I was reminded of this when considering the selection of articles for republication.[3] Any historian is embarked upon a two-fold task: the recapturing, to the best of his or her ability, of a vanished past and, consciously or unconsciously, the reflection of his or her own times.

The articles grouped under "Imperialism" might not have been undertaken without the impact of the Vietnam War: scholars fight wars with the weapons available to them. The articles grouped under "Ideology" represent more diverse interests, though these lend themselves to some sub-groupings. There is, moreover, in racism more than a little overlap between "Imperialism" and "Ideology." "Classism, Racism, and Sexism" are condemned today; often enough in a ritualistic fashion. They share the common denominator of exploitation, and, in one fashion or another, I have dealt with all three factors. I have noticed, however, that classism now tends to be slighted. That is a mistake.

If not untouched by the events and ideas of my times—its *Zeitgeist*, if you will—my relationship to it has been dialectical, for I have both participated in it and reacted against it. History, after all, is not something you look back upon from a secure vantage point in the present. That very present, after all, is rapidly turning into history. Historians, like all their contemporaries, weither they like it or not, live in history.

Before moving on to the discussion of particular concerns, allow me to take opportunity of republication to pay some long-overdue debts, both academic and non-academic. I have been extraordinarily fortunate in my teachers, and I wish to thank them. I have also been fortunate in my students, though they, with one exception, have been too numerous to name.

At the University of Pittsburgh as an undergraduate, between 1955 and 1959, I had as instructors the Schmannite Hugh Cleland, James T.C. Liu who ended up at Princeton, and the marvelous C.H. George, the only Early Modern historian whom I would still rank with Natalie Davis. They and others must have done their jobs well, for upon graduation I had a fellowship to Berkeley, one to Harvard, and a Woodrow Wilson Fellowship. For reasons I can no longer recall, it was decided that I take the Wilson to Columbia before moving on to Harvard. It was at Pitt that I also discovered that I could learn from my fellow students, and not only the Jews among them who had read far more books than I had. The brightest and best-read of these fellow-students, Ella Fogel, would later become my first wife and a first-rate Chinese historian. Cleland also put me in touch with Michael Harrington, an Irish-American whose ideological path had preceded my own.

The year at Columbia was something of a disaster, for I was torn between Morningside Heights and Greenwich Village. I have scant recall of the historians I encountered, but do recall the hours in the Village debating the finer points of Marxist theory with Harrington in a diner which no longer exists, across the street from a theater which no longer exists but which then carried a plaque stating that Clemanceau had once practiced medicine on that site, and doing the same in the much more rowdy atmosphere of the White Horse Tavern, with its mixed clientele of longshoremen and intellectuals.

September, 1960 brought marriage and the move to Cornell. Here again some teachers were extraordinary. Especially outstanding were Knight Biggerstaff, the China specialist, and Mario Einaudi, Professor of Political Theory, who sharpened even further my interest in the Hegelian strain within Marxism. Although I did not work with him, I was also very impressed with George Kahin, the U.S.'s leading academic opponent of the Vietnam War. Fellow students also came into the picture: Ella, of course, but also Greg Calvert, Henry Copeland, Eric Hansen, and Henry Heller.

Although he occasionally served as an academic, the greatest non-academic teacher of the Cornell years was Soejatmoko, Indonesian revolutionary, diplomat, and scholar. By then, of course, the Vietnam War was in full swing. Perhaps the richness of the Cornell Southeast Asian holdings alone would have carried me in that direction, but I continue to believe that the impact of a filthy war played the pivotal role in the selection of a dissertation topic having to do with the role of the French in the Far East. During research in Paris I encountered Sanford Elwitt, eventually a colleague and the author of two fine books on the Third Republic.[4] He became my best friend and remains this historian's historian. In any event by 1966 I had completed the dissertation, "French Imperialism and the Lyon Mission to China," from which many of my early articles are derived. Perhaps I should have turned it into a book, but that would have required more research. Perhaps I am at best a decent short-distance runner or, far worse, an intellectual dilettante. I leave it to the reader of this collection of articles to decide.

In my first teaching post, at Wayne State University in Detroit, I encountered yet another non-academic master, Roman Rosdolsky who was working away at what became the great *The Making of Marx's "Kapital"* (1977). What a life: the retreat with the Red Army from Poland, the years at the Marx-Engels Institute, the years in Auschwitz, the wanderings, the settling in Detroit where his wife worked for the UAW and he pursued his scholarship. Broken in health, but an incredible sense of humor. At Wayne I also encountered the very conservative and very wise Sinologist Paul Michaud, the first Québecois I had run across. Some conservatives do deserve respect. The following year at Western Reserve brought acquaintance with the fine Latin Americanist Robert Randall, a cowboy, turned merchant seaman, turned scholar.

I arrived in Montréal in September, 1968. The discovery there was Alan Adamson who, though now aged, still possesses one of the most acute minds and sharpest tongues that I have encountered. I also came in contact with members of the so-called Heath Project, a textbook project which was never completed. Still, our meetings were the equivalent of a high-powered post-graduate seminar, and I retain my respect for Pierre Boulle, the late Michel Grenon, Fred Krantz and Camille Limoges. Although not a member of that group, Harvey Schulman also deserves mention as a superb teacher. Not only of undergraduates, for this Cornell Ph.D. learned from him while teaching with him. That completes the list of great teachers.

I also got to rub shoulders with other outstanding scholars. I did not know the Sinologist Jean Chesneaux well enough to include him on the list of debts owed. My one-time colleague George Rudé was a fine craftsman, a quality not to be dismissed, but I cannot recall him teaching me much. He, like other good colleagues—Fred Bode, Carolyn Fick, and Franziska Sholesser—probably made unnoticed contributions to my education. They also served primarily as models of academic probity, a quality in short supply at Concordia University. Another deserves mention: Eugene Genovese, a fine scholar and in ways that he would not recognize, let alone acknowledge, one of the wretched of the earth.

Before the pieties are fulfilled, one other scholar must be noted, and this time a student. Louise Gavard has recently made a major contribution to the most decisive change in my thinking since I became a Marxist decades ago. Whatever Marxism's current vicissitudes, many of them, intellectual and otherwise, due to the follies of Marxists, historical materialism remains for me the *only* historical method, and, thus, perhaps, I found it relatively easy to assimilate a feminist materialism. Of course, many others have crowded a long, rich, and reasonably happy life, but this is an introduction to a collection of scholarly articles, not the memoirs which would have to include the marriages, the university and departmental politics, and some assorted trivia and which might yet appear, perhaps in fictionalized form.

Imperialism

French imperialism in the Far East brought together my interests in China and France. As a founder of the Chinese Communist Party, later purged as a Trotskyist, used to argue, there were only two civilizations, for only the Chinese and the French could cook vegetables properly. French imperialism also involved my interest in exploitation and its protean forms. The dissertation focused on a Lyonnais Mission to China at the end of the last century and led into a concern with what I called Municipal Imperialism. The thesis, in brief, had it that, while the mass of the French population, as well as even the bankers, possessed little interest in the colonies, the productive and commercial elites of certain cities did and assumed pivotal roles in regard to particular areas of the empire. Lyon was interested in the Far East because of the importance of silk, Marseille in proximate North Africa, Bordeaux in West Africa as a market for cheap booze, Lille in anywhere where cotton might be grown and cotton textiles marketed. Such cities disguised conflicts among themselves, particularly in regard to the tariff issue, by invoking in Paris nebulous ideals, especially the *mission civilisatrice.*

I dismissed this celebrated "mission" as, much like "the white man's burden," so much ideological hogwash and took few notes on it. Much later, when working on *Civilization and its Discontented*, I would regret that decision: I undoubtedly by-passed some fine passages illustrating the uses to which the highly ideologically-charged concept of civilization has been put. Still, at the time it was fashionable among students of imperialism to argue that the French had scant, if any, economic stake in empire, and I wished to set the record straight. Perhaps a young man's vulgar materialism also entered into the matter. More seriously, I was insufficiently the historical materialist at the time in one important respect. I neglected to differentiate among merchant, industrial, and finance capital and to explore the relations among them.

My focus was on Lyon in a story which I eventually carried up unto the eve of World War II. The first two articles in this collection detail that story. The first, "Roots of French Imperialism in the Nineteenth Century: the Case of Lyon," is so badly flawed that I considered replacing it with "Les racines de impérialisme français en Extrême Orient" or even "L'Impero coloniale francese" which essentially tell the same story. A French or Italian text, however, would have appeared odd in publication in English.[5] A responsible editor should not have published that first article, but the basic fault is mine. It has to do with footnoting. There are far too many of them. That could be put down to a young scholar, advancing a radical thesis, wishing to bring as much support to it as possible. It can also be ascribed to the pedantry which marks all too many dissertations. Still, with all of the caution, too many of the footnotes are imprecise, and the system itself clumsy. But however tempting, I have foregone making changes in any of the articles in this collection, save one, and in that one for reasons explained below. I was aided in that decision by my visual condition, macular degeneration, which rules out any further library work.

By the time the second article, "Lyonnais Imperialism in the Far East, 1900—1938" appeared, seven years later, I was more firmly in control of the material. The footnotes are more streamlined and the style better, but, of course, the focus was narrower. Incidently, as should be apparent from the list of "Papers and Publications" appended to this essay, I have worked in a fashion which, while it entailed a certain amount of repetition, allowed me to explore various dimensions of particular problems.

Yes, the focus was on Lyon. While challenging the thesis of Municipal Imperialism, a younger French scholar has recently said: "He remains the *père spirituel* of our works, with all the Freudian complexes implied."[6] I replied to him that Freudian complexes might even make for progress in scholarship, but I am enough of a Québecois, not to mention an Irish-American, to be disturbed by spiritual fatherhood. Far more disturbing was his book, *Un Lyonnais en Extrême-Orient: Ulysse Pila, Vice-roi de l'indochine*. A man whom I had portrayed, in the politist scholarly terms, as an imperialist gangster had become an entrepreneurial hero, a pioneer in that globalization of the world economy which I still insist upon calling "imperialism." That in itself is supposed to reflect an old-fashioned "Manichean" view of matters.[7] But is it so Manichean to insist that the globe has been and is still inhabited by exploiters and exploited? Invocations of Mircia Eliande only obfuscate a question well put by Lenin: Who Whom?[8] Who does What to Whom? → *Lone Star*

The next article, "Colonial Reformism Before 1914: The Case of the *Revue Indigène*," focuses upon efforts to reform colonial "abuses." It is a short piece and possibility the slightest in this collection. It bears the marks of having been first presented as a paper. It might also reflect the pitfalls of relying upon a single source: in this case the run of a single journal. Still, the historian works with the sources available to him or her.[9] The *Zeitgeist* again? Perhaps in the treatment of the opium problem. It was, after all, roughly the time of the American "war on drugs," but I have no conscious recollection of being influenced by this now failed undertaking. Of possibly more relevance was the establishment of committees which were designed to do nothing, except to keep their members busy and enhance their self-importance, something which I was familiar with from Concordia, though the ploy is a standard feature of all bureaucratic life.

The piece does have importance in that it makes the point that the "abuses" of any system are likely to be intrinsic to it. Certainly this has been the case with imperialism. As with the proponents of class reconciliation, colonial reformers can be quite ideologically sincere, for one is seldom more sincere than when apparent morality and self-interest coincide. Sincerity, moreover, has little to do with correct political analysis: there were, after all, plenty of sincere Nazis. Implicit in the article is a problem which the Left perrenially confronts: opposition to any reform can be stupid, but a devotion to reform as such often precludes the consideration of any prospect of radical transformation. Accomodation to all reforms *within* a system precludes the transcendence of that system, but total opposition to a system too often ends in easy moralizing and political impotence. The key questions have to do with who is doing the reforming and who benefits from it. Incidently, it is mildly amusing that the last reference in the article should be to Hegel, for while the dialectic informs, with greater or lesser skill, all of these articles, explicit reference to it very seldom appears.

Although its underlying theme is imperialism, the following article, "French Far Eastern Policy in the 1930s," is more narrowly a study in diplomatic history. I discovered that diplomatic history is more difficult to write than it might appear. What one diplomat said to another is often as dry and sterile—not to mention, dishonest—as its reporting. Although one might personally prefer the Popular Front's Yvon Delbos to the more shady Georges Bonnet, they both tended to operate within what were perceived as the same very real constraints. In face of a dynamic Japanese imperialism, the French were in a ludicrously weak position in the Far East. Just how they got there is explained in the first article of this collection. Whether they *should* have been there is another question altogether. The point is that, as a result of the workings of capitalism, they *were* there and had to confront the issue of what was to be done. A stagnant imperialism might well be preferable to a dynamic one, but I rather doubt that their Vietnamese subjects wasted much sympathy on them. Incidently, geography tends to outlast human generations, and so, given the subject matter, the Gulf of Tonkin inevitably enters the story, but also perhaps the *Zeitgeist*.

The article returns us implicitly to a quarrel which began with the very appearance of history in the West: should one cast one's net widely, as Herodotus did, or focus more narrowly on politics in Thucydides' fashion? Ideally, of course, history should be approached as a totality. That, however, becomes increasingly difficult to do in this age of the monograph. Still, if forced to choose, throughout much of my life, I would have favored Herodotus. Although hints of my dawning suspicions of historical cultural anthropology had appeared as early as my treatment of "the problematic bourgeosie," I was still somewhat surprised to find myself arguing to the Canadian Historical Association in June, 1991 that Heroditus was the first postmodernist historian. After all, *The Persian Wars* is filled with fascinating details in regard to necrophilia among the Egyptian priesthood, temple prostitution in Babylonia, and even the Sythians as "the Other." One critic on the panel, after admitting that she had not bothered to read Herodotus, also proclaimed that she knew that temple prostitution was more important than the wars themselves. A strangled cry from the audience: "Yeah, but there were a lot of dead Greeks and Persians." This only a few months after the end of the Persian Gulf War. The critic had announced earlier that she would be the victim, for she was the youngest member of the panel, a woman, and a sociologist. I allowed that I had no difficulty with the first two categories, but might have trouble with the third. In any event, the *Zeitgeist* again: post-modernism and identity politics, to both of which I will have to return to below.

The next article, "Racism and Imperialism: French Views of the 'Yellow Peril,' 1894—1914," confronts one manifestation of the ideological element integral to imperialism. Racism, however, extends beyond imperialism and, as the article seeks to make clear, racist arguments can even be invoked against imperialism. Whatever form racism takes, its bottom line remains the justification of discrimination, exploitation, and sometimes mass murder.

Perhaps the *Zeitgeist* is also here, for the article was published at a time when the East Asian economic "miracle" was again stirring fears in the West. It also might do so in another fashion. The arguments of the last few pages are too telescoped. Or perhaps simply confused. The article ends in 1914, and at the time of writing I had no patience with Karl Kautsky's theory of ultra-imperialism. If I were to re-do it in this age of globalization, I would pay more attention to that notion, without, however, necessarily accepting it.

The format of the article is something of a technical curiosity. The pagination symbols of the sources (e.g., p., pp.) are missing, but that might simply be due to the whim of the editor. Or it might have something to do with the way in which the journal appeared: on *microfiche* rather than in printed form. Even scholars are touched by technological change. In the age of the typewriter, editorial requests for changes and revisions often entailed the re-typing of an entire manuscript. The computer has changed that for the better. But again the dialectic of progress: the computer has also allowed for the rapid publication of mountains of academic garbage.

Ideology

The concept of ideology has exercised far better minds than my own. Still, my own reflections on the matter might yet appear.[10] Be that as it might, I have spent years exploring, in teaching and publishing, various dimensions of the matter. For our purposes here, those dimensions might be here grouped roughly into The Politics of Reconciliation, and Psychological Man.

The vision of human concord reaches back beyond Roman temples to the Bible and forward to a society from which exploitation will finally have been banished. But in a society from which oppression has not been banished, that vision lies open to ideological manipulation. One manifestation of such manipulation was explored in my very first article, "Auguste Comte: Prophet of Reconciliation and Reaction." There was a problem with the piece: it appeared in *Science & Society*, deemed by some of my former Schmannite Trotskyist comrades as a Stalinist journal. Certainly close to, if not under the control of, the American Communist Party, but that post-Hungary party was in such disarray that I am not sure "Stalinist" was an accurate description. In any event, throughout my teaching career I continued to use the Schmannite idea of "bureaucratic collectivism" to describe the Soviet betrayal of Marxism. But in reviewing my articles for republication, I was struck by the extent to which the Soviet system may actually have been the realization, minus the capitalists, of Comteanism: the same scientific positivism, the hierarchy with the party members or commissars as the new "priests of Humanity," and the ex-seminarian, Josif Djugasheviii (Stalin) as Supreme Pontiff. In that issue of the journal, incidentally, appeared a review by the Englishman, George Rudé.

Having spent years teaching at Concordia University, where I enjoyed the company of that learned gentleman as an esteemed colleague, I returned to the reconciliation theme in the Rudé *Festschrift*. There I made my view of Concordia, a botched institution, fairly explicit: "The great square telescopes a history in its names: *place Louis XV, place de la Révolution, place de la Concorde.*" If *Concorde* was a Thermidorian ideological swindle, "Concordia" masked a squalid reality which eventually led to quadruple murder. Be that as it might, the larger message was a warning against calls for reconciliation launched from above. The issues involved should determine the permissible levels of conflict, but conflict is inevitable within a classist, racist, and sexist society.

The only hitherto unpublished article in this collection follows. It introduces several articles devoted, in one fashion or another, to Psychological Man. It has had a strange history. I wished, with the department's approval, to try out the arguments in a seminar. It is true that one learns as one teaches. That was not to be. The Academic Priorities Committee objected to the course title. "Man" was the rub: I had collided with identity politics. Viewing the matter as one of academic freedom, I wrote in protest, on June 7, 1990, to the highest academic officer of the university. I drew her attention to my qualifications for teaching the course. I mentioned *bürokretinismus* and, as I was addressing a biologist, the dangers of Lysenkoism. I ended on what was for me a conciliatory note: "Still, pathologists and healers have learned from each other."

I received a reply dated July 16, 1990: "In general I find your letter offensive and unbecoming to a professor in any university...It is impolite, intemperate and unacceptable in its tone and some of its implications." The Vice Rector, Academic continued: "Should you however, seriously wish to discuss the issues of the gender of language, employment equity, etc., I shall be glad to engage in such. However it would be important for you to do some reading on this issue, especially by writers/authors/researchers upon how this issue impacts in a negative manner." So an illiterate as the highest academic officer. I replied to her reply on July 23, 1990: "My position remains unchanged: without academic freedom, there is no university."

Although it reveals the kind of incompetence which contributed to multiple murders, the vital issue here remains one of academic freedom. In these days of identity politics, which make for successful careerism, but which is self-defeating for oppressed groups in that it largely precludes effective coalitions and ends in ineffective political narsicism, academic freedom is in trouble. It is highly unlikely that today a Voltaire, who managed to offend Christians, Jews, and Moslems, would find an academic post in North America. Not that he would be interested.

I still remain somewhat uneasy with the "Psychological Man" effort. Intellectual abstractions strut, collide, embrace within it. And abstraction is indeed necessary. History, after all, is made up of modes of production. But, in fact, one very seldom encounters pure modes of production. Far more frequent are messier social formations in which a particular mode of production is likely to be predominant. Intellectual constructs are necessary, but I rather miss the flesh and blood of living presence. That might simply be a matter of personal preference, but "Psychological Man" might have benifited from student in-put.

In any event, despite the Vice Rector's kind offer of reading material, I had confronted the matter of sexism in "The Problematic Bourgeoisie" and would return to it in *Civilization and Its Discontented*. The latter work in particular fuelled my hostility to feminist "essentialism." The purported female qualities denigrated in the nineteenth century are now being lauded by the essentialists for their own reasons. Pendulums can and do swing. Today were I not handicapped (visually challenged, you know), I would turn my research attention to the matter along lines mapped out by scholars like Colette Guilaumin and Nicole-Claude Mathieu, towards whose work I was directed by Louise Gavard who is cited in the only footnote introduced into the "Psychological Man" article since the late 80s. If one must be a feminist, as every right-thinking man must be today, I would much prefer to be a feminist materialist than a feminist essentialist. Like social reconciliation and colonial reformism, essentialist feminism is, consciously or unconsciously, an ideological swindle.

After looking at that problematic bourgeoisie, basically a review article, the next piece, "Economy, Society, and Psyche: the Case of Pierre Janet," treats of more strictly psychological concerns, viewed in light of ideology. The piece has its flaws: as Sanford Elwitt advised, I should have done more with Janet's late industrial psychology. Incidently, the ability to give and to accept harsh criticism is one of the basic tests of friendship, and not only among scholars. I never did follow up with the promised study of Pierre Janet's uncle, Paul. Sheer laziness? Or boredom? I do seem to recall Paul's *La famille, leçons de philosopie* as one of those male-written tracts of ideological drivel which littered the nineteenth century. The reference to Bergson (fn. 66) is gratuitous, quite possibly mistaken, and a passing indication of my hostility to all forms of *Lebensphilosophie*. Perhaps it can be arged that, as with the Comte article, I did not pay enough attention to the subject's chronological development.

One could have done more with that in books rather than articles. The dilettante? It should be apparent that, despite all my suspicion of Janet's economic imagery, I am more sympathetic to Janet than to Freud. He knew something which most of the inhabitants of the era of psychological man have yet to learn: the limitations of his craft. Incidently, at the time I was writing, I had scant personal experience of the economy of energy and the effects of exhaustion. I do now.

"Social Psychology as Political Ideology: The Cases of Wilfred Trotter and William McDougall" follows. It grew out of a paper prepared for the Rudé colloqiium in the fall of 1976. "Races, Hordes, Herds, Classes, Mobs and Crowds," which sought to honor that great historian of the crowd, George Rudé. In the article I dealt with two figures upon whom Freud drew when sketching his own social psychology. Neither was of continuing importance, but they did have a certain significance in their times. The Paine-Burke parallels might be a trifle forced, but they do seek to relate these figures to an older tradition with which Rudé was throughly familiar. Although I disagree with his ideas, my preference obviously lies with Trotter, the surgical crarftsman, rather than McDougall, the eugenicist with an interest in psychical research. With the article ending with reference to William Jensen and Richard Herrnstein, the *Zeitgeist* had again intruded.

Although I devoted a paper to him and although he makes some minor appearances in some of the articles reproduced here, I never did get around to dealing with another figure who influenced Freud's social psychology, the odiously racist Gustave Le Bon. Possibly the recognition that a treatment of Le Bon might make Emile Durkheim, far more intelligent, influential, and dangerous, look good. Orthodox Freudians, of course, would see in my scattered treatments of their master instances of resistance. Perhaps. In fact, I respect him—as the last great exponent of a tradition of thought which began with Hobbes, as possibly the last great bourgeois ideologist. My more immediate fascination with his system, however, lies in the pivotal role played by the Viennese in the emergence of Psychological Man.

Ten articles selected from thirty years of work, and I am an essentially lazy man. A short-distance runner? Yet I am not unacquainted with work: learning, research, writing, and teaching. Alexander Herzen who, despite his distaste for Marx, I continue to revere, once remarked: "We have no prayers; we have work. Work is our prayer."[11] I leave it to others to judge that work.

Notes

1. Carl E. Schorske, *Fin-de-siècle Vienna: Politics and Culture* (New York: Alfred A. Knopf, 1980), p. xxii.

2. *Ibid*, p. xxiv. For his own earlier concerns, see Carl E. Schorske, *German Social Democracy, 1905-1917: The Development of the Great Schism* (New York: John Wiley & Sons, 1965); the first edition appeared in 1955. Although very different, both books are equally good, the mark of a fine historian.

3. A complete listing of my papers and publications can be found at the end of this essay.

4. Anford Elwitt, *The Making of the Third Republic: Class and Politics in France* (Baton Rouge: Louisiana State University Press, 1975) *The Third Republic Defended: Bourgeois Reform in France, 1880-1914* (Baton Rouge: Louisiana State University Press, 1986). Contrary to most contemporary historians, the notion of class did not embarrass Sanford.

5. For a list of my papers and publications, see the list which follows this essay.

6. Jean Francois Klein, "De la Compagnie Lyonnaise à l'Union Commerciale d'Indochinoise: Histoire de'une Stratégie d'Entreprises," *Cahiers d'historie*, XL, 3-4 (1995), pp. 349-72, fn. 38, p. 360.

7. Jean-François Klein, *Un Lyonnais en Extrême-Oreint: Ulysse Pila, "vice-roi de l'Indochine" (1837-1909)* (Lyon: Editions Lyonnaise d'Art et d'Histoire, n.d.), p. 5.

8. *Ibid.*, p. 158.

9. I very much doubt that "Faces of Truth and the Sociology of Knowledge," not included here, would have appeared without the publication of the University of Toronto's magnificent edition of Mill's *Collected Works*. The piece makes the point that both Liberals distanced themselves from what appeared to be implicit in their systems: Mill, from determinism, Mannheim, from relativism. What a difference a century makes.

10. That will depend upon whether or not my *Social and Intellectual History of Europe Since the Seventeenth Century* ever appears. Several reasons may work against such an appearance. The transformation of lectures, given over thirty years, into book format, it is both unoriginal and idiosyncratic. Unoriginal in that I have shamelessly plundered the works of better historians than myself. Idiosyncratic in that a unfashionable Hegelian Marxism pervades it. It is, moreover, much too massive, perhaps nothing more than a good Victorian read, and there are today few Victorian readers. In any event, the publishing giants have show no interest in it. Concentration in the publishing industry and post-modernist taste, not unconnected with each other, will probably work together to prevent its appearance. That is hardly a matter of conspiracy, but is rather a sign of where things are in the late twentieth century.

11. *My Past and Thoughts: The Memoirs of Alexander Herzen* (New York: Alfred A. Knopf, 1973), p. xviii.

IMPERIALISM

1

ROOTS OF FRENCH IMPERIALISM IN THE NINETEENTH CENTURY: THE CASE OF LYON[1]

Why, demanded Jules Cambon in 1894, should Lyon, "famous for its wisdom, its moderation, its prudence, manifest such an ardent interest in colonization?"[2] The next year, the vice-president of the Chamber of Commerce of Lyon, Auguste Isaac, added: "That Marseille, Le Havre, Bordeaux, Nantes, and even Rouen, are centers of colonial enterprise is understandable, but why Lyon?"[3] Lying at the confluence of the Saône and the Rhone, the city was justly famous for its commercial enterprise; but Lyon was also further from the ocean than any other major city in France. This alone would make the local interest in overseas affairs worth comment.

Religious fervor, for which Lyon was also renowned, played a major role in directing the attention of her citizens abroad. During the Restoration a new interest in foreign missions appeared. Pauline Jaricot, the daughter of a local silk magnate, began to gather a small group about her.[4] With the goal of aiding the missions as a means of making reparation for the outrages of the Revolution, they founded in 1818 a branch of the Propagation de la Foi, an association created by the Société des Missions étrangères to encourage support for its missions. Four years later, expanding horizons beyond a single missionary organization, a group of Lyonnais founded the Oeuvre de la Propagation de la Foi. Despite initial troubles, the association flourished and, although it spread its work to other nations, remained rooted in France. The bishop of Avignon could declare with some accuracy in 1873: "The Oeuvre de la Propagation de la Foi is eminently patriotic...It speaks above all, with the name of God, that of France.[5] Within France, the Oeuvre continued to be financially based in Lyon.[6]

If Lyon was not sparing in funds for the missions, neither was it frugal with its sons. The diocese had "blood and gold to place at the service of its beliefs."[7] Two missionary orders, the Maristes de Lyon and the Missions Africaines de Lyon, were founded in the city during the nineteenth century.[8] Under the July Monarchy, Jesuits from the Lyon province of the Society established themselves in Syria.[9] The Far East was not neglected.[10] Père Tabert worked in Cochinchina, Daguin in Mongolia, Retord in Tonkin. Many missionaries lost their lives. Père Bonnard met martyrdom in Tonkin. Jean Pierre Néel was decapitated in China on Febrary 18, 1862. For the French the site of his death became the Monts du Lyonnais. The struggle between France and China over Tonkin produced new victims. On May 20, 1883 Gaspard-Claude Bechet was decapitated in Tonkin. Six French priests, three of them from Lyon, perished between December 25, 1883 and January 6, 1884. As late in the century as 1898 Mathieu Berthelot was killed in Kwangsi province in China. Lesser honours than martyrdom also distinguished the missionaries from Lyon. In the last decade of the century the Bishop of Chengtu, the Provicar Apostolic of Western Tonkin, and the Apostolic Vicar of Laos came from Lyon. The city had reasons to be proud of the "colonizers of souls" it had spread through the world.[11]

Missionaries and their supporters were not the only Lyonnais, however, to concern themselves with overseas activity. The city's major industry in the nineteenth century, the manufacture of silken textiles, confronted serious problems both in securing a dependable supply of raw silk and reliable markets for the finished products.[12] These factors led to the development of a markedly imperialist orientation, expressed in the undertakings of particular business firms and the concerns of the local geographical society. But it was the Chamber of Commerce of Lyon which most clearly formulated the imperialist point of view and strongly supported concrete plans for expansion. By 1895 its vice-president was probably justified in calling it "the most colonial of the [French] Chambers of Commerce."[13]

The Chamber's espousal of imperialism began with an address to the king in July, 1830 that stressed the value of founding establishments in Algeria.[14] In the subsequent debate over the future of Algeria, the Chamber vigorously supported retention of the new acquisition.[15] The Société de Colons lyonnaises, formed in 1835, detected great promise in the new colony.[16] Algeria would provide an outlet for domestic discontent, something with which Lyon was all too familiar.[17] It would supply French factories with raw materials.[18] Of vital interest to Lyon was the prospect of developing Algerian sericulture.[19] Although the production of raw silk in Algeria was ultimately to prove disappointing, other interests were developed, among them the Société agricole lyonnaise du Nord de l'Afrique.[20] Substantial Lyonnais holdings in Algeria and Tunisia were consolidated as the century advanced.[21] Under the Second Empire, the thrust inland from the African littoral received support. In 1862 members of the Lyon Chamber of Commerce acted as hosts to a delegation of Turgeg chieftains with whom they discussed the possibilities of developing the commerce of the Sahara.[22] Four years later the Chamber provided a subsidy for Le Saint, who was being sent by the Société de géographie de Paris to explore equatorial Africa.[23] By the sixties imperialism had become vital to the existence of Lyon's industry. With the outbreak of pebrine in French sericulture in 1852, the production of raw silk in France plummeted, and the manufacturers of Lyon were forced to look elsewhere for it.[24] Shortly after the outbreak of the disease the firm of the old Saint-Simonian Arlès-Dufour began to inform its customers of the promising condition in Syria.[25] French concerns established cocoloneries there and by their employment of Maronite Christians lent another dimension to France's claims to the protection of Christians in the Middle East. The Druse-Maronite hostility, erupting into massacre, harmed these establishments and led to France's intervention of 1860.[26] Syrian silk, however, was not the only incentive for involvement in the region. As early as 1847 the Lyon Chamber of Commerce had voted five thousand francs in support of studies on the piercing of the isthmus of Suex, a project especially dear to Arlès-Dufour.[27] In 1865 members of the Chamber visited the Suez site and again were present at the opening of the canal in 1869.[28]

Beyond Suez lay the Far East, the world's greatest silk producing area. The industry in Lyon had considered China, first with fear and then with polite indifference, as a possible competing centre of production.[29] The catastrophic impact of pebrine on French sericulture forced reconsideration. Paul Chartron had an agent in Shanghai from 1854. Victor Pignatal established a branch of his firm at Chefoo in 1862. These silk merchants would be among the founders of the Crédit Lyonnais.[30] In 1860 the Lyon Chamber of Commerce voted resolutions favouring the creation of a steamship line trading with the Far East and the founding of a bank there.[31] These recommendations were swiftly acted upon. Late in the same year the Comptoir d'Escompte opened its first foreign branch in Shanghai. The next year the French state signed a contract with the Messageries maritimes providing for a monthly departure for the Far East. In the 1860s China came to rival Italy as a source of raw silk for Lyon.[32]

The city jealously guarded its increasing stake in the China trade. On February 22, 1870, the president of the Chamber of Commerce wrote to the Minister of Agriculture and Commerce about the Alcock Convention, Article XII of which allowed for an increase in the Chinese duty on the export of silk. He requested that "the representative of France in China receive the instructions required for him to oppose an increase in the duties on silks being exported and to refuse the concessions which the Chinese had obtained from the British envoy."[33] In a subsequent letter he underscored Lyon's concern with Chinese silk: "We attach…very great importance to this revision of the Treaty of Tientsin, for it is silk which forms the principal element of our commerce with China. Further, the use of Chinese silk is necessary to the work of our looms. Under this double relationship, we have a more direct interest than England in the question of the increase of duties on the export of silks, and we must be especially alert that this tax is not increased."[34]

The exercise of such pressure contributed to the growth of the silk trade. In the 1870s, despite a major crisis in the local industry, Chinese silks assumed a commanding position in Lyon. They accounted in 1877 for 42.07 per cent of the total amount of raw silk received from all sources.[35] By 1888 France, primarily Lyon, was possibly consuming two-thirds of the silks exported from China.[36] The importance of this commerce gave the city a vital interest in China while presenting France with a continuing unfavourable balance in its trade with that nation.

However, in southeast Asia, France was slowly acquiring a hold over Indochina, reinforcing Lyon's concern with China and offering, among other advantages, a possible means of reversing the adverse trade balance. In pursuit of more exact information about the new colony of Cochinchina, the Lyon Chamber of Commerce asked a M. Bonnevay[37] to investigate it.[38] The acquisition of Tonkin could not fail to interest Lyon, its major firms having been among the first to invest in the Banque de l'Indochine.[39] Addressing the local

Société d'Economie politique in 1884, Ulysse Pila stressed the advantages which could flow from the acquisition of Tonkin. With the spectacle of the crisis resulting from the failure of the Lyon-based Union générale immediately before him, he evoked a dark picture of a France "on the eve of a terrible economic crisis" unless she expanded abroad.[40] As Pila's generalizations did not assuage the need for more exact information, the Chamber of Commerce decided to commission Paul Brunat "to explore the new Asian colony from the commercial point of view."[41] Brunat's encyclopedic report, submitted to the Chamber on February 18, 1885, dealt with such Tonkinese products as rice, sugar, silk, cotton, textiles, paper, tea, spices, medicines, dyes, woods, resins, and tobacco.[42]

Not content to concern itself with Tonkin and the prospects of trade with south China moving through it, the businessmen of Lyon also looked to the older stake in Sino-French relations. The treaty ending the conflict between France and China provided for the conclusion of a commercial convention between the two countries. The task of negotiating it was confided to M. Cogordan, an official of the Ministry of Foreign Affairs who originally hailed from Lyon.[43] On the night prior to his departure for the Far East, he was the guest of honour at a banquet given by the Chamber of Commerce. There Cogordan expressed his willingness "to serve the great Lyonnais commercial interests."[44]

He was obviously unprepared for what followed. The Chamber's vice-president revealed that in 1884 Félix Faure, Under-Secretary of Navy and Colonies, had secretly requested its views on modifications to be wrought in the Sino-French treaty of 1858.[45] The reply of the Chamber was then read to Cogordan. He could only observe that "the moment has not yet come to strip this communication of its confidential character."[46] But the concrete demands of the commercial and industrial magnates of Lyon were not to be avoided that evening. While it was recognized that "by the very fact of being a Lyonnais, M. Cogordan has known for a long time the *desiderata* of our commerce of silks and silken fabrics," he was reminded of them at length.[47] The views of the Chambre syndicale des Soieries were presented.[48] M. Giraud, on behalf of the Syndicat des marchands de soie, argued that the major concern of the French negotiator should be the suppression of the internal Chinese duties.[49] M. Morel, a Lyonnais director of the Hongkong and Shanghai Banking Corporation, and Ulysse Pila agreed with Giraud.[50] Cogordan, of course, could not satisfy all these demands, and the final treaty was bitterly attacked by colonialists.

Such attacks in part reflected frustration in face of the anti-colonial reaction which had set in after the defeat at Langson (March 28, 1885). Yet despite the disinterest, if not hostility, of the mass of the French population to expansion, Lyon did not abandon imperialism. In 1884 Ulysse Pila had founded a branch of his firm in Tonkin. Two years later he opened up trade with the Chinese province of Yunnan.[51] Although this undertaking did not immediately prosper, Pila's position in Tonkin was far from hopeless.[52] "Under the auspices of the most honorable houses" of Lyon, the Société des Docks de Haiphong had been founded in 1886.[53] Pila was its president. His fellow activists in the ranks of the local geographical society, G. Cambefort and G. Saint-Olive was also officers.[54] After encountering various problems, it opened its first installations in 1889.[55]

In France itself the Chamber of Commerce of Lyon pursued the protection and expansion of Lyonnais interests in Indochina and China. In 1886 it received from the Resident General of Tonkin a collection of samples of the protectorate's silken fabrics.[56] Three years later it held a reception for the uncle of the Vietnamese monarch.[57] That year the Chamber was also receiving, through the local geographical society, information on central China and Tibet from a Lyonnais who was supposedly exploring the area on behalf of the Russian government.[58]

The role of the geographical society was not accidental. Lyon initiated the basically imperialist geographical movement of the 1870s with the founding of the first such provincial society.[59] The local business community stood behind the geographical society, with the Chamber of Commerce a major source of financial support.[60] Although the listing of professions is often incomplete, the geographical society's membership lists contain the names of many of the city's more prominent entrepreneurs.[61] Of major interest to the local business community was such information as that forwarded to the society by the Apostolic Vicar of Korea and that contained in the atlas of sericulture prepared under its auspices.[62]

In the last decade of the century a combination of threat and well-being drove the business community of Lyon both to continue along what were by then traditional imperialist lines and to open new avenues of expansionist endeavour.[63] In both the old and the new undertakings the Chamber of Commerce played the central role. It continued to provide a subsidy for the geographical society.[64] Pila, a member of the Chamber of Commerce, was vice-president of the society.[65] He was also a vice-president of the Paris-based Union coloniale française. Founded in 1893, this organization received an annual subvention of 1,000 francs from the Lyon Chamber of Commerce.[66] With a contribution of 1,000 francs, the Chamber in 1896 became one of the founding members of the colonialist Comité Dupleix.[67] Two years later a smaller subsidy went to the Comité de Madagascar.[68]

The problems of imperial education also occupied the Chamber of Commerce. Lyon's Ecole supérieure de Commerce, founded in 1872, had encouraged a concern with expansion.[69] But this was no more sufficient for Lyon than the program of the Ecole coloniale in Paris. The founding of the latter in 1889 had provoked a slashing report drafted by Pila for the Chamber of Commerce. He complained that the Chambers of Commerce had not been consulted about the founding.[70] Charging the new school with possessing a monopoly of colonial posts for its students, he argued that this discriminated against provincial and colonial youth.[71] The Chamber of Commerce resumed the attack in 1895; it wanted the termination of what was again described as the Parisian institution's institutions virtual monopoly of colonial positions.[72] It asked the competition for these positions be opened to "students of other colonial schools, and notably the one which we wish to create at Lyon."[73]

When negotiations with the Academy of Lyon and the local Ecole supérieure de Commerce for the founding of a program of colonial studies came to little, the Chamber decided to sponsor its own series of courses.[74] In January, 1899, Paul Doumer, Governor General of Indochina, offered an annual subvention of 30,000 francs for such a program.[75] The following July the Chamber itself provided 10,000 francs in support of colonial courses.[76] Although

Pila accepted the program, it fell far short of his ideal arrangement. He had envisioned a series of regionally based colonial schools, oriented more towards commerce than administration and specializing in instruction on the colonial area most relevant to the region where each school was located.[77]

Disappointed on this score, Pila nevertheless had several major successes to his credit in the last decade of the century. He was the organizer of the large Colonial Exposition held in Lyon in 1894.[78] In justification of the decision to hold the exposition, the Chamber of Commerce had reviewed Lyon's colonial history, deciding that "this natural tendency has assumed a very great strength as a result of an abundance of Lyonnais capital, the importance of the export industries and even the feeding of a dense population."[79] Another motive behind expansion was suggested at the opening of the exposition when the mayor of the city, aware of the increasing restlessness of French labour, outlined a program of social imperialism: "Colonial expansion will increase the public wealth, will give impetus to the industry of the nation, and will attenuate the crises born of suffering and misery. In place of a chimerical and harmful dream, it will realize the equality which honours not a lowering of some individuals but the raising of the entire nation to a higher degree of prosperity and morality."[80] The *mission civiisatrice* was not forgotten, although the president of the Chamber of Commerce gave it a typically Lyonnais twist: "The sole *raison d'être* of colonial conquest is to bring peoples more justice and science in their government and in the exploitation of their riches."[81] The exposition, with its exhibitions and the distinguished visitors which it attracted, provided a focus for the Lyonnais imperialism of the last decade of the century.

Lyon's imperial endeavours, however, were remarkably diffuse in this period. In 1891 the Chamber of Commerce sent a representative on a mission of investigation to the French Congo.[82] The next year the Chamber gave a reception for Charles Rouvier, then on his way to take up the post of Resident General in Tunisia. Rouvier obliged his hosts by assuring them that he would devote "the greatest care to the protection of Lyonnais interests in Tunisia."[83] A deputy of the Chamber toured Tunisia in 1896.[84] The next year, introducing a speaker then in France on a mission for the Tunisian government, a member of the Chamber of Commerce remarked that no other city had "proportionately furnished as many *colons* to Tunisia."[85] By the end of the century seven firms interested in the exploitation of Madagascar had their head offices in Lyon.[86] The Comptoir lyonnais d'Abyssinie was founded in 1899.[87]

Even so, Africa was hardly the key region in the colonial preoccupations of Lyon. The Far East still held primacy of place for the city. The interests there were carefully cultivated. The Chamber of Commerce in 1891 gave a banquet for Jean de Lanessan, who was departing the next day to assume his functions as Governor General of Indochina.[88] Pila read a report at the affair. Silk could be produced in Tonkin, he declared, indeed the very type which Lyon was now purchasing in Italy.[89] Pila also stressed the advantages of making direct contact with China through Tonkin.[90] Exchange between the south of China and France's possession could be encouraged by the construction of a railroad from Hanoi to Yunnan and by the provision of freer trade between the French colony and the Chinese empire.[91] A similar banquet was held on February 16, 1895 in honour of Lanessan's successor, Armand Rousseau. Auguste Isaac, vice-president of the Chamber, drew attention to Lyon's particular interest in Asia.[92] He informed Rousseau that "China has always exercised a fascination on our Chamber. We have asked the government of the Republic to favour there the attempts at a pacific and commercial penetration of the southwest."[93] Isaac was followed by Pila, who, repeating the same message, declared that "of all the parts of the world which have been opened in recent times to French expansion, the Far East has most seduced the ambitions of the commerce of the Lyon region."[94] Pila gave Rousseau to understand that he would not be leaving Lyon behind when he arrived in the Far East.[95] He then urged the construction of two railroads which he believed would allow France to dominate the trade of the western provinces of China.[96] The stage was being set for the despatch of a major mission to these areas.

Pila, acting for the Chamber of Commerce, organized this exploratory mission.[97] Invitations to participate in it were accepted by the Chambers of Commeerce of Lille, Roubaix, Roanne, Bordeaux, and Marseille. The Chamber of Commerce of Lyon mobilized government support for it. Leaving France in 1895, the expedition spent two years in the Far East, visiting Indochina and the provinces of south and western China. While it was still conducting its investigations, the Lyon Chamber welcomed the Chinese statesman, Li Hung-Chang, to the city. The president of the Chamber pointed out to him that, owing to the importance of the silk trade, "very few cities" had as much claim as Lyon to his "attention and sympathy."[98] The aims of the mission then in China were described to Li.[99] Whatever Li thought privately of this program, he expressed his happiness at visiting Lyon because of its ties with his country.[100]

The mission bore fruit. The Compagnie lyonnaise indo-chinoise was founded in 1898 to promote trade with China and economic development in Indochina.[101] Its president was Pila and two former members of the mission were its representatives in Tonkin.[102] The same year the Société cotonnière de l'Indochine was founded with Pila on its board of directors.[103] He was also involved with the Société des Ciments Portland artificiels de l'Indochine, which was founded in the following year.[104] The Compagnie lyonnaise indo-chinoise possessed exclusive rights to the sale of both the textile and the cement firms.[105] After the return of the expedition, Pila also concerned himself with plans for Anglo-French cooperation in the exploitation of the supposed wealth of Yunnan.[106] He was not, however, connected with yet another undertaking resulting from the mission, the Société lyonnaise de Colonisation en Indo-Chine.[107]

These concerns, along with others such as the Société des Docks et des Houillères de Tourane, led the business community of Lyon to take pride in its imperialist achievements.[108] By the end of the century the city alone had invested an estimated 255,000,000 francs in the empire.[109] The largest single amount of this sum, between sixty and eighty million francs, was invested in Indochina.[110] As the citizens of Lyon were and are reticent about their investments, such figures can be only approximations. What is clear is that during the nineteenth century the business community of Lyon developed an interest in economic imperialism which complemented the religious impulse towards expansion.

Notes

1. *French Historical*, Studies, VI, l (Spring, 1969), pp. 78-92.

2. Jules Cambon, Address, "Exposition coloniale de Lyon -- inauguration," Chambre de Commerce de Lyon, *Compte rendu des travaux, Année 1894* (Lyon, 1894), pp. 194-224.

3. Auguste Isaac, "Réception de M. Rousseau, Gouverneur général de l'Indochine," Chambre de Commerce de Lyon, *Compte rendu, 1895* (Lyon, 1896), pp. 234-55.

4. On Pauline Jaricot and the Oeuvre de la Propagation de la Foi, see David Lathoud, *Marie Pauline Jaricot, I, le secret des origines de la Propagation de la Foi* (Paris, 1937), and Marie-Andrée Sadrain, "Les Premières Années de la Propagation de la Foi (1820-1830)," *Revue d'histoire des missions*, l6e Année (Sept. 1939), pp. 321-48; (Dec. 1939), pp. 554-79.

5. Quoted in André Retif, "Les Evêques français et kes missions au XIXe siècle," *Etudes*, CCLXXXXV (Dec. 1952), pp. 362-72.

6. "Détail des aumones transmisés par les diocèses qui ont contribué à l'Oeuvre en 1895," *Annales de la Propagation de la Foi: Recueil périiodique des lettres des évêques et des missionaires des deux mondes et de tous les documents relatifs aux missions et à l'Oeuvre de la Propagation de la Foi, Collection faisant suite aux lettres édifiantes*, LXVIII (1896), pp. 166-87; "Détail des aumones transmisés par les diocèses qui ont contribué à l'Oeuvre en 1896," *Annales*. LXIX (1897), 165-86;"Compte rendu de l'Oeuvre de la Propagation de la Foi, 1897," *Annales*, LXX (1898), 163-85; "Compte rendu de l'Oeuvre de la Propagation de la Foi, 1898," *Annales*, LXXI (1899), 163-86; "Compte rendu de l'Oeuvre de la Propagation de la Foi," *ANNAles*, LXXII (1900), 163-87.

7. Adrien Launay, *Nos missionaires, précedés d'une étude historique sur la Société des Mission étrangères* (Paris, 1886), p. 159.

8. Comité départemental du Rhône, *La Colonisation lyonnaise* (Lyon, 1900), pp. 152-53.

9. Dominique Chevallier, "Lyon et la Syrie en 1919; les bases d'une intervention," *Revue historique*, CCXXIV (Oct.-Dec. 1960), 275-320.

10. The following information was derived from largely hagiological works: Comité départemental du Rhône,*La Colonisation lyonnaise*, pp. 150-51; Launay, *Nos missionaires*, p. 160; Jean Escot, *Le bienheureux Jean-Pierre Néel et ses compagnons martyrs des monts du lyonnais au Kouy-Toheou* (Lyon, 1951); Valerien Groffier, *Héros trop oubliés de notre épopée coloniale* (Lyon, 1928), pp. 477, 501-3; "Le Muerte de M. Berthelot et les épreuvres des Chretiens du Koung-si," *Les Missions catholiques*, XXX (June 24, 1898), pp. 289-92; Ulysse Pila, Rapport, "Mission d'exploration commerciale au Chine," Chambre de Commerce de Lyon, *Compte rendu, 1895* pp. 297-35; "Tonkin occidentale," *Les Missions catholiques*, XXX (Jan. 14, 1898), pp. 15-16.

11. Maurice Zimmermann, "Lyon colonial," *Lyon et le région lyonnaise en 1906, II, Economie sociale -- agriculture -- commerce -- industrie -- transports -- navigation -- aérostation* (Lyon, 1906), 230-83.

12. These factors are treated at some length in John F. Laffey, "French Imperialism and the Lyon Mission to China" (unpublished Ph.D. dissertation, Department of History, Cornell University, 1966).

13. Quoted in Maurice Zimmermann, "Lyon et la colonisation française," *Questions diplomatiques et coloniales*, IX (June 15, 1900), 705-17; X (July 1, 1900),1-21, 708.

14. *Ibid.*

15. Zimmermann, *Lyon et la région Lyonnaise en 1906*, II, 238.

16. Zimmermann, *Questions diplomatiques*, p. 708.

17. Louis-Francois Trolliet, le président de la Société des Colons de Lyon, *Mémoire sur la nécessité et sur les avantages de la colonisation d'Alger* (Lyon, 1835), p. 4.

18. *Ibid.*, p. 2.

19. *Ibid*, p. 8.

20. Zimmermann, *Questions diplomatiques*, p. 717.

21. Zimmermann, *Lyon et la rion lyonnaise en 1906*, II, 262-66.

22. Comité départemental du Rhône, *La Colonisation lyonnaise*, pp. 11-14.

23. And in 1875 the Chamber subscribed five thousand francs to help to support Paul Soleillet's attempt to establish commercial relations between Algeria and Senegal by way of the Sahara. *Ibid.*, p. 14.

24. The last good harvest of cocoons in France for more than a decade took place in 1855, when 19,800,000 of them were gathered. Even then, however, it took eleven kilograms of cocoons to produce onew kilogram of raw silk whereas it had taken only nine in 1851. The harvests of the succeeding years were disastrous: 7,500,000 in 1856 and 1857; 9,000,000 in 1858 and 1859; 8,000,000 kilograms in 1860; 5,800,000 in 1861 and 1862; 6,000,000 in 1863 and 1864; and 4,000,000 kilograms in 1865. E. Pariset, *Histoire de la fabrique lyonnaise; étude sur le régime social et économique et l'industrie de la soie, depuis le XIVe siècle* (Lyon, 1901), pp. 338-39.

25. Chevallier, "Lyon et la Syrie," p. 282.

26. E. Emerit, "La Crise syrienne et l'expansion économique française en 1860," *Revue historique*, CCVII (April-June 1952), 211-32.

27. E. Pariset, *La Chambre de Commerce de Lyon; étude faite sur les registres de ses délibérations* (Lyon, 1899), 193.

28. *Ibid.*

29. Paul Pelliot, *L'Origine des relations de la France avec la Chine, le premier voyage de "l'Amphitrite" en Chine* (Paris, 1930), pp. 67, 74; Pierre Bonnassieux, *Les Grandes Compagnies de commerce; étude pour servir à l'histoire de la colonisation* (Paris, 1892), pp. 340-43; Justin Godart, *L'Ouvrier en soie, monographie du tisseur lyonnais* (Lyon, 1899), pp. 208-09; Pariset, *Fabrique lyonaise*, p. 297.

30. Jean Bouvier, *Le Crédit lyonnais de 1863 à 1882, les années de formation d'une banque de dépôts* (Paris, 1960), I, 106.

31. Chambre de Commerce de Lyon, *Commerce de la France avec la Chine: délibération prise sur le rapport de M. Rondot, délegué de la Chambre, Séance du 12 janvier 1860* (Lyon, 1860), pp. 25-26.

32. "Mouvement de la Condition des soies de Lyon depuis 1860 par provenances," Chambre de Commerce de Lyon, *Compte rendu, 1900* (Lyon, 1901), n.p.

33. Louis Guerin to the Minister of Agriculture and Commerce, Feb. 22, 1870, Chambre de Commerce de Lyon, *Rvévision du traité de Tien-tsin avec la Chine: lettres à S. Exc. le Ministre de l'Agriculture et du Commerce* (Lyon, 1870), pp. 4-6.

34. Louis Guerin to the Minister of Agriculture and Commerce, May 3, 1870, *Ibid.*, pp. 10-11

35. Chambre de Commerce de Lyon, *Compte rendu des operations de la Condition des soies de Lyon pendant l'année 1895* (Lyon,1896)), p. 14.

36. Castonnet des Fosses, "La Chine industrielle et commerciale," *Bulletin de la Société géographie de Lyon*, VII (April-June 1888), 331-65.

37. The documents do not always provide full names.

38. Comité départemental du Rhône, *La Colonisation lyonnaise*, p. 14.

39. Henri Baudoin, *La Banque de l'Indochine* (Paris, 1903), p. 25.

40. Ulysse Pila, *Le Tonkin et la colonisation française* (Lyon, 1884), p. 33.

41. Paul Brunat, *Exploration commerciale du Tonkin: rapport presenté à la Chambre de Commerce de Lyon, Séance du 18 février 1885* (Lyon, 1885), p. v.

42. *Ibid.*, pp. 27-51.

43. "Traité de commerce avec la Chine: mission de M. Cogordan," Chambre de Commerce de Lyon, *Compte rendu, 1885* (Lyon, 1886), pp. 167-76.

44. *Ibid.*

45. *Ibid.*

46. *Ibid.*, p. 169.

47. *Ibid.*, p. 168.

48. *Ibid.*, p. 173.

49. *Ibid.*, p. 169.

50. *Ibid.*

51. Ulysse Pila, "Le Régime douanier de l'Indochine, communication faite à la 6e section, le 18 décembre," *Recueil des délibérations du Congrès colonial national -- Paris, 1889-90*, II, Rapports de commissaires. Documents annexes (Paris, 1890), 345-54.

52. By 1889 Pila's steamboat line to Hongkong had been discontinued, the Nam Dinh branch of the firm had been closed, and that at Hanoi was on the verge of suspension. Ibid., 352-53.

53. "Société des Docks de Haiphong," Chambre de Commerce de Lyon, *Compte rendu, 1888* (Lyon, 1889), pp. 249-51.

54. Alfred Bonzon, *Manuel des sociétés par actions de la région lyonnaise* (Lyon, 1893), p. 293.

55. The government of Indochina eventually purchased the installations at an excellent price. J. Chailley-Bert, *Dix années de politique coloniale* (Paris, 1902), pp. 122-23.

56. "Enchantillons des tissus de soie du Tonkin," Chambre de Commerce de Lyon, *compte rendu, 1886* (Lyon, 1887), p. 68.

57. "Réception de la Mission annamite," Chambre de Commerce de Lyon, *Compte rendu, 1889* (Lyon, 1890), pp. 251-55.

58. "Explorations de M. Martin dans la Chine centrale et le Thibet," *Ibid.*, 63-64; "Mort de l'explorateur Martin," Chambre de Commerce de Lyon, *Compte rendu, 1892* (Lyon, 1893), p. 217.

59. Donald V. McKay, "Colonialism in the French Geographical Movement," *Geographical Review*, XXXIII (April 1943), 214-32; Agnes Murphey, *The Ideology of French Imperialism, 1871-1881* (Wash., D.C., 1948).

60. In 1878 the geographical society of Lyon received these subventions: Conseil général du Rhône, 250 francs; Conseil municipal de Lyon, 3,000 francs; Chambre de Commerce de Lyon, 1,000 francs; Ministre d"Instruction publique, 900 francs; total, 5,150 francs. "Situation financière, 31 décembre 1878," *Bulletin de la Société de géograhie de Lyon*, II (1878), 496-97.

61. "Liste des sociétaires," *Bulletin de la Société de géographie de Lyon*, V (1884), 631-74.

62. F. C. Ridel, "Lettre, 25 août 1875," *Bulletin de la Société de géographie de Lyon*, I (Jan., 1876), 278-82; Léon Clugnet, *Géographie de la soie, étude géographique et statistique sur la production et le commerce de soie en cocon* (Lyon, 1877).

63. For a more detailed exploration of the situation of the Lyon silk industry in the last decade of the century, see Laffey, "French Imperialism," pp. 104-16.

64. "Actes de la société: assemblée générale du 10 décembre 1898," *Bulletin de la Société de géographie de Lyon*, XV (Jan. 1, 1899), 289-316; "Actes de la société: assemblée générale du jeudi 7 décembre 1899," *Bulletin de la Société de géographie de Lyon*, XVI (Jan. 1, 19000), 97-123.

65. "Nomination annuelle du bureau, séance du comité d'action du 11 décembre 1896," *Bulletin de la Société de géographie de Lyon*, XIV (Jan. 1, 1897), 98.

66. "Souscription à l'Union coloniale française," Séance du 8 février 1894, Lettre du 20 fevier, Chambre de Commerce de Lyon, *Compte rendu, 1894*, p. 174; "Souscription en faveur de l'Union coloniale française," Séance du 1er avril 1897, Lettre du 3 avril 1897, Chambre de Commerce de Lyon, *Compte rendu, 1897* (Lyon, 1898),p. 225; "Subvention à l'Union coloniale française," Séance du 10 février 1898, Chambre de Commerce de Lyon, *Compte rendu, 1898* (Lyon, 1899), p. 326; "Union coloniale française (Allocation de la Chambre), Chambre de Commerce de Lyon, *Compte rendu, 1899* (Lyon, 1900), p. 352.

67. "Comité Dupleix: Souscription de la Chambre," Chambre de Commerce de Lyon, *Compte rendu,1896* (Lyon, 1897), p. 314.

68. "Souscription en faveur de Comité de Madagascar," Chambre de Commerce de Lyon, *Compte rendu, 1896* (Lyon, 1897), p. 327. The Chamber had already provided 2,000 francs

for the Comité de l'Afrique française. "Souscription en faveur du Comité de l'Afrique française," Chambre de Commerce de Lyon, *Compte rendu, 1891* (Lyon, 1892), pp. 399-400.

69. Ganneval, professeur à l'Ecole supéreiur de Commerce de Lyon, "La Colonisation moderne, conférence du dimanche 27 novembre 1887," *Bulletin de la Société de géographie de Lyon*, VII (Sept.-Dec. 1887), 183-84.

70. "Création d'une école coloniale," Chambre de Commerce de Lyon, *Compte rendu, 1890* Lyon, 1891), pp. 331-37.

71. *Ibid.*, p. 335.

72. "Privilège de l'Ecole coloniale de Paris," Chambre de Commerce de Lyon, *Compte rendu, 1895*, pp. 256-61.

73. *Ibid.*

74. "Création à Lyon d'une chaire d'études coloniales," Chambre de Commerce de Lyon, *Compte rendu, 1894*, p. 173; "Projet de création à l'Ecole de Commerce d'une section d'enseignement coloniale," Chambre de Commerce de Lyon, *Compte rendu, 1895*, pp. 272-73; Zimmermann, *Lyon et la region lyonnaise en 1906*, II, 247.

75. "Organisation du cours d'enseignement colonial," Chambre de Commerce de Lyon, *Compte rendu, 1899*, pp. 332-48.

76. *Ibid.*, p. 333.

77. Ulysse Pila, *Vingt ans de progrès colonial: nécessité d'un enseignement colonial, conférence faite à la Société d'Economie politique de Lyon* (Lyon, 1900), p. 29. If the thesis of Municipal Imperialism is accepted, then Pila's proposal made sense.

78. "Exposition coloniale de Lyon Lyon en 1894," Chambre de Commerce de Lyon, *Compte rendu, 1893* (Lyon, 1894), pp. 193-200.

79. *Ibid.*, p. 195.

80. Gailleton, Address, *Ibid.*, Chambre de Commerce de Lyon, *Compte rendu, 1894*, pp. 200-04.

81. Edouard Aynard, Address, *Ibid.*, pp. 206-15. Another member of the Chamber provided much the same definition of the *mission civilisatrice*: "To civilize people in the modern sense of the word is to teach them to work in order to acquire, to spend, and to trade." Auguste Isaac, Address, "Réception de M. Doumer, gouverneur général de l'Indochine," Chambre de Commerce de Lyon, *Compte rendu, 1901* (Lyon, 1902), pp. 470-98.

82. "Mission commerciale au Congo française," Chambre de Commerce de Lyon, *Compte rendu, 1891*, pp. 398-99.

83. "Réception de M. Charles Rouvier, résident général à Tunis," Chambre de Commerce de Lyon, *Compte rendu, 1892*, pp. 204-08.

84. "Déégation de M. Teste en Tunisie," Chambre de Commerce de Lyon, *Compte rendu, 1896*, pp. 307-12.

85. Louis Chavent, Address, "Conférence sur la Tunisie," Chambre de Commerce de Lyon, *Compte rendu, 1897*, pp. 219-22.

86. Zimmermann, *Questions diplomatiques et coloniales*, p. 718.

87. Comité départemental du Rhône, *La Colonisation lyonnaise*, p. 98.

88. Lanessan, then a deputy from the Seine, had addressed Lyon's geographical society in 1888, acknowledging that "it is from here, from Lyon, that the first colonists carried to Indochina...their capital and their wise experience in business." Lanessan in his capacity as Governor General was back in Lyon for the inauguration of the Colonial Exposition of 1894, where he drew attention to the millions of Indochinese awaiting French products. Jean de Lanessan, "L'Expansion coloniale de France, ses intérêts dans l'Extrême Orient, Conférence du 25 mars 1888," *Bulletin de la Société de géographie de Lyon*, VII (July-Aug., 1888), 473-88; Jean de Lanessan, Address, Chambre de Commerce de Lyon, *Compte rendu, 1894*, pp. 218-19. Returned to France, Lanessan was elected a deputy by a Lyonnais district in 1898 and became Minister of Navy in Waldeck-Rousseau's cabinet.

89. Ulysse Pila, Report, Chambre de Commerce de Lyon, *Séance extraordinaire du 28 mai 1891: réception de M. de Lanessan, Gouverneur général de l'Indochine, rapport de M. Ulysse Pila sur*

son second voyage d'études commerciales au Tonkin, Banquet offert par la Chambre de Commerce de Lyon (Lyon, 1891), pp. 6-27.

90. *Ibid.*, p. 21.

91. *Ibid.*, pp. 18, 21.

92. Auguste Isaac, Address, Chambre de Commerce de Lyon, *Compte rendu, 1895*, p. 237.

93. *Ibid*, p. 241.

94. Ulysse Pila, Address, *Ibid.*, pp. 242-53.

95. "...you will recognize in the country you have been called upon to administer...[that] the Lyonnaise dominate both commerce and the administration, and that most of the works undertaken or accomplished are of Lyonnaise creation or have been participated in by the Lyonnais region: I will cite to you the Houillères de Tourane, the Docks de Haiphong, the public works of the city of Haiphong, these last under the direction of M. Malon, a Lyonnais, the Syndicat lyonnais d'études pour l'Indo-Chine, the farm of the Croix Cuvelier, under the direction of M. Thomé. a member of the council of the protectorate, also a Lyonnaise..." *Ibid.*

96. *Ibid.*, pp. 251-52.

97. For the mission, see Laffey, "French Imperialism," pp. 251-400.

98. Edouard Aynard, Address, "Réception de S.E. Li Hong-chang, Ambassadeur extraordinaire de s. M. l'empereur de Chine," Chambre de Commerce de Lyon, *Compte rendu, 1896*, pp. 460-70.

99. *Ibid.*, p. 464.

100. Li Hung-chang, Address, *Ibid.*, pp. 465-66.

101. Alfred Bonzon and J. J. Girardet, *Manuel des sociétés par actions de la région lyonnaise* (Lyon, 1901), pp. 519-20.

102. Zimmermann, *Questions diplomatiques et coloniales*, pp. 7-8.

103. Bonzon and Girardet, *Manuel*, pp. 517-18.

104. Zimmermann, *Lyon et la région lyonnaise en 1906*, II, 274.

105. Comité départemental du Rhône, *La Colonisation lyonnaise*, p. 121.

106. Michel Brugière, "Le Chemin de fer du Yunnan; Paul Doumer et la politique d'intervention francaçaise en China (1889-;902)," *Revue d'histoire diplomatique*, 77e Année (July-Sept. 1963), pp. 262-78.

107. Bonzon and Girardet, *Manuel*, p. 542.

108. An important coal vein at Non San had been ceded to a Chinese, In 1889 he sold the concession to the Société des Houillèrea de Tourane, which had been founded in Lyon. Fires in the shafts and lack of capital drove the concern intto dissolution in 1894. Four years later the Société des Docks et Houillères de Tourane, with Pila as its president, took over the concession. Comité départemental de Rhône, *La Colonisation lyonnaise*, pp. 112-14.

109. *Ibid.*, p. xviii.

110. *Ibid.*

2

LYONNAIS IMPERIALISM
IN THE FAR EAST: 1900-1938[1]

Influential citizens of the French city of Lyon embraced the cause of expansion during the nineteenth century. Religious zeal led to the founding of the Oeuvre de la Propagation de la Foi during the Restoration, and local Catholics continued to lend fervent support to overseas missionary endeavors. But even when the religious impulse towards expansion stood at its zenith, the Lyonnais did not overlook the more concrete advantages to be secured through the acquisition of Algeria and the opening of China to Western trade.

Economic motivation took on far more importance during the second half of the century when the devastation of French sericulture by pebrine forced the magnates of the silk industry, the most important local industry and the only French industry dominant in the international market, to look elsewhere for new supplies of raw silk. The Far East, the world's greatest silk-producing region, became the focus of attention, and the Lyon Chamber of Commerce, the most effective local organization devoted to the cause of imperialism, supported the opening of Japan, called for the wringing of new concessions from China, and backed the acquisition and development of Indochina. Just as within the larger pattern of French municipal imperialism the business communities of Bordeaux and Marseille acquired vital stakes in West and North Africa, so also Lyon's business community came to play a pivotal role in French undertakings in East Asia where the Lyonnais soon pushed their activities beyond the confines of the all-important silk trade.[2]

East Asia continued to be of central concern to the Lyonnais in the years separating the turn of the century from the end of the Third Republic. Throughout this period they worked to extend and defend their stakes in formal and informal empire in the region. But these tasks now proved more arduous. Developments of global significance, the First World War and the Depression, along with more specific developments in East Asia, created unprecedented problems. Despite their distinct identities, the dimensions of these problems, whether defined in terms of space or time, tended to overlap. The Lyonnais faced different challenges in colonial Indochina, semi-colonial China, and fully sovereign Japan, but as time passed, these challenges increasingly impinged upon each other. If in many respects the years prior to 1914 witnessed the workings of tendencies already apparent in the previous century, those following the outbreak of the First World War saw the unfolding of a series of crises which ultimately sapped the Lyonnais position in the Far East. These crises overlapped to such an extent that no neat temporal division can be established among them, but, in general terms, whereas the Lyonnais managed to cope with the problems confronting them throughout the period between the outbreak of the war and the onset of the Depression, in the 1930s events overwhelmed them, and the silken threads of empire, spun between France and the Far East in the nineteenth century, began to snap.

Few hints of the changes of the 1930s existed before 1914. When the Boxer Rebellion provided the French government with an opportunity to consider the revision of France's commercial accords with China, the Lyon Chamber of Commerce took advantage of the ocasion to review the general situation in China, which it described with its usual imperialist flair as a country "where respect for the truth has never existed." The results of the treaty of Shimonoskei, from the Lyonnais perspective, had proved disappointing, and they hoped that the display of foreign power involved in crushing the Boxers would lead to a more sincere enforcement by the Chinese of the existing treaty arrangements. The Chamber denounced the *likin*, the internal exactions levied on goods after customs charges had been met. Believing that the problem would be solved with the construction of railways in China, relegated the solution to the future, it rejected the idea of raising Chinese customs charges from a five to a fifteen per cent *ad valorem* level in return for Chinese promises to root out the *likin*, and proposed the staffing of Chinese tax offices with European personnel. The Lyonnais also attacked the obstacles still placed in the way of the development of foreign manufacturing in China. They rightly insisted that they shared these concerns with the nationals of other powers, and their only complaint about Chinese interference with specific French interests involved difficulties placed in the way of the introduction of sea salt from Annam and Tonkin into Yunnan.[3]

These views appeared remarkably mild, at least when contrasted with earlier Lyonnais formulations of their aims in China. Moderation had been forced on them at the end of the nineteenth century when their ambitious plans in regard to south and western China, rooted in older commercial concerns and best summed up in the mission despatched to China by the Chamber of Commerce immediately after the Sino-Japanese War, suffered a check when caught between the new interest of Parisian financiers in investments throughout China and the threat to traditional Lyonnais ties with the British posed by the aggressive expansionism espoused by Paul Doumer when he assumed the Governor Generalship of Indochina.[4] While he shared the Lyonnais unease about Doumer's adventurist proclivities, the Foreign Minister, Théophile Delcassé, rejected their optimistic estimates of the potential worth of the projected French sphere of influence, and, in commenting on the American Open Door Note in the Chamber of Deputies, he fell back upon the position of the financiers in arguing that China should be kept "open to the free struggle of intelligence and capital of the entire world."[5] The Lyonnais adjusted to the change in policy, and within a few years the president of the local Chamber of Commerce could be found urging the advantages of the Open Door on a visiting Manchu prince.[6]

Despite the limits on Chinese duties imposed by the Western powers during the nineteenth century, the Lyonnais still complained about the workings of the Chinese tariff.[7] Their grievances reflected their concern with the China market. If the fascination with projected sales of their silken commodities partook of economic myopia, their larger concern with this market made economic sense, for the balance in Franco-Chinese trade weighed heavily against the French. Lyonnais imports of Chinse raw silk created and sustained this adverse trade balance. Throughout the first decade of the twentieth century the Chinese silks registered at Lyon's Condition des Soies averaged annually 37.52 per cent of the totals from all sources of supply.[8] Here lay the real stake of the Lyonnais in China, and, if the silk trade did not hold out promise Parisian bankers detected in railway development and government loans, it played a vital role in the prosperity of Lyonnais industry during the *belle époque* when its profits reached unprecedented levels. Confident of their commanding position in the Chinese silk trade, the Lyonnais could afford to turn their attention to other imperialist undertakings, notably the French thrust into Morocco.[9] The complications arising from the Moroccan affair, especially the international crisis of 1911, even partially diverted their aattention from the Chinese revolution of that year, which in any event did not interfere greatly with the silk trade.[10]

Confidence about the basic strength of their position in China, along with the defeat at the end of the nineteenth century of their larger plans for China, allowed the Lyonnais to devote more attention to Indochina. The Chamber of Commerce did not hesitate to bring to the notice of the government such matters as the need to reinforce the military units serving on the Tonkin-China border.[11] It also backed the Exposition held in Hanoi in 1902 and on several occasions welcomed Indochinese missions visiting Lyon.[12] More important, it entertained Governor Generals of the Far Eastern colony at affairs which allowed these high officials to outline their policies in face of the questions, complaints, and suggestions of the members of the Chamber and their constituents. Couched in terms of the most exquisite *politesse*, such sessions involved exchanges among equals, for whatever the official powers of the Governor-General and the strength of his political support in France, in Lyon he had to confront a wealthy and politically influencial business community which regarded the Far East as its special preserve.

Paul Doumer spent a hectic day in the city on May 30, 1901. Meeting in the morning with members and staff of the Chamber's colonial education program before taking a tour of local establishments concerned with imperialist enterprise, he assured them of his continuing support for their activities and discussed Indochinese-Chinese relations with them.[13] At the reception held for the Governor-General, Auguste Isaac, president of the Chamber of Commerce and an increasingly important figure on the national political scene, stressed Lyon's ties with the Far East, dismissed the spectre of "the yellow peril," condemned the neo-mercantilist sentiments astir in France, defined the importance of Indochina to the mother-country in terms of its intrinsic worth and its value as a "base of operations," and urged the completion of a railway link between the valleys of the Red River and the Yangtze.[14] Aware of Lyonnais unease about some of his ideas, Doumer showed remarkable caution in his reply.

He defended his regressive fiscal policies by arguing that the Indochina population paid less in the way of taxes than the population of France and that, if taxes had been increased under his rule, the increase had allowed his administration to introduce a series of improvements which stimulated the growth of native income. Doumer stressed that the French conquest of the Chinese provinces neighbouring Indochina would come about through railway development and the activities of French doctors, educators and engineers, a view differing from his previous projection of the staging of a new Fashoda, a confrontation with Great Britain on the Upper Yangtze from which, this time, France would emerge victorious, and the interventionist plans he had spawned during the Boxer Rebellion. With the greater part of the Far Eastern silks reaching Lyon transported in English vessels and with Great Britain constituting Lyon's greatest foreign market, such moderation was well-advised. He even went so far as to soften his neo-mercantilist views in the light of the inclinations of his his audience and admitted that, should particular metropolitain industries prove unable to compete in a protected colonial market, a case might be made for establishing those same industries in the colony.[15] Such concessions to the occasion did not disguise the fundamental tension between the Anglophobe and protectionist attitudes of Doumer and the Anglophile and *laissez faire* views of the Lyon Chamber, and, all in all, despite the service rendered the Lyonnais in supplying funds for Chinese language instruction in the city, they provided a warmer welcome when his successor, Paul Beau, a former Minister to China, visited on October 28, 1905.

Once again Auguste Isaac ran through Lyon's traditional links with the Far East before going on to thank Beau for continuing Doumer's educational subsidy and to invite him to engage in a frank discussion of the present and future of Indochina.[16] Ulysse Pila, whose wealth and power earned him the unofficial title of "Viceroy of Indochina," carried the burden of discussion for the Chamber. Turning to the general situation in the Far East, Pila sought to allay the fears of a Japanese threat to Indochina spawned during the Russo-Japanese War: he insisted that, with the return of peace to the Far East, France's good relations with Great Britain allowed the country to benefit from the Anglo-Japanese alliance without placing in jeopardy the Franco-Russian alliance. Pila also emphasized the changes taking place in China and argued for the continuation of the Open Door Policy.

Having moved into investment after establishing his fortune in the silk trade, he rejoiced in the pivotal role foreign investment would play in the creation of a new China, but he did not abandon completely his older concerns, for he worried about whether French merchants and industrialists would be able to reap benefits commensurate with those of French bankers. This brought him back to his old fixation on Yunnan. Pila admitted that in the past he had exaggerated its wealth, but he stressed the importance of its mineral resources, warned against any Chinese offers to purchase the Yunnan section of the Hanoi-Yunnan-fu railway, and urged the extension of the Banque de l'Indochine's activities into the Chinese province. Coming to Indochina, Pila implicitly condemned Beau's predecessor: excessive attention had been paid to railway development at the expense of the colony's agricultural development.

Special attention, Pila asserted, should be paid to the encouragement of sericulture.[17]

Beau agreed with Pila in general terms, but the Govedrnor-General cautioned him about exaggerated expectations about what the colonial administration could accomplish in the agricultural sphere.[18] Such practical concerces re-emerged that evening at the banquet held in Beau's honor by the Chamber of Commerce, but, as befitted the occasion, some of the diners sounded more lofty notes: French imperialists, after all, could never sit down to a good meal and good wines without the *mission civilisatrice* surfacing at some point. Here ideological commitments, rather than smothering more concrete objectives, seemed to promise their fulfilment. Raising the native to the dignity of a civilized man, in Auguste Isaac's view, meant elevating him to the status of someone "who understands the services rendered him and is accustomed to pay for them."[19] Beau himself pointed to his efforts to attract Chinese students, then flocking to Japan, to French schools in Indochina and to place French teachers in Chinese universities as practical applications of the dictates of the *mission civilisatrice* and signs that France could contribute as much to the "moral evolution" as to the "economic transformation" of China.[20]

One measure of the changes which had taken place in the Far East between the visits of Doumer and Beau to Lyon lay in the amount of attention paid to Japan on the latter occasion. The Lyonnais viewed Japan primarily in economic rather than political terms. Just as in the case of China, the balance in trade with Japan weighed against the French, and once again the silk trade, with imports of Japanese silks fluctuating between 16.00 per cent and 22.50 per cent of the annual totals in the first decade of the century, accounted for this problem.[21] Although it forced the Lyon Chamber to lump Chinese and Japanese figures together, the Russo-Japanese War did not interfere substantially with this trade: 55.20 per cent of the silks reaching Lyon's Condition des Soies in 1905 came from the Far East.[22] The war, however, confirmed Japan's status as a fully independent power. Consequently, the decision of the Japanese government, on August 4, 1910, to terminate the Franco-Japanese commercial accord of 1896 could hardly have come as much of a surprise. The French Ministry of Commerce, in preparing for the negotiation of a new agreement, asked the Lyon Chamber for its views on the matter. The Chamber took advantage of the request to comment on Japan's relationship to China, and, after evaluating the changes occurring in the Far East, it decided that the annexation of Korea worked against Japan's assuming a commanding position in the China market and that the coming "profound transformation in China" would make that country into a "formidable competitor" rather than a "benevolent client" of Japan. More important, the Chamber deplored the ultra-protectionist character of the Japanese tariff of 1910 and suggested that the French government make use of the Japanese stake in the French market for raw silks, interest in French investment, and concern with the importation of Indochinese rice in order to prevent any increase in the Japanese duties on silken commodities. It urged, moreover, the use of these same factors to protect Lyonnais interests in Indochina. Such a course of action implied hard bargaining, and it did not necessarily entail the abandonment of their usual insistence on freer tariff policies in the colonial sphere. It marked, however, the first small step away from the *laissez faire* position which had distinguished the Lyon Chamber from the Chambers of Commerce of other French textile-producing centres. Concluded on August 19, 1911, the new treaty provided for some reductions in the minimum levels of the Japanese tariff and for the reciprocal extension of most favoured nation status. Indochina, at least for the moment, was excluded from its application.[23]

Despite the problems which arose in the early years of the twentieth century, the Lyon business community felt free to indulge in self-congratulation at the International Exposition held in the city in 1914: the silk industry, the local mainstay of imperialist effort, had prospered more than usual during the *belle époque*, and, well aware of the relationship between this prosperity and imperialism, the president of the Chamber of Commerce took pride in drawing the attention of Raymond Poincaré, the president of the republic, to the role played by the Lyonnais in in French expansion overseas.[24] The outbreak of the war, however, placed all in doubt; the initial economic disruption forced the Lyon textile manufacturers to take what comfort they could in the increasing sales of black crêpe.[25] Yet, contrary to expectation, conditions began to improve, and, despite the loss of some foreign markets and sources of supply, heightened freight rates, increased insurance charges, cargo restrictions and a plethora of government regulations, the silk industry fared well in the war. The difficulties of maritime transport did not even interfere greatly with the supplies of raw silk reaching Lyon from the Far East: Lyon's Condition des Soies received from China and Japan, respectively, 52.45 per cent and 14.59 per cent of its 1915 total, 44.78 per cent and 14.51 per cent of its 1916 amount, 50.53 per cent and 23.36 per cent of its 1917 sum, and 45.62 per cent and 32.98 per cent of its 1918 amount.[26] The war did, however, prevent the Chamber of Commerce devoting its usual close attention to events in the Far East, though in 1916 two developments, both ominously bringing Japan further into the Indochinese picture, roused concern in Lyon.

With war losses mounting swiftly, some Frenchmen suggested the sale of Indochina to Japan in return for increased military support. Auguste Isaac, a former president of the Chamber of Commerce, and Henri Brenier, the leader of its mission to China in 1895, denounced the idea in the press.[27] If nothing came of this evanescent notion, the Lyonnais faced a more difficult problem when France's ally, Japan, asked for the extension to Indochina of the duties provided for in the 1911 commercial accord. The request roused fierce opposition in France and Indochina. The Chambers of Commerce of Paris, Rouen, Nantes, Marseille and Beauvai, the Union coloniale, the Comité des forges, the Chambre syndicale des constructeurs d'automobiles, the Chambre syndicale de bonneterie de Troyes, the Chambers of Commerce of Saigon and Hanoi, and the government of Indochina, all came out against it. The war had accelerated a change in economic attitudes, for the protesting parties now included, along with the traditional proponents of neo-mercantilism, groups which earlier had supported freer trade policies. The Lyon Chamber of Commerce, a traditional bastion of free trade, had wavered when confronted with the negotiation of the 1911 accord, and now it invoked arguments, scorned in the past, to justify a refusal to fulfill the Japanese request. The Lyonnais proclaimed that the coming return of the Alsatian cotton industry would require protected colonial markets. It charged the Japanese with favouring the domestic market rice from their Korean and Formosan colonies at the expense of Indochinese rice. The Chamber also emphasized the gravity of the potential Japanese economic threat to Indochina: Japanese bankers would follow Japanese merchants to the colony, and the inability of the French to cope with a Japanese economic offensive would discredit them in the eyes of the native populations. The Lyonnais proposed, in place of meeting the Japanese request, the implementation of special tariff arrangements designed to favour French commodities in Indochina and Indochinese products in France.[28] Always flexible in matters involving the interests of its constituents, the Chamber soon dropped the latter part of this suggestion and, aware of what might happen to imports of silk from non-colonial sources, in 1919 it backed the stand taken by the Michelin rubber company against the government's favouring, at the expense of rubber from foreign sources, the entry into the domestic market of Cochinchinese rubber.[29] However important this reservation, in 1916 the Lyon Chamber took a momentous step on the path leading to the awkward position of the 1930s: "The Lyon Chamber of Commerce has liberal principles, but duty requires it to sacrifice them, sometimes with regret, to the immediate interests of the Lyonnais."[30]

The Lyonnais could not detect a return to "normalcy" at the end of the war, for behind the soaring sales of their silken commodities lay the loss of the Russian market, rising tariffs abroad, labour unrest and the introduction of the eight-hour day at home, wild fluctuations in the values of world currencies, the increasing competition offered by synthetic textiles, and the heightened rivalry of other centres of silk manufacturing. Despite these problems, and in part because of them, the Lyonnais silk magnates, like other good imperialists, soldiered on. If agitation for the acquisition of Syria and support for Albert Sarraut's comprehensive plan for colonial development occupied much of their time in the years immediately after the war, they did not overlook their old stakes in East Asia.[31] Indeed, during the 1920s these stakes became all the more important as exports of Levantine silks to France failed to re-gain their pre-war levels, nationalist unrest shook Syria and Morocco, and attempts to implement the Sarraut plan bogged down. But the forces of change had also taken root in the Far East, and the Lyonnais gradually became aware that here too the old imperialism faced new problems.

Moving beyond the provision of Chinese-language instruction in the colonial education program it patronized on the local scene, the Chamber involved itself with other educational endeavors in regard to China during the post-war years. It played a role in the transformation of a medical and technical school (founded by Germans in the French Concession of Shanghai before the war) into the Institut franco-chinois d'industrie et de commerce.[32] It provided support for missionary efforts to spread technical and commercial education.[33] The Chamber also encouraged the founding in Lyon of the Institut franco-chinois.[34] Other relations with the Chinese, at least initially, appeared to proceed on much the same basis as in the pre-war period. The Chamber continued to protest against *likin* charges.[35] Replying to a 1923 inquiry from the

Minister of Commerce and Industry about possible changes in the Chinese tariff, it accepted specific duties, as long as they met the five per cent standard, observed that the reduction of duties crossing the Tonkin-China border had not appreciably benefited Indochina, opposed the Chinese idea of introducing a five per cent surtax on luxury items like silken commodities, and once again called for the abolition of the *likin*.[36] The Lyonnais also continued to be good hosts. In 1921 the Chamber entertained a Chinese mission largely composed of Shanghai merchants and two years later a mission headed by the aging Chang Chien.[37]

Business as usual suffered a severe shock in 1924. The Chamber of Commerce informed Edouard Herriot, the mayor of the city who was then serving as Premier and Minister of Foreign Affairs, about the interference with the silk trade arising from the strike of the Chinese employees of the European commercial houses in Canton, and the apparent threat to the lives and goods of the French community in that distant city. Herriot, in reply, assured the Chamber that French lives were not in danger and that the French consul, along with other foreign diplomats, was attempting to end the strike.[38] As the Chinese revolution of the 1920s continued to unfold, the Chamber in 1925 lent its support to the complaints of the local Union des Marchands de Soies about the disruption of trade at Canton and the sinister influence being exercised by the Russians on the Chinese revolutionaries.[39] In early 1927, with the Northern Expedition sweeping towards Shanghai, the Chamber demanded and received from the Minister of Foreign Affairs assurances that the government had taken all the measures necessary to protect French lives and goods.[40] The Lyonnais also worried somewhat that the Chinese upheaval would lead to renewed rivalry among the powers in China.[41] The Lyonnais fears proved exaggerated in both respects: the Kuomintang shortly showed itself to be no more interested in social revolution than the foreign imperialists, and the internal social turmoil did not unduly exacerbate rivalry among the great powers. At the height of the decade's revolutionary unrest, the percentages of Chinese silks registered at Lyon's Condition des Soies climbed from in constant progression from 43.70 per cent in 1924 to 54.20 per cent in 1927.[42]

The Lyonnais did not go wholly untouched by the changes in China. The Kuomintang, whatever its failings, represented new nationalist forces, and this boded ill for French efforts aimed at developing a larger share of the China market. The Lyon Chamber, disturbed by a rumoured thirty per cent increase in Chinese duties on silken commodities, protested in August, 1927 against any violations of the existing tariff arrangements.[43] The issue became more acute the following year. Writing to the government, the Chamber pointedly remarked that it had learned from the press that France and China stood on the verge of concluding a new commercial accord. It wanted more precise information on how the new Chinese duties would affect Lyonnais exports of silken goods, automobiles and perfume. Recognizing that the time had passed for effective intervention in regard to this accord, the Chamber acidly inquired whether it should forward its views on the commercial accord to be concluded subsequently between China and Indochina. The government replied that the continuing negotiations made precision difficult, but that the new Chinese duties would be markedly higher than those of the past. The Chamber then wrote to the Minister of Commerce, on January 2, 1929, to complain that it had not been consulted about the negotiations. The government responded that the accord had been concluded on December 22, 1928, that details in regard to specific items still had to be worked out, and, with a brusqueness never before encountered by the Lyonnais in their dealings with officialdom in regard to Far Eastern affairs, that the Chamber of Commerce could find the provisions of the accord in the *Journée industrielle* or the *Moniteur officiel du commerce*.[44]

The difficulties encountered in semi-colonial China during the first post-war decade reinforced Lyonnais concern about colonial Indochina. The Lyonnais, who had been among the first to invest in the Banque de l'Indochine, obviously had every interest in supporting the renewal of its privileged status.[45]

Efforts at encouraging the development of Indochinese sericulture, which seemed to offer the possibility of partially freeing Lyon from dependence on Chinese and Japanese sources of supply, proved less successful.[46] Such interests explain the courtesies extended to the puppet emperor of Vietnam during his 1922 visit to Lyon.[47] A year earlier practical concerns had also mixed with *politesse* in the reception held for Maurice Long, the Governor-General of Indochina. Senator Jean Coignet, a magnate of the local chemical industry and a former president of the Lyon Chamber, ran through Lyon's ties with the colony, its bright prospects, the Chamber's gratitude for the continuing subsidization of its Chinese-language program and recent Lyonnais activities in China and Japan.[48] Long emphasized the new geo-political importance of the Pacific region and pointed with pride to the role of the Lyonnais in developing the colony's coal deposits, the importance of its rice production, and its social stability at a time when "anarchy" ruled Russia and the Japanese confronted troubles in Korea.[49] Auguste Isaac, another former president of the Chamber and now Minister of Commerce and Industry, stressed the need to develop the production of such raw materials as silk and cotton in the colonies in order to guarantee supplies for domestic industries.[50]

In 1923 the Chamber welcomed another Governor-General, Martial Henri Merlin, to the city. The Chamber's president rehearsed the old score for him: the importance of Lyonnais interests in the colony and the necessity for sericultural development.[51] Merlin provided his audience with what it wanted to hear: praise for their past achievements in the colony and promise of "the most complete support and the surest advice" for others willing to carry "their capital, their experience, their intelligence to the colony."[52] Two years later the newly-appointed Alexandre Varenne arrived in the city to be entertained by the Chamber of Commerce. Once again the Chamber drew the attention of the new imperial proconsul to the extent of Lyonnais interests in Indochina and the need to encourage the development of sericulture there.[53] Varenne introduced a note of caution: the First World war had increased unrest outside Europe, and he expected to have to walk a narrow line between granting too little or too much to native populations who, if not on the verge of rebellion, still demanded change.[54]

As might have been expected, Varenne's reforms ended up encompassing too little to satisfy the Vietnamese and too much to win support from the vested colonial interests, and his successor, Pierre Pasquier, returned to older and harsher policies. The Lyonnais business community, however, yielded to few in toughness, and when, on November 27, 1928 the Governor-General met in a study session with members of the Chamber of Commerce and other local notables interested in the colony, he confronted demands for the extension to the colony of the government subsidies for domestic sericulture, the protection of the Indochinese market for silken commodities against a Japanese intrusion, a crackdown on the smuggling into the colony of Chinese and Japanese commodities, the suppression of a new Indochinese levy on the import of goods from all sources, and several more minor measures designed to better the position of the French, especially the Lyonnais, in the colony.[55] After a lunch attended by Edouard Herriot, various local parliamentary figures and "representatives of the principal societies engaged in business relations with Indochina," the Chamber's president noted with satisfaction Pasquier's willingness to meet the desires of the Lyonnais before launching once again on the relation of Lyon's links with the colony.[56] Pasquier, in turn, thanked the Lyonnais for what they had done for Indochina in the past and, more to the point, for what they would do in the future. He promised that, should he have need of directives in the future, he would turn to Lyon.[57]

The Lyonnais did not bring the Japanese problem to Pasquier's attention by accident. Japan still supplied Lyon with significant amounts of raw silk, with Japanese imports constituting, for instance, 22.32 per cent and 9.58 percent of the total amounts of registered in 1919 and 1925 at the local Condition des Soies.[58] This factor alone made it worth while in 1921 to entertain the French ambassador to Japan, Paul Claudel, though the banquet held for the noted writer tended to turn into a tour down memory lane for the local Old China Hands.[59] The Chamber also proved willing to contribute to French cultural undertakings in Japan, to express genuine horror at the ravages of the 1923 earthquake, and to provide an economic mission to Japan with a subsidy.[60] Yet they could not entirely suppress unease about Japan. Although the Lyonnais continued to reject the idea of special favours for Indochinese products in the French domestic market, their commitment to the protection of the Indochinese market quickened after the war.[61] The Japanese, rather than the British, had become the leading commercial threat, and, when confronted with the rumour that they intended to take advantage of the Washington Conference to request a further opening of that market to their exports, the Lyonnais reaffirmed the position taken in 1916.[62] To make matters worse, the Lyonnais also had to worry about the Japanese introduction in 1924 of a one hundred per cent *ad valoren* surtax on imported luxuries and the prospects of new negotiations over the renewal of the 1911 treaty.[63] In face of the latter threat, the Chamber of Commerce still insisted that the minimum level of duties of the French tariff should not be extended to Japanese products entering Indochina.[64]

Seven years were to pass before the French and Japanese governments reached agreement on a new commercial convention, and in the interval the onset of the Depression transformed the situation of the Lyonnais silk magnates: whereas before 1929 they continued to enjoy a fluid prosperity and managed to hold their own overseas, the onslaught of the economic crisis cast all in doubt at home and abroad. If the Depression had less of an immediate impact in France than in more industrialized nations, the importance of international markets for

Lyon quickly brought its effects home to the city. As early as 1929 the Lyonnais complained of a glut of raw silk on the market, and by 1935 the amount of silken commodities produced in Lyon bared reached half of the total produced in 1913.[65] Lyonnais silken exports reached that year a value of roughly 540,000,000 francs, and, computing in terms of the 1935 franc, this sum represented a seventy per cent decline from the 1913 figure of 1,850,000,000 francs and a drastic drop from the 3,250,000,000 of 1928.[66] The crisis, viewed from the perspective of the Chamber of Commerce, only deepened the following year when Léon Blum's Popular Front government took power. Not until 1938, when the Chamber greeted the Munich accord with delight, could the Lyon Chamber take comfort in the more conservative governmental policies pursued at home and abroad, and even then such comfort could not be extended to cover the condition of the silk trade and industry.[67] The economic troubles of the silk magnantes, like their previous prosperity, depended on developments in several spheres, and however encouraged the Chamber of Commerce may have been by changes on the domestic political scene and in German-French relations, by late 1938 these changes did not in themselves compensate for the loss of foreign markets or other troubles which dogged the Lyonnais in different parts of the globe during the 1930s. The Lyonnais position in the Far East, for instance, rapidly weakened during this troubled decade.

The Chinese tariff continued to rouse concern. In 1929 the Chamber of Commerce pressed the French government to make sure that the Chinese authorities carried through on their commitment to suppress the *likin*. Although it recognized the difficulties inherent in the Chinese situation, the Chamber, stopping just short of suggesting the cancellation of the 1925 grant of customs autonomy, thought that France or, better still, all the concerned powers, should bring pressure to bear on the Chinese government to secure this goal. The Minister of Foreign Affairs informed the Chamber that French diplomatic efforts aimed at the abolition of the *likin*, but he did not appear to be much interested in the type of energetic action proposed by the Lyonnis.[68] The caution of the French government, from the Lyonnais perspective, simply invited the Chinese to take advantage of the situation, and two years later the Chamber returned to the charge. It complained that the Chinese had raised their duties on many items to forty-five or fifty per cent *ad valorem* levels. Aware of similar complaints from both the local Syndicat des fabricants de soieries and the Syndicat des acheteurs de soieries, the Chamber wrote again to the Ministers of Commerce and Foreign Affairs later in the year to protest against a rumoured Chinese increase to levels between sixty-five per cent and eighty percent. Suggesting that French diplomats threaten the Chinese with reprisals, it held out the strong stand taken by Italy as an example of the line which should be pursued. The Ministers responded that the complaints possessed, "at least for the moment," no foundation in fact.[69] The Lyonnais paranoia of 1931 may have been misplaced, but in 1932 the Chinese did raise their duties on a variety of commodities, including silken products, and the Lyon Chamber, once again urging reprisals, had the bitter satisfaction of pointing out to the Ministers of Foreign Affairs and Commerce that its fears of the previous year had been realized. This time the Ministers indicated their willingness to consider some action.[70] The situation, however, did not improve, and in 1934 the Chamber, after having noted that Chinese rates now reached one hundred per cent, wrung from the Minister of Commerce the vague promise that its views would be considered in connection with the negotiations with the Chinese over the tariff question.[71]

The Chamber had a chance to voice its discontent in 1936 when Emile Naggiar, a Lyonnais by upbringing and education and the new ambassador to China, stopped in Lyon on his way to the Far East. At a study session held on the morning of April 2, the Chamber's president attempted to drive home to the diplomat the seriousness of the situation by pointing out that between 1928 and 1935 French imports of Chinese silks had fallen from a value of 1,374,887,000 francs to 84,407,000 francs and the value of exports to China had declined in the same period from 58,148,000 francs to 652,000 francs. But when a representative of the Syndicat des fabricants de soieries lodged the inevitable complaint against the high Chinese duties, the ambassador, while promising to do what he could for the Lyonnais, directed his audience's attention to a matter heretofore studiously ignored in the Chamber's complaints to the government: the Chinese attempt to defend themselves against Japanese aggression and, in face of this threat, the attractiveness of the idea of falling back on increased duties on "French novelties."[72] The ambassador's *faux pas*, the introduction of a note of political realism into the discussion, was graciously overlooked at the luncheon which followed, The Chamber's president went through the ritual invocations of the old ties with the Far East, and, in adding the personal touch much appreciated by Lyon's Old China Hands, he pointed out that he had first met the new ambassador twenty-three yeas ago in China. He also reminded his audience that the Minister of Foreign Affairs had requested that the press should not be informed of Naggiar's visit.[73] The days in which the Lyon Camnber jauntily conducted its own "open diplomacy" had drawn to an end.

While endeavouring in face of the Depression to keep the China market open to their own commodities, the Lyonnais also struggled to keep other markets closed to foreign competition. Viewed from the Lyonnais perspective, the Japanese economic threat in particular took on awesome proportions during this period. As early as 1932 the Chamber of Commerce, acting on behalf of the Syndicat des fabricants de soieries, criticized the push of Japanese textile exporters into the Asian, Australian, South African, Canadian, American, Egyptian and Moroccan markets.[74] Two years later it supported the demand of important members of the International Silk Federation for the establishment of a quota system for Japanese products.[75] The intrusion of the Japanese into French colonial markets especially disturbed the Lyonnais, for the Depression rendered those markets all the more important. In 1934 the Lyon Chamber, acting in conjunction with local silk manufacturers, the Moroccan government and the Marseille Chamber of Commerce, protested against Japanese, as well as Italian, "dumping" in Morocco and suggested the introduction of a quota system there.[76] The suggestion, however, collided with the Act of Algeria's provision of the Open Door for Morocco, and, given the French commitment to the sanctity of international treaties during the inter-war period, the French government worked slowly in attempting to secure the agreement of other powers to the favouring of French conamodities within the protectorate. The delay left the Lyonnais to worry that in the meantime the Japanese would secure a commanding position in the Moroccan market.[77] Japanese "dumping" in Lebanon and Syria also concerned them, though here the picture appeared brighter, for only members of the League of Nations benefited from the minimum level of duties in these Mandates, and, as the Chamber pointedly reminded the Minister of Commerce in 1935, Japan had abandoned the League.[78]

Important as the Japanese commercial offensive of the 1930s may have appeared in areas as distant from the home islands as Morocco and the Levant, it took its sharpest edge, from the Lyonnais perspective, in regard to Indochina. It was not, however, the only Indochinese matter of concern to the Lyon Chamber during the 1930s. Although trade remained the issue of key importance, several other matters were discussed in a 1934 study session with Eugène-Louis-René Robin, yet another Governor-General. The value of the piastre, public works, the application of French regulations governing explosives, the electoral regime of the colony's Chambers of Commerce, spinning and sericulture, all received attention.[79] Sericulture, in particular, had been a subject of earlier concern, with the Lyonnais now pressing for the extension to Indochina of the kind of subsidies which they had once fought against in France.[80] But reflecting a shift away from a primary concern with supplies of raw silk to markets for silken products, the protection of the Indochinese market received the greatest amount of attention or, as the Chamber's president coyly put it after lunch, the Lyonnais wished that Indochina's proximity to other countries should not distort "the family relationships" which the colony enjoyed with the mother country, "without which it would not be what it is."[81]

This note had been struck before and would be struck again. The Lyonnais worried about smuggling.[82] But legitimate trade, especially Japanese trade, also constituted a threat. The Chamber of Commerce's attempts to protect the Indochinese market appeared to have achieved some success, for the new Franco-Japanese commercial accord, concluded in May, 1932, contained provisions designed to defend the privileged position of French silken commodities in the colonial market, even though it did extend to the Japanese the minimum rates of the general French tariff.[83] Within months such benefits proved ephemeral. Writing to the Ministers of Colonies and Commerce in 1933, the Chamber complained not only of Chinese competition in Indochina, but also about the advantages lent the Japanese by the devaluation of the yen and the extension of the minimum duties. The Chamber cited official statistics to make its point: whereas the imports into the colony of French silken and blended fabrics had fallen from 34 per cent of the total of these goods in 1930 to 8.1 per cent in 1932, the Japanese share had climbed in the same period from 9.45 per cent to 55 per cent. The writing on the wall appeared in the statistics for December, 1932: Japanese imports made up 83.00 per cent of the amount. Faced with this situation, the Lyonnais urged the introduction of a 50 per cent surtax, or at the very least a thirty-five per cent surtax, in order to allow local manufacturers to recapture a larger share of the market. The colonial government rejected this demand, though it moved to establish a quota system for foreign products.[84]

Not only did the colonial administration draw the line at introducing the ultra-protectionist measures favoured by the Lyonnais, but in 1936 it endeavoured to reduce existing customs charges. The Lyon Chamber of Commerce protested. Petitioning the Governor-General, the Minister of Colonies and the deputy from Cochinchina, it outlined the devastating effect of the projected reduction on sales of Lyonnais textiles in the colony and offered itself as the defender of Indochinese artisans whose livelihoods Chinese and Japanese competition threatened with extinction. The Chamber urged the modification of the new measures and a delay of in any implementation until the consequences of the extension of the Popular Front's reforms to Indochina had become known. The government agreed to suspend the reduction in duties for several months, and in 1937 prolonged this delay.[85] The Chamber of Commerce, in other words, scored a minor victory against a Popular Front government which again and again showed itself willing to back down in face of the pressures exerted by vested colonial interests.

Besting a weak ministerial combination came easier than besting the Japanese. The sales of Lyonnais commodities in Indochina did not increase appreciably in the years immediately before the outbreak of the Second World War. In the same years, moreover, renewed Japanese aggression in China interfered with the silk trade.[86] The Lyon Condition des Soies registered 411,933 kilograms of Chinese silk in 1938, hardly a figure to be compared with even the 950,293 kilograms of 1933, let alone the 2,586,767 kilograms of 1913.[87] Although at war with China, the Japanese still found it possible in 1938 to supply Lyon with 1,057,160 kilograms, a sum which compares more or less favourably with the 1,246,902 kilograms of 1913.[88] Given their other problems with the Japanese, the Lyonnais could not have taken much comfort in the extent to which they remained dependent upon them for raw silk supplies.[89]

The Lyonnais, of course, had not set out to create this situation. Initially they had hoped to make use of Japanese silk worm eggs to revitalize domestic sericulture, and, given the conditions of times, the Bonapartist government of the Second Empire had little difficultly in forcing the Japanese to lift their ban on the export of these eggs.[90] The revival of French sericulture, however, came more from the research of Louis Pasteur than from foreign silk worm strains. The Lyonnais welcomed the revival, but, as good *laissez faire* liberals, resolutely fought the efforts of domestic serciltural interests to gain tariff protection and government subsidies. Liberal principles in this instance, as in so many other cases, rested upon solid material interests: the Far East during the last decades of the nineteenth century came to constitute Lyon's chief source of supply of cheap and high quality silk. Entrepreneurs like Ulysse Pila, whose hallowed memory continued to be invoked after his death in 1909, carved out fortunes in the silk trade before diversifying their interests in the Far East and in France itself. But conditions changed in the twentieth century. Pila would not have recognized the world confronted by his son, Fernand, when serving as French ambassador to Japan during the 1930s. Indochina, where the elder Pila developed interests in trade, mining and cement, was in deep trouble. The informal empire of the Lyonnais in China, spun largely out of silk, was in even more serious difficulties. Japan had become economically competitive and militarily aggressive. The forces which shortly would carry Japanese troops to Indochina were perhaps already implicit in this situation. The retreat of the Lyon Chamber of Commerce to its mercantilist positions of the *ancien régime*, in any event, exacerbated Franco-Japanese relations.

Some changes would have taken place in the best of circumstances. However great the achievements of the Lyon's silk industry, its eminence was somewhat anomalous even in the nineteenth century. Its domination of the international market reflected in part France's relative industrial backwardness in the new age of iron and steel, and, despite the increasing interest of Lyonnais manufacturers in the mass market, their products remained at a disadvantage *vis-à-vis* cotton textiles. Inevitably, in the twentieth century, new industries, in this case metallurgy, automobile manufacture and chemical production, assumed increased importance in Lyon itself. Yet historical changes seldom take place in the best of circumstances, and the trials and tribulations of the silk magnates prior to the end of the Third Republic must also be seen in terms of the competition offered by foreign manufacturers, the rise of synthetic textiles, the impact of the First World War, the post-war wave of protectionism, the inflations and currency fluctuations in the 1920s and the onslaught of the Depression which lent increased strength to practically all of the preceeding factors.

Such developments affected Lyonnais imperialism in Eastern Asia where, despite continuities like the dependence on raw silk from this source of supply and the inability to develop a flourishing sericulture in Indochina, the forces of change also came to outweigh the factors buttressing the *status quo*. One major change came at the dawn of the twentieth century when the Lyon Chamber retreated from championing the vision of a sphere of influence in the Chinese south and adopted the Open Door idea favoured by the Parisian bankers. This change accurately reflected the balance of power within the ranks of the French *haute bourgeoisie*, and, given the diversification of their Far Eastern interests late in the nineteenth century, the Lyonnais had relatively little difficulty in making the adjustment. Other changes presented greater challenges after 1914. The Lyonnais had taken the Boxer rebellion in their stride, but in the 1920s they had to worry about the threat of social revolution in China. Welcoming Paul Doumer to the city at the beginning of the century, the Lyonnais Chamber's president denounced protectionism and the "yellow peril" psychosis, and, in line with preoccupations reaching back to the conquest of Cochinchina, vaunted the real and potential ties between Indochina and China. These positions were abandoned after 1914. With the supply of raw silks from the Far East secured at the expense of continuing adverse balances in French trade with China and Japan, the Lyonnais devoted more attention to gaining a larger share of the China market and guaranteeing a market for their products in Indochina. Domestic production of silken goods in China placed definite limits on what the Lyonnais could sell there, and even the circumscribed market for their luxury products inevitably suffered from internal social turmoil, the use made of tariff autonomy by the Kuomintang, and, in the end, Japanese aggression. To their credit, the Lyonnais avoided resort to "yellow peril" fantasies, but by the 1930s they had come to fear even Chinese competition in the Indochinese market. The Japanese, however, constituted the main threat there. The Chamber of

Commerce, in face of this menace, took its first step towards protectionism in 1916, and by the 1930s it adopted the ultra-protectionist stand so often excoriated during the previous century. By then, Indochina's proximity to other Far Eastern nations, once presented as an advantage, had become a liability in Lyonnais eyes.

To make matters worse, not only could the Lyonnais no longer influence changes taking place in East Asia, but the French government could do little in coping with them. A new note of acrimony, consequently, entered the exchanges between the Chamber of Commerce and the French government: the Lyonnais grew increasingly petulant and querulous, and the government found it increasingly difficult to disguise its impatience with Lyonnais complaints. Another new note also entered Lyonnais expressions of concern with the Far East, and the tone of Lyonnais accounts of their interests and achievements there changed. Such recitations still served to remind visiting dignitaries that they would have to take Lyonnais concerns into consideration when dealing with the peoples of the Far East, but by the 1930s they also served as ritualistic incantations aimed at raising the spirits of the past and banishing the spectres of the present.

Notes

1. *Modern Asian Studies*, 10, 2 (1976), pp. 225-248.

2. John F. Laffey, "Les racines de l'impérialisme français en Extrême-Orient," *Revue d'histoire moderne et contemporaine*, XVI (April-June 1969), pp. 282-99.

3. "Revision des traités de commerce avec la Chine," *Compte rendu des travaux de la Chambre de Commerce de Lyon, Année 1902* (Lyon, 1903), pp. 256-61. Henceforth this annual publication will be cited as *C.R.T.C.C.L.*. These volumes were always published in the year after the deliberations and the events described in them had taken place. The date included in the cituation will be the date in the title and not the date of publication.

4. The objectives of the mission included the determination of whether Szechuan could be attached to a French "sphere of commercial or direct political influence." Chambre de Commerce de Lyon, *La Mission lyonnaise d'eploration commerciale en Chine 1895-1897* (Lyon, 1898), p. vii.

5. November 24, 1899, *Journal Officiel (Chambre de Députés)*, p. 499.

6. Auguste Isaac, Discours, "Réception de la mission impériale chinoise (27 avril 1906)," *C.R.T.C.C.L.*, *1906*, pp. 262-7, 264-5, 265.

7. "Tarif des douanes chinoises (conversion des droits sécifiques sur les soieries en droits 'ad valorem')," *C.R.T.C.C.L.*, *1903*, pp. 127-33.

8. "Mouvement de la Condition des soies de Lyon, *C.R.T.C.C.L.*, *1904*, p. lxxviii; "Mouvement de la Condition des soies de Lyon," *C.R.T.C.C.L.*, *1906*, p. 64;"Mouvement de la Condition des soies de Lyon," *C.R.T.C.C.L.*,*1910*, p. 60. These percentages include small amounts of Indochinese silk.

9. "Mission au Maroc de M. Mouliéras," *C.R.T.C.C.L.*, *1900*, p. 383; "Réception de la mission marocaine," *C.R.T.C.C.L.*, *1901*, pp. 504-5; "Comité du Maroc (Sousciption)," *C.R.T.C.C. L.*, *1904*, p. 171; "Mission d'exploration commerciale au Maroc, 197 Rapport de M. Alfred Charmetant," *ibid.*, pp. 343-95; "Réception de la mission marocaine," *C.R.T.C.C.L.*, *1909*, pp. 385-6; "Renseignements sur le Maroc," *C.R.T.C.C.L.*, *1912*, p. 424; "Organisation de l'Office cherifien," *C.R.T.C.C.L.*, *1914*, p. 364.

10. "Exposé de la situation industrielle et commerciale de la circonscription de la Chambre de Commerce de Lyon pendant l'année 1911," *C.R.T.C.C.L.*, *1911*, pp. 1-60, 7.

11. "La Situation en Indo-Chine," *C.R.T.C.C.L.*, *1909*, pp. 386-7.

12. "Exposition de Hanoi en 1902-1903," *C.R.T.C.C.L.*, *1902*, pp. 332-3; "Réception de la mission tonkinoise," *C.R.T.C.C.L.*, *1900*, pp. 381-2; "Réception de la mission laotienne," *ibid.*, pp. 382-3; "Réception de la mission annamite," *C.R.T.C.C.L.*, *1902*, pp. 321-3; "Mission indo-chinoise à Lyon," *C.R.T.C.C.L.*, *1906*, pp. 267-8; "Mission indo-chinoise à Lyon," *C.R.T.C.C.L.*, *1908*, p. 290.

13. "Réception de M. Doumer, governeur généal de l'Indochine," *C.R.T.C.C.L.*, *1901*, pp. 470-98.

14. Auguste Isaac, Discours, *ibid.*, pp. 473-82.

15. Paul Doumer, Discours, *ibid.*, pp. 483-98.

16. Auguste Isaac, Discours, "La Colonisation en Indo-Chine—Réception de M. Beau, governeur général de l'Indo-Chine (Rapport de M. Ulysse Pila)," *C.R.T.C.C.L.*, *1905*, pp. 204-53, 204-8.

17. Ulysse Pila, Rapport, *ibid.*, pp. 208-25. For Pila's various undertakings, see Laffey, *Revue d'histoire moderne et contemporaine*, pp. 291-8.

18. Paul Beau, Discours, *ibid.*, pp. *C.R.T.C.C.L.*, *1905*, pp. 226-8.

19. Auguste Isaac, Discours, *ibid.*, pp. 231-8, 235-6.

20. Paul Beau, Discours, *ibid.*, pp. 238-43, 235-36.

21. See fn. 7.

22. See fn. 7.

23. "Convention de commerce entre la France et le Japon," *C.R.T.C.C.L.*, *1911*, pp. 277-82. For the general position of the Chamber in regard to colonial tariff policy, see "Commission du régime douanier colonial," *C.R.T.C.C.L.*, *1909*, pp. 383-4; "Régime douanier colonial," *C.R.T.C.C.L.*, *1910*, pp. 251-7; "Régime douanier colonial," *C.R.T.C.C.L.*, *1911*, pp. 267-72.

24. Jean Coignet, Discours, "Réeption de M. Poincaré, Président de la République," *C.R.T.C.C.L.*, *1914*, pp. 472-82, 476-80, 479.

25. "Exposé de la situation industrielle et commerciale de la circonscription de la Chambre de commerce de Lyon pendant l'année 1914," *ibid.*, pp. 1-51.

26. "Mouvement de la Condition des des soies de Lyon," *C.R.T.C.C.L.*, *1919*, p. 82. The Chinese percentages include small amounts of Indochinese silk.

27. Auguste Isaac, Discours, "Réception de M. Maurice Long, gouverneur général de l'Indochine, le 7 janvier 1921," *C.R.T.C.C.L.*, *1921*, pp. 697-711, 706-11, 710.

28. Régime douanier appliccable en Indo-Chine aux produits japonaise," *C.R.T.C.C.L.*, *1916*, pp. 232-7.

29. "Régime douanier du caoutchouc de provenance étrangère," *C.R.T.C.C.L.*, *1919*, pp. 254-5.

30. *Notes sur la Chambre de commerce de Lyon à usage de ses membres* (Lyon, 1937), p. 10.

31. "Création du Comité lyonnais des intérêts français en Syrie," *C.R.T.C.C.L.*, *1919*, pp. 350-4; "Mission en Syrie. Réception du Général Gouraud," *C.R.T.C.C.L.*, pp. 400-55; "Projet de loi relatif à la mise en valeur des colonies françaises," *C.R.T.C.C.L.*, *1922*, pp. 606-13.

32. "création d'une école d'enseignement technique à Shanghai," *C.R.T.C.C.L.*, *1919*, pp.473-5; "Création d'une ole d'enseignement technique à Shanghai,' *C.R.T.C.C.L.*, *1920*, pp. 549-52.

33. "Subvention en faveur d'une Ecole professionelle à Pekin," *C.R.T.C.C.L.*, *1920*, pp. 470-1; "Ecole des hautes études industrielles et commerciales de Tien-tsin," *ibid*, pp. 471-2; "Ecole des hautes études industrielles et commerciales de Tien-tsin," *C.R.T.C.C.L.*, *1927*, pp. 521-2.

34. "création d'une Université chinoise à Lyon," *C.R.T.C.C.L.*, *1921*, pp. 629-30.

35. "Relévement du tarif douanier chinois," *C.R.T.C.C.L.*, *1919*, pp. 268-9.

36. "Revision du tarif douanier chinois," *C.R.T.C.C.L.*, *1923*, pp. 246-8.

37. "Mission chinoise en France," *C.R.T.C.C.L.*, *1921*, pp. pp. 106-7; "Réception de la mission commerciale chinoise," *C.R.T.C.C.L.*, *1923*, pp. 578-9.

38. "Protestation du commerce de la soie contre la grève des Chinois de Canton," *C.R.T.C.C.L.*, *1924*, pp. 30-1.

39. "Entraves au commerce de la soie à Canton," *C.R.T.C.C.L.*, *1925*, pp. 27-8.

40. "Protection des intérêts français en Chine," *C.R.T.C.C.L.*, *1927*, pp. 26-7.

41. "Exposé de la situation industrielle et commerciale de la circonscription de la Chambre de commence pendant l'année 1927," *ibid.*, pp. 673-819, p. 678.

42. "Mouvement de la Condition des soies de Lyon," *ibid.*, p. 826.

43. "Application par le Gouvernement de Nankin d'une taxe 'ad valorem' à l'importation des marchandises étrangères," *ibid.*, p. 313.

44. "Traité de commerce franco-chinois," *C.R.T.C.C.L.*, *1928*, pp. 251-4.

45. "Renouvellement du privilège de la Banque de l'Indochine," *C.R.T.C.C.L.*, *1922*, pp. 572-3.

46. "Exposé sur la sériciculture en Indo-Chine," *C.R.T.C.C.L.*, *1920*, pp. 153-4; "Développement de la sériciculture en Indochine," *C.R.T.C.C.L.*, *1922*, pp. 194-5; "Développement de la sericiculture en Indochine," *C.R.T.C.C.L.*, *1923*, p. 49; "Développement de la sericiculture en Indochine," *C.R.T.C.C.L.*, *1924*, pp. 29-30.

47. "Visite de l'Empereur d'Annam au musée des tissus," *C.R.T.C.C.L.*, *1922*, p. 805.

48. Jean Coignet, Discours, "Réception de M. Maurice Long, gouverneur général de l'Indochine, le 7 janvier 1921," *C.R.T.C.C.L.*, *1921*, pp. 697-711, 698-701.

49. Maurice Long, Discours, *ibid.*, pp. 701-6.

50. Auguste Isaac, Discours, *ibid.*, pp. 706-11.

51. Louis Pradel, Discours, "Réception de M. Merlin, gouvrneur général d'Indochine; de M. Garbit, gouverneur général de Madagascar, et de M. Carde, gouverneur général de l'Afrique occidentale française, *C.R.T.C.C.L.*, *1923*, pp. 558-72, 550-65.

52. Martial Heni Merlin, Discours, *ibid.*, pp. 570-2.

53. Louis Pradel, Discours, "Réception de Alexandre Varenne, gouveneur général de l'Indochine, et de M. Antonetti, gouveneur de l'Afrique Equatoriale française," *C.R.T.C.C.L.*, *1925*, pp. 368-80, 369-74.

54. Alexandre Varenne, Discours, *ibid.*, pp. 376-80.

55. "Réception de M. Pasquier, gouverneur général de l'Indochine," *C.R.T.C.C.L.*, *1928*, pp. 387-90.

56. Louis Pradel, Discours, *idid.*, pp. 387-90.

57. Pierre Pasquier, Discours, *ibid.*, pp. 390-1.

58. "Mouvement de la Condition des soies de Lyon," *C.R.T.C.C.L.*, *1919*, p. 82; "Mouvement de la Condition des soies de Lyon," *C.R.T.C.C.L.*, *1927*, p. 827.

59. "Réception de M. Paul Claudel, ambassadeur de France au Japon," *C.R.T.C.C.L.*, *1921*, pp. 720-6.

60. "Athénée français de Tokio," *C.R.T.C.C.L.*, *1923*, p. 50; "Cataclysme du Japon," *ibid.*, pp. 525-6; "Mission économique au Japon," *C.R.T.C.C.L.*,*1924*, p. 403; "Désignation d'un pensionnaire à la maison franco-japonaise de Tokio," *C.R.T.C.C.L.*, *1925*, pp. 443-5.

61. "Régime douanier du caouchouc," *C.R.T.C.C.L.*, *1922*, pp. 408-12; "Application à l'Indochine des coefficients de majoration des droits de douaine," *C.R.T.C.C.L.*,*1921*, p. 385; "Application des coefficients de majoration des droits de douanie à l'Indochine," *C.R.T.C.C.L.*,*1922*, pp. 425-8.

62. "Régime douanier applicable en l'Indochine aux produits japonais," *C.R.T.C.C.L.*, *1921*, pp. 383-4.

63. "Institution d'une taxes de 100% 'ad valorem' sur les marchandises de luxe importées au Japon," *C.R.T.C.C.L.*, *1924*, pp. 229-31; "Eventualité de renouvellement de la convention du commerce entre la France et le Japon," *C.R.T.C.C.L.*,*1925*, pp. 198-205.

64. "Eventualité de renouvellement de la convention du commerce entre la France et le Japon," *C.R.T.C.C.L.*, *1925*, pp. 198-205.

65. "Exposé de la situation industrielle et commerciale de la circonscription de la Chambre de commerce de Lyon pendant l'année 1929," *C.R.T.C.C.L.*, *1929*, pp. 599-743, 599; "Exposé de la situation industrielle et commerciale de la circonscription de la Chambre de commerce de Lyon pendant l'année 1935," *C.R.T.C.C.L.*, *1935*, pp. 359-412, 366.

66. *Ibid.*

67. "Séance du 6 octobre," *C.R.T.C.C.L.*, *1938*, pp. 51-3; "Exposé de la situation industrielle et commerciale de la circonscription de la Chambre de commerce de Lyon pendant l'année 1938," *ibid.*, pp. 309-72, 309-14, 317-29.

68. "Application du traité de commerce franco-chinois du 22 décembre 1929," *C.R.T.C.C.L.*, *1929*, pp. 225-6.

69. "Tarif douanier chinois," *C.R.T.C.C.L.*, *1931*, pp. 180-83.

70. "Augmentation du tarif douanier chinois," *C.R.T.C.C.L.*, *1932*, pp. 202-3.

71. "Exchanges commerciaux avec la Chine," *C.R.T.C.C.L.*, *1934*, pp. 230-1.

72. "Réception de M. Naggiar, ambassadeur de France en Chine," *C.R.T.C.C.L.*, *1936*, pp. 53-7, 53-5.

73. Morel Journel, Discours, *ibid.*, pp. 55-7.

74. "Concurrence japonaise dans l'industrie textile," *C.R.T.C.C.L.*, *1932*, pp. 178-80.

75. "La concurrence japonaise," *C.R.T.C.C.L.*, *1934*, pp. 203-7.

76. "Régime douanier marocain." *ibid.*, pp. 223-4.

77. "Régime douanier du Maroc," *C.R.T.C.C.L.*, *1935*, pp. 240-3; "Régime douanier du Maroc," *R.R.T.C.C.L.*, *1936*, pp. 138-9.

78. "Importation des soieries japonaises en Syrie et au Liban," *C.R.T.C.C.L.*, *1935*, pp. 250-1.

79. "Réception de M. Robin, gouverneur général de l'Indochine," *C.R.T.C.C.L.*, *1934*, pp. 30-4, 30.

80. La sériciculture en Indochine -- Allocation d'une prime pour les soies grèges exportées d'Indochine en France et aux colonies," *C.R.T.C.C.C.L.*, *1929*, pp. 14-6.

81. Moreel Journel, Discours, *C.R.T.C.C.L.*, *1934*, pp. 31-4, 34.

82. Tarif douanier indochinois et contrebande en Indochine," *C.R.T.C.C.L.*, *1929*, pp. 211-20; "Tarif douanier indochinois et contrebande en Indochine," *C.R.T.C.C.L.*, *1930*, pp. 206-12; "Contrebande des tissus de royonne japonais en Indochine." *C.R.T.C.C.L.*, *1935*, pp. 248-9.

83. "Protection contre la concurrence japonaise des tissus de soie français importés en Indochine," *C.R.T.C.C.L.*, *1932*, pp. 186-7.

84. "Protection contre la concurrence japonaise des tissus de soie française importés en Indochine," *C.R.T.C.C.L.*, *1933*, pp. 203-6.

85. "Incidence des lois douanières du mois d'octobre 1936 sur les exportations de soieries en Indochine," *C.R.T.C.C.L.*, *1936*, pp. 139-41; "Incidence des nouvelles lois douanièrs sur les exportations de socieres en Indochine," *C.R.T.C.C. L.*, *1937*, pp. 122-3.

86. Difficultés éprouvées par le commerce frano-chinois du fait des évéventements de l'Extrême-Orient," *C.R.T.C.C. L.*, *1937*, p. 292.

87. "Condition des soies," *C.R.T.C.C.L.*, *1938*, pp. 264-72, 270.

88. *Ibid.*

89. "Exposé de la situation industrielle et commerciale de la circonscription de la Chambre de commerce de Lyon pendant l'année 1938," *ibid.*, pp. 309-72, 314.

90. E. Pariset, *Histoire de la fabrique lyonnaise. Etude sur le Régime social et économique et l'Industrie de la Soie à Lyon, depuis le XIV siècle* (Lyon, 1901), p. 340.

3

COLONIAL REFORMISM BEFORE 1914: THE CASE OF *REVUE INIGÈNE*[1]

F rench colonial theory and to a lesser extent practice underwent significant change in the middle of the first decade of the twentieth century.[2] Although never fully implemented and never without critics, a tendency towards colonial assimilation—that assimilation of policies and practices in the colonies to those of the mother country—had characterized the earlier decades of the Third Republic. But the scandals arising in the French Congo, the course and outcome of the Russo-Japanese War which seemed to reveal the precariousness of the hold over Indochina, and, more generally, the feeling that the extensive empire had so far produced very little of what had been expected from it, all suggested that a new orientation was very much in order. By late 1905 the Colonial Minister, Etienne Clémentel, could call for the implementation of a policy of association rather than assimilation. The new orientation would be endorsed enthusiastically by colonialist journals and congresses, for it seemed to make both idealistic and practical sense: if it demanded respect for the native traditions of the peoples of the empire, it also rested upon a calculation that they could be better controlled through their own elites. But given the diversity of the indigenous populations and the differing forces of change to which they were exposed, the associationist orientation never acquired the symmetry of the assimilatinist tendency. Consequently, in the years between 1906 and 1914, colonial practice remained very much in flux and colonial theory remained very much a matter of debate.

At the beginning of this period, in January, 1906, the *Revue Indigène* appeared. It was founded and edited by Paul Bourdarie, a colonial publicist most familiar with French Sub-Saharan and North Africa. He offered the support of his journal to all those who sought the improvement of the living conditions of the native populations over whom France had come to rule. In his view, such improvement required the fulfilment of several conditions:

- First, he called upon the colonial administrations to foster independent peasant proprietorship among the native populations;
- Second, he believed that the French should welcome the emergence of indigenous bourgeoisies, Indeed, they should encourage such a development

by not requiring, either legally or culturally, that such groups abandon their own traditions, religious or otherwise;

- Third, he and his collaborators, self-proclaimed "professors of social hygiene," committed themselves to the defence of the collective and individual rights of the natives.[3]

Perhaps most importantly, they also proclaimed that the improvement of the condition of the natives required their education. While its contents would have to vary in relation to the state of development of the specific indigenous group and in relation to social status within that group, this education was to aim at, most generally, the provision of "the two levers of civilization: the *sense of the future*, through which races raise themselves, and the *sense of foresight*, through which individuals perfect themselves."[4]

Given the nature of this program, Bourdarie expected, accurately enough, collision with "interests and prejudices."[5]

The interests had to do primarily with the stake of the *colons* in large land holdings and cheap labour. A more widely spread racism buttressed these economic interests. Hence, if the programme of the *Revue Indigène* was to succeed, both interests and prejudices would have to be overcome. But the struggle would be worth the effort, for victory in it would not only aid the indigenous populations, but also the metropolitan population. In other words, a prosperous empire would provide French industry with protected markets, and booming industry would benefit the mass of the French nation. Seen in light of such social imperialist considerations, the concerns of the *colons* were but petty, selfish, and short-sighted. Still, once they had come to understand that their real interests were "inseparable" from those of the natives, even the *colons* had a role to play in this imperial scheme.[6] In brief, despite the hatred which the *Revue Indigène* provoked in some colonial circles, Bourdarie and his collaborators remained firm imperialists, a fact further attested to by their support for expansion into Morocco; their suspicions of the Pan-Islamic ploys of Wilhelm II; their adulation of the colonial military heroes, Gallieni and Lyautey; their enthusiastic welcoming of Raymond Poincaré to the presidency; and their careful distancing of their own criticisms of the empire from those of the socialists.

Critical of the empire as it existed, they had no quarrel with the idea of empire. Rather than wishing to dismantle it, they wished to reform it. They wanted to correct "abuses," a word which constantly recurs in their journal. But to recognize their imperialist commitment is not to call into question either their genuinely humanitarian sentiments or the validity of their trenchant criticism of existing colonialist beliefs and practices. Colonial reformism, however, possessed inherent limitations and contradictions, some of which sprang from conditions and events over which the colonial reformers had little or no control. At least such seems to be the lesson of the positions taken by the *Revue Indigène*'s contributors in regard to Indochina.

While the region never came close to attracting the attention devoted to France's North African holdings, the problems which bedevilled Indochina could not be ignored. Indeed, an article in the second issue of the review detected, among the Vietnamese, "seeds of revolt and separation."[7] If the French wished to retain a hold over this population, reforms would have to be implemented. And given the outcome of the Russo-Japanese War, as well as the changes taking place in China and Siam, that would have to be done quickly. Always stressing the need for reforms, the *Revue Indigène* devoted attention to matters like the inadequacy of the indigenous language skills to be found at all levels of the colonial administration, but most dangerously among the magistrates who had to rely on native interpreters; the excessive number of minor French officials; the need for educational institutions which would provide rudimentary skills for the mass of the population and introduce the offspring of the elite to Western notions of science and progress; the vexed issue of the language of instruction; the economic role played by Chinese migrants to the detriment of the Vietnamese and French alike; the racism so widely spread among the French of Indochina; the possibility of making greater use of Vietnamese troops; and the heavy burden of taxation imposed upon the Vietnamese.[8] Obviously, one cannot explore all such matters here, but a discussion of the review's campaigns against the colonial government's opium and alcohol monopolies and its responses to outbreaks of unrest in Indochina should provide some indication of the limitations of colonial reformism.

The opium question was brought to the attention of the *Revue Indigène* in 1906 when, as part of a belated effort at reform, the Manchu government of China decreed that "within a period of ten years the evils arising from foreign and native opium be equally and completely eradicated."[9] The following year the Government of India agreed to reduce progressively the export of opium to China until it would be completely ended in 1917, provided that equal reductions took place in the Chinese production of the narcotic, These developments were not without implications for Indochina where the colonial government purchased opium from both China and India and, after processing, sold it through a monopoly.

Recognizing that attempts to suppress sales in Indochina would threaten the colonial government's finances, Bourdarie and his supporters still argued: "The suppression of the opium habit would have for the European colonies of Asia the best consequences from the point of view of the native populations who, delivered from a passion most unhealthy for the individual and dangerous for his descendants, would acquire, along with the moral liberty of the individual, a greater economic and social capacity."[10] Acknowledging the complexity of the problem, they asked for the opinions of those deemed competent to judge the matter. More specifically, the review wanted to know about the kinds of administrative measures which would best contribute to suppression, the kinds of taxes which should be introduced to replace the government's lost income, and the prospects for cooperation among China, England and France in the eradication of the opium peril. While awaiting the results of these inquiries, contributors pre-judged the matter when they complained, rightly enough, of the reluctance of the colonial administration to take meaningful steps against the use of the drug in Indochina.

The December, 1907 issue of the review was devoted solely to the opium question. Bourdarie began with a ringing declaration of faith in the seriousness of the Chinese effort to stamp out domestic cultivation. Short accounts of the drug and its history followed. When it came to discussion of the global centres of production and consumption, it had to be noted that the distillery of Saigon, which purchased its opium from India, sold on the average 45,000 kilograms of finished product annually and that the distilleries of Tonkin, drawing upon the internal upland regions and especially the Chinese province of Yunnan, sold 84,000 kilograms annually. These sales bought nineteen and a half million francs into the coffers of the Indochinese government in 1905, and the projection for 1907 stood at twenty-one million francs. As the total budget of the colony stood at this point somewhat short of eighty million francs, the matter deserved further scrutiny.

Going back to 1860, when the French first moved into Cochinchina and "one did not profess the same humanitarian sentiments as today," an effort was made to explore the history of the monopoly.[11] The conclusion was clear. And depressing. It had to be admitted that "the opium monopoly has always been the most important of the indirect taxes of first Cochinchina, then Annam-Tonkin, and finally of united Indochina."[12] It also had to be acknowledged that the opium monopoly constituted "one of the most perfect administrative organisms of the colony, it is indeed the only indirect tax which functions well and which causes the administration no vexations."[13] Its only real defect lay in its immorality. Bad enough in Indochina, the ravages of addiction had spread from there to the French ports and then to Paris. A case of addiction in Toulon had even led to espionage. Empire had in a unwanted sense come home, and, hence, the case for suppression of the monopoly appeared to be all the stronger.

Faced with the Chinese initiative and some criticism of the monopoly in the Chamber of Deputies, the metropolitan government seemed willing to move towards suppression. The Colonial Minister had asked the Governor General of Indochina, Paul Beau, to examine the ways in which to end the problem. Beau himself had something of a reputation as a colonial reformer, and some of his measures had won the approval of the *Revue Indigène*. But he ruled out any immediate and complete suppression of the monopoly. He believed that such an action would only provoke discontent among the natives, that it would be impossible to enforce prohibitions until China had stamped out production, and that it would create major fiscal problems for the colony. All that resulted from the ministerial intervention was an order forbidding the use of the narcotic by officials and the formation of a committee to study the problem. Given the composition of the committee, the *Revue Indigène* expected little from it.

Bourdarie and his supporters probably expected more from those who responded to their call for expert opinion. If so, they could only have been disappointed, But they had the courage to run extracts from the largely negative responses, Joseph Chailley, colonial activist and deputy, was blunt: he did "not see the necessity of sacrificing to a need for purely humanitarian demonstration the 12 or 14 million francs that opium brings in yearly to the Indochinese treasury."[14] Another deputy argued, rightly enough, that alcohol constituted a far more serious danger than opium in France. Jules Harmand, old Indochina hand, former ambassador to Japan, and a leading colonial theorist, thought the problem to be "essentially of an administrative and financial order" and, hence, one which should be dealt with at the level of the colonial rather than the metropolitan government.[15] M. Z. did not think that the use of opium could be wiped out in either Indochina or China. He suggested that China had duped Europe and especially England: *"In ten years there no longer be English opium in China, but everybody will be smoking Chinese opium."*[16] Albert de Pourvourvile, another old

Indochina hand, arrived at much the same solution as the colonial government: the price of opium should be raised in order to discourage consumption and a committee should study, without undue haste, this complicated matter. M. Y., an Indochinese official, favoured suppression and suggested that the lost revenues could be made up by a tax on umbrellas and parasols, now items of mass consumption whereas once they had been emblems of mandarinal dignity. Only M. X., described as an "Indochinese personality," provided a somewhat detailed programme for meeting the budget problem, but he doubted that a "satisfactory solution" could be achieved.[17]

If they could hardly rejoice in the results of their inquiries, Bourdarie and his friends put a brace face upon matters. They simply ruled out the comparison between alcoholism in France and opium addiction in the colonies, of course, they opposed alcoholism in France and in the colonies, but that had nothing to do with the issue at hand. Confronting that issue, they refused to doubt the seriousness of the Chinese government's intention to wipe out opium cultivation. They praised England's costly willingness to respond to the Chinese effort. And even if China and England were to withdraw from the struggle, they urged that France move ahead alone to protect the native populations and officials and officers from the ravages of the drug. More specifically in regard to Indochina, they argued that the monopoly should be phased out in a progressive series of steps and that the lost revenues be made up out of budgetary economies and taxes on tobacco and luxury items.

The committee of investigation in Indochina went some way, a very short way, to meet such demands: if it clung to the policy of purportedly discouraging use through raising opium prices, it at least entertained the notion of introducing a tobacco tax and a lottery to replace the income which might be lost to the colony's budget. But as the latter options were not put forward as recommendations, let alone implemented as policies, the *Revue Indigène* remained dissatisfied. It continued to bring to the attention of its readers the spread of addiction within France. And if such notes failed to generate sufficient horror, one could and did turn to the opium dens of London's sinister dockside. One also now had to consider the damages inflicted by the opium derivative, morphine, and this colonialist journal began to pay attention to regulations governing pharmacology. It also opened its pages to conflicting views of the Chinese campaign against the drug: whereas one doctor argued that, whatever the sincerity of the government's wishes, it confronted enormous difficulties when it came to enforcing its will, another medical man commended the effectiveness of its measures. But the matter was thrown into further doubt by the Chinese revolution of 1911. Always more at ease with reformers rather than revolutionaries, Bourdarie and his collaborators noted ruefully that this upheaval had disrupted, at least momentarily, the Chinese struggle against opium.

Throughout this period contributors to the review placed special hope in what could be accomplished through international conferences aimed at dealing with the problem. Noting sadly that French "scepticism accords badly with the idea of a purely humanitarian and social struggle," they welcomed the conference held in 1909 in Shaihai at American initiative.[18] They deplored, however, the weakness of the French position at this conference. But the Shanghai meeting did lead to another conference which, on January 23, 1912, produced The Hague International Opium Convention which outlined some ways of moving gradually to the suppression of all use of opium, morphine and cocaine. The French delegates signed this document. But they did so with the reservation that ratification might have to be obtained from their protectorates and dependencies. In effect, this left the Indochinese government with a veto over measures aimed at suppression. The reformers had lost on the opium issue.

They scarcely fared better when it came to alcohol. Very much opposed to the excessive use of alcohol throughout the empire, Bourdarie and other reformers could only find the situation in Indochina especially outrageous. Since 1897 the monopoly of distillation and sales had been held by a small number of French firms, and each Indochinese province had to buy a fixed amount of their products every month. According to the review, not only did the natives dislike these products, but they resented not being able to use their own alcohol for ritual purposes. Moreover, the taxes on alcohol continued to increase. And the procedures, involving informers, raids and imprisonment, through which the government struck against those engaged in illegal distillation and consumption especially outraged the Vietnamese. As one critic commented ironically, "It seems difficult to make the Annamite understand that the benefit of civilization consists in selling him at high cost a product of prime necessity under the pretext that it is necessary to support a crowd of agents to permit French industrialists to make a fortune rapidly."[19]

The review, however, did not discount the power and influence of those devoted to making such fortunes. It noted that among the major stockholders in the Alcohols Fontaine, the most important concern, could be found officials serving in Indochina or who had served there. Evidence of connivance between the private interests and the public powers could be found in the administration's forcing, at a time of famine, the Tonkinese provinces to purchase alcohol on credit—"with enormous guaranteed interest for the monopoly."[20] Influence of a somewhat different sort was exercised in France itself: when in 1908 the colonial publicist, Albert de Pourvourville, launched a new journal devoted to Indochinese affairs, it shared the same address and telephone number with the Alcohols Fontaine.

The situation appeared to improve, however, when in 1909 Governor General Klobukowski announced that the contracts with the firms which shared in the monopoly would not be renewed upon their expirations. As the Fontaine contract would not expire until 1913, the *Revue Indigène* predicted continued native discontent. But at least the colonial administration seemed to be headed in the right direction. Hence, the shock and disappointment was all the greater when in early 1913 Governor General Sarraut, who had been perceived as a genuine reformer, decided to postpone the ending of the Fontaine contract for another ten years. In the eyes of the *Revue Indigène*, the word of France had been betrayed for 500,000 francs a year. And only a small fraction of this sum would reach a government which still approached the issue in purely fiscal terms when, in fact, it was very much a political matter. The declaration that the colonial government intended to lessen the discontent provoked by the activities of its agents through lowering monopoly prices in order to make them more competitive with contraband prices only provoked derision. Moreover, if the administration really intended to increase opium prices in order to discourage consumption, then the lowering of alcohol prices could be seen as a means of encouraging consumption. Once again the obsession with revenue had interfered with the implementation of sound policy. And once again the cause of reform had been defeated.

Whereas some commentators directly linked the assassination of two French officers in Hanoi in 1913 to the extension of the alcohol contract, others connected it, more generally, to years of colonial misrule. In any event, as their self-proclaimed defender, the *Revue Indigène* registered all such manifestations of native discontent. But there were acceptable and unacceptable expressions of such discount. In 1908, in the wake of tax riots in Annam, the review urged leniency and, describing him as "especially devoted to the French cause," protested against the arrest of a native reformer, Phan Chu Trinh.[21] The arrest in the same year of the naturalized Gilbert Chieu did not lead to a similar protest, but it did provoke reflections on how best to deal with members of a newly emergent elite who, if their legitimate aspirations remained unsatisfied, could gravitate towards subversion. The case of De Tham, the primitive rebel who again rose against the French in 1908, also attracted considerable attention, attention compounded when he managed to hold out until 1913, With the campaign against him taking on both squalid and farcical features and the casualties mounting, the *Revue Indigène* tried to learn more about what had prompted the rising: did De Tham simply seek to take advantage of the admittedly unsettled conditions in northern Tonkin or had the colonial government reneged on the conditions of peace established with him in 1897?

The wave of unrest in 1908, highlighted by the attempt at poisoning the Hanoi garrison, forced the review to devote closer attention to Indochinese conditions. It explained the disturbances in light of intrigues on the part of Japanophiles; unrest in China which encouraged "piracy" in an Indochina which lacked the troops necessary to bring it under control; and "a pacific movement—(with accidents)—of native protest against the fiscal regime, monopolies and taxes."[22] Attacking the hysterical response of many of the French residents of Indochina to the events of 1908, the *Revue Indigène* denied vehemently the charge that its own criticisms of the situation had contributed to the unrest. In any event, the editors had their own notions of how matters should be handled:

- *Strike hard* at those guilty of the Hanoi plot, the fomenters of revolt, and also against those of our compatriots who by lack of discipline (military men or officials) or by actions (civilians) compromise the security of the protectorate.
- *Pardon quickly* the numerous natives whom governmental incoherence has left exposed to all suggestions and all seductions.
- *Correct as quickly as possible* our errors of taxation and administration since they are the efficient cause of disaffection.[23]

But that last proposal would be all the more difficult to implement in that one confronted "thousands of abuses which have enormous importance in the eyes of an increasingly exasperated population."[24]

The bombing of the Hanoi café in 1913, with the deaths of two French officers and a Vietnamese, brought about another reconsideration of the old problems. Once again the editors had to provide explanations of what had happened. They first presented the event as an "accident of colonial policy which does not involve the loyalty of the mass of the population."[25]

"Accidents," incidently, appear almost as frequently as "abuses" within the pages of this journal. But agitation also had to be taken into account, agitation fuelled in part by measures like the extension of the alcohol contract. The defects of the French security arrangements, as well as the racist virulence of the local French press, had also made their own contributions to a tragic occurrence. Such explanations, however, could not disguise a new note of frustration: Bourdarie and his friends remained committed to reforms in Indochina, but they now had a greater sense of the obstacles which they confronted. They were now even prepared to consider the arguments of Onémise Reclus' work of 1904, *Lâchions l'Asie, Prenons l'Afrique*, a work which had been seldom mentioned hitherto, and then in passing, in the review.

Yet Bourdarie could recall that, in the very first issue of the journal, he had called for French economic preponderance in the Asian holdings, but also for "complete autonomy" to be "given progressively to those colonies and the reconstitution of the Annamese, Laotian and Siamese nationalities in order to oppose the Chinese and Japanese nationalities."[26] The *Revue Indigène* had certainly worked for reform in Indochina, but the Southeast Asian colony had never been as important to it as the North African possessions. The loss of Indochina would be painful, but the failure to arrive at meaningful reform in so many areas, not just in regard to opium and alcohol, forced one to consider that possibility.

Faced with the problems posed by Indochina—and, indeed, by all of the Asian empire—Bourdarie and his limited number of supporters proved themselves to be both too sophisticated and not sophisticated enough. Too sophisticated in that their social imperialist programme eclipsed the understanding of *colons*, officials and ideologues blinded by the more immediate interests and prejudices. Not sophisticated enough in that their deep commitment to the empire blinded them to the structural faults intrinsic to it on the eve of World War I. Consequently, they criticized "abuses" and invoked "accidents." Although never as sentimental as their opponents charged, their humanitarianism cannot be placed in doubt. The criticisms voiced by their journal had its uses at the time, and certainly historians have every reason to be grateful to them. But given the course which history was to take in the twentieth century, perhaps these colonial reformers would have done well to reflect upon a remark of Hegel's in regard to the Catholic Church on the eve of the Reformation: "A corrupt state of things is very frequently represented as an 'abuse'; it is taken for granted that the foundation was good—the system, the institution itself faultless—but that the passion, the subjective interest, in short the arbitrary volition of men has made use of that which in itself was good to further its own selfish ends, and all that is required to be done is to remove these adventitious elements."[27]

Notes

1. Serge Courville and Philip Boucher (eds.), Proceedings of Eleventh Meeting of the French Colonial Historical Society, Québec, May 1985 (Lanham: University Press of America, 1987), pp. 159-69.

2. For an account of this shift, see Raymond Betts, Assimilation and Association in French Colonial Theory, 1890-1914 (New York: Columbia University Press, 1961).

3. Paul Bourdarie, "L'Idée indigène," La Revue Indigène, III (Janvier 1908), pp. 1-5, p. 3. Hereafter La Revue Indigène will appear as RI.

4. "Remerciements et Précisions," RI, I (Février 1906), pp. 25-26, p. 26. All emphases in this article appear in the sources cited.

5. "Notre programme," RI, I (Janvier 1906), pp. 1-7, p. 2.

6. Etienne Marsan, "Les 'Questions indigènes' et les futurs congrèses coloniaux," RI, I (Novembre 1906), pp. 182-88, p. 186.

7. Georges Froment, "La polique indigène en Indo-Chine," RI, I (Mars 1906), pp. 53-58, p. 53.

8. There is a lacuna in the wide sweep of criticism which is puzzling—that is, an almost complete silence on the part of the review's contributors in regard to the land concession system in effect in Tonkin, a system which by the end of the first decade of the century had provoked considerable criticism in other quarters, including other colonialist quarters. For this problem, see John F. Laffey, "Land, Labour, and Law in Colonial Tonkin Before 1914," Historical Reflections / Réflexions historiques, II, 2 (Winter,1975) pp. 223-93; and John F. Laffey, "Imperialists Divided: The Views of Tonkin's Colons Before 1914," Histoire sociale / Social History, IX, 19 (May, 1977), pp. 92-ll3.

9. Quoted in W.W. Willoughby, Opium as an International Problem: The Geneva Conferences (Baltimore: The Johns Hopkins Press, 1925), pp. 14-15.

10. La Direction, "Enquête sur le problème international et social de l'opium en Asie," RI, II (Juillet 1907), pp. 233-36, p. 234.

11. "Opium en Indo-Chine," RI, II (Décembre 1907), pp. 455-61.

12. Ibid., p. 456.

13. Ibid., pp. 460-61.

14. "Extraits de quelques Correspondances," Ibid., pp. 489-93, p. 490. Characterizing the review's investigation of the opium problem as "very impartial," Chailley responded to it at greater length in 1908. He argued that the only result of the campaign to end the monopoly would be the reduction of the revenues of Indochina by a fifth. The cultivators and smugglers of Yunnan would be the only ones to benefit from such a measure, for, in his view, opium production in China could not be wiped out. Indeed, he very much doubted that the Chinese government, which derived badly needed income from it, wished to do so. According to Chailley, that government simply wanted to reduce imports from India. As for the ravages of the drug in the colony, he believed them to be exaggerated. Its chief consumers were the Chinese of Saigon and Cholon, always something of an object of envy and fear on the part of Frenchmen concerned with Indochina. In his view, the Vietnamese could scarcely afford it, and the European consumers were few. Its abuse by French officials could be controlled by a third offense bringing dismissal. J. Chailley, "L'opium et le budget de l'Indo-Chine ," RI, III (Mars 1908), pp. 104-09, p. 104.

15. "Extraits de quelques Correspondances," RI, II (Décembre 1907), pp. pp. 489-94, p. 492.

16. Ibid., p. 493.

17. Ibid., p. 492.

18. Gia Dinh, "La Conférence de l'Opium," RI, IV (Août 1909), pp.163-69, p. 163.

19. Gia Dinh, "L'Annamite et le Régie," RI, II (Août 1907), pp. 284-91, p. 290.

20. Jean Ajalbert, "Le régime de l'alcohol en Indochine," RI, iv (Juin 1909), pp. 257-62, p. 259.

21. "Annam," RI, III (Mai 1908), p. 195.

22. La Direction, "La crise indo-chinoise," RI, III (Août 1908), pp. 281-85, p. 282.

23. Ibid., p. 285.

24. Gia Dinh, "Parlons de l'Indo-Chine," RI, III (Août 1908), pp. 293-98, p. 296.

25. La Direction, "Le problème indochinoise," RI, VIII (Mai 19l3), pp. 309-22, p. 313.

26. Ibid., p. 316. For confirmation, see Paul Bourdarie, "La Politique de l''Association," RI, I (Janvier 1906), pp. 1-12, p. 8. The idea of such a "reconstitution" was very likely launched initially to counter fears of a Pan-Asian bloc dominated by Japan which resulted from the Japanese victory over Russia, See John F. Laffey, "Racism and Imperialism: French Views of the 'Yellow Peril,' 1894-19l4," Third Republic / Troisième Rublique, I, 1 (spring, 1976), pp. 4-52.

27. Georg Wilhelm Friedrich Hegel, The Philosophy of History (New York: Dover Publications, 1956), p. 412.

4

FRENCH FAR EASTERN POLICY IN THE 1930s[1]

The completion in 1986 of the *Documents diplomatiques français, 1932-1939* permits a review of French Far Eastern policy during the troubled time characterized by J. B. Duroselle as *"la décadence."*[2] This massive documentary collection, however, still does not provide a full picture of the forces which shaped French East Asian policy in the years before the outbreak of the Pacific War. Understandably focussed upon European developments, it begins and ends, from the Far Eastern perspective, *in media res*; that is, after the outbreak of the Manchurian crisis and before the Japanese occupation of Indochina. Moreover, like other compilations of what statesmen and diplomats said to each other, this one slights economic factors and, though to a lesser extent, the role of public opinion.[3] Even taken in their own terms, the documents perhaps reveal more about what others said and did to the French than about what they themselves accomplished. That points to a more fundamental problem, for one can question whether anything so gelatinous as the French responses or lack thereof to developments largely beyond their control can even be described as "policy." Still, although much more work in archives and private papers will be necessary before the entire story can be pieced together, these documents do shed light upon what passed for French policy in East Asia during the years before the outbreak of World War II.

If the Far East was never of central concern to the Quai d'Orsay during the inter-war years, some attention had to be paid to it in light of France's status as a great power, considerations of trade and investment, and the imperial stake in Indochina. During the 1920s, despite massive turmoil in China and stirring of unrest in Indochina, the accords resulting from the Washington Conference—the Four Power Treaty (December 13, 1921), the Naval Armaments Treaty (February 6, 1922), and the Nine Power Treaty (February 8, 1922)—seemed to have established a framework which, providing for some degree of cooperation among the imperialist powers, guaranteed stability in the region. However, as the decade waned, the nominal unification of China, as well as the onset of the Depression, began to pose new problems. Shortly thereafter, Japanese aggression not only overturned any semblance of an East Asian *status quo*, but began to interact with developments in Europe in a fashion which threatened the entire treaty structure upon which French security rested. While harsh security measures still worked to ensure control over Indochina, the French position in the Far East steadily eroded during the 1930s. Two phases marked this process: the first, lasting from mid-1932 to mid-1937, can be characterized in terms of pessimistic passivity; the second, running from the outbreak of the Sino-Japanese conflict in mid-1937 to that of the European war in early September 1939, in terms of ineffectual reactions to an unfolding nightmare. Informing both phases, however, were certain continuities: the impotence intrinsic to a vastly over-extended imperial commitment, an inability to reach meaningful accords with other powers interested in the preservation of stability in the East Asia, and a combination of arrogance and fear deeply rooted in racism.

Although the initial Japanese move into the area had taken place months before, the Manchurian crisis remained unresolved when the *Documents diplomatiques français* begins. The Japanese aggression, the investigations and conclusions of the Lytton Commission, the creation of the puppet state of Manchukuo, and the more general ramifications of the crisis could not be ignored by the French. Possessed of their own interests in East Asia, they would also be subjected to pressures exerted by other interested parties. Already conducting their own para-diplomacy, Japanese military men proved remarkably persistent in this regard. In early July 1932 the Vice Minister of War suggested to the ambassador in Tokyo that Japan would need capital to develop Manchuria and only France could supply it. The next day the Japanese military councillor at the Geneva Disarmament Conference urged that, if France backed Japan before the League, the way would be open to a mutually beneficial arrangement whereby France would be strengthened against Russia and Indochina protected against Communism, and Japan would acquire the European ally it had lacked since the Washington Conference. Two months later, when the Japanese Minister of War visited Admiral Berthelot aboard his flagship, he emphasized the advantages of closer and closer rapprochement.[4]

The French reacted to such proposals with the greatest reserve. As René Masigli explained to the military councillor in Geneva, France had to consider not only relations with Japan, but also those with other nations, especially the United States at a time when the war debt issue had become pressing, and, more generally as a signatory of the treaty establishing the League, could not "contract engagements which would be in contradiction with the principles of this pact."[5] Both problems were real enough. Seeking to rally support for the Stimson Doctrine, the Americans seemed to have made their position brutally clear when their representative at the Geneva Conference declared in what was purported to be a confidential interview for journalists: "If when it comes to the application of the Nine Power Treaty, France avoids compromising her relations with Japan, then the United States, to which German armaments matter little, has no interest in damaging her relations with the Reich."[6] The Chinese, for their part, stressed not only the violation of their rights, but also the extent to which "the sanctity of and inviolability of international treaties is in danger."[7] Given such conflicting pressures, a French diplomat could explain to a Japanese colleague that his country's policy involved "the desire to remain faithful to the League of Nations Treaty while taking into great account the special interests of Japan."[8] But however significant the French concern with those "special interests," the Japanese definition of their scope made it all the more impossible to square that particular diplomatic circle. Still, it turned out that the American position was by no means as firm as had been suggested in Geneva. Eight days after the proclamation of a Japanese protectorate over Manchukuo (September 15, 1932), not a single Western power had presented official observations to the Japanese government, a delay which the French Chargé d'affaires in Tokyo realized would weaken any subsequent protests. Clearly peace itself, rather than the treaty obligations designed to secure such peace, was becoming of paramount importance.

The crisis, however, could not simply be wished away. Indeed, it deepened with the submission of the Lytton Report to the League on October 4, 1932. Confronted with the Report, the French delegation was clear enough about the goals which it would seek to realize:

- To safeguard the authority of the League of Nations and procedures of the pact;
- To lead, in a form to be determined, the United States and the Soviets to participate in a definitive settlement;
- To gain time, the Japanese not being presently disposed to adopt the fundamental solutions with which one could present them, and time would incline them more to conciliation in light of the growing seriousness of the economic and financial crisis through which they are passing.[9]

These goals provoked the consideration of various courses of action at the Quai d'Orsay. If the notion of accepting the Report in its entirety was dismissed quickly enough, the ideas of the British representative at the League, Sir Eric Drummond, received closer attention, but only to be also rejected. The preferred option envisioned the League Assembly approving the conclusions of the Report and inviting the signatories of the Nine Power Pact, as well as Germany and the Soviet Union, to intervene in the Sino-Japanese dispute, with Assembly opposition to the recognition of Manchukuo to be balanced by a condemnation of boycotts and a downplaying of the kind of political and economic aid for China which Drummond had championed.

The French frustration with the situation found expression, along with darker sentiments, in a memorandum prepared by the Asia-Oceania section of the Quai d'Orsay in mid-January, 1933. It began with history or what purported to be such:

> The first years of the XXth century witnessed the zenith of the worldwide expansion of the white race. The fall of Port Arthur marked its first recoil and the Treaty of Portsmouth consecrated for, for the first time, a victory of the yellows over the whites. After that came the World War, with the antagonism of the great white nations, with some defeated and others weakened, while China and Japan, without having fought, appeared at Versailles among the conquerors of Germany and Austria. A permanent member of the League Council, Japan found itself promoted to the first rank among the great powers and called upon to intervene in the settling of European affairs.[10]

Certain concessions did have to be made to the Japanese: they had not really involved themselves in European affairs, could complain justifiably about the Chinese, and did need outlets for their population and commodities. The problem lay with their military men who, borrowing from the "blood and iron" prescriptions of Bismarck, had committed themselves to a "methodical programme of an unrestrained imperialism."[11] More fundamentally, "however perfect the utilization by Japan of Western technique, nothing of the moral and intellectual discipline of the West had penetrated the Japanese mentality."[12]

Hence, it had to be concluded that Japanese reaction to a League condemnation would be violent, and French interests in East Asia would be affected by it. Those interests were defined in territorial, political, economic and moral terms. If Japan constituted a threat to French, British and American possessions in the region, there was also, from the French perspective, yet another danger:

> It would be both unjust and imprudent to give the blame incurred by Japan the significance of unreserved approval of Chinese claims and methods. Besides it would be dangerous to encourage any solution which would involve the reorganization, with or without Japan, of a unified and disciplined China, which would constitute an immediate danger on the very frontier of Indochina.[13]

Turning to the political dimension of the situation, the Foreign Ministry's experts explained that the Japanese overtures of the previous summer had been rejected because they ran counter "to all the principles of general policy consecrated, since the war, by the signature of France."[14] Economic problems were discounted: French investors in Japan had no cause for complaint, and the stake in trade with Japan was considerably less than that of Great Britain. Recognizing that increased tension between Japan and France would affect adversely that nebulous element central to the rhetoric of many French imperialists, the Asia-Oceanis section wasted no time on sentimentality: "These intellectual interests, however precious, cannot be compared with a question which places at risk the general policy of France."[15] The Quai d'Orsay, in brief, recognized the paramount significance of the existing treaty structure, but with the important qualification that France had no interest in a stronger China.

As was often the case in regard to Far Eastern matters, while French diplomats might propose, others disposed: the spring of 1933 witnessed Japan's withdrawal from the League and, when returning from Geneva, Foreign Minister Matsuoka's disquieting stop in Berlin. Still, the French government seems to have accepted the situation of its representative in Japan who observed that "short of really effective economic sanctions, which none of the great powers appear disposed to adopt, it is inopportune to seek in half measures, without real import but still humiliating for the Japanese, new satisfactions for the League of Nations."[16] The Japanese problem, however, would not go away. Their expansion continued in the northern Chinese provinces where their army purportedly promised "to deliver the country from servitude to white foreigners."[17] Like the British and the Americans, the French expressed concern over this development. But they were hardly prepared to do anything about it. When the Chinese requested the aid of the three powers in ending the continuing conflict, the French Minister in China urged caution upon an already suitably cautious Foreign Minister. France was, of course, in favour of "a *suspension of hostilities*" but had "to avoid...any participation in a combination which would pre-judge the fixing of the border between China and Manchuria."[18] With Chiang Kai-shek and T.V. Soong locked in a bitter struggle for power within the Kuomintang, the domestic condition of China only reinforced this sense of the need for caution.[19] Paris, in fact, received the same advice from its diplomats in China and Japan: do nothing for the time being. The wisdom of such counsel seemed to be confirmed when peace of a sort came to East Asia with the signing, on May 31, 1933, of the Tangku Truce.

The Sino-Japanese problem still refused to disappear. Against a background of continuing tension, the Chinese stepped up their efforts to obtain Western aid. In mid-July a Colonel Pei, a personal secretary of Chiang Kai-shek, spent an evening with the French Chargé d'affaires in Nanking. Presumably speaking for Chiang, he presented a compromise with Japan as inevitable, but stressed the need for Western aid in order to realize domestic reforms. Complaints about French conduct, or the lack thereof, followed; whereas the other Western powers had tried to adjust to the changes in China, France had remained "immobile, uncertain, and distant."[20] When asked what might be done to correct this "regrettable error of interpretation," the Colonel replied that Chiang wished "to confide to France the economic and military organization of the Northwest provinces, as an advanced bastion against the disintegration of these regions by Soviet or Japanese influences."[21] Turning to domestic politics, Pei emphasized the close ties between Chiang and Soong. While the Minister in China had cause to doubt the closeness of those bonds, he still though it possible that, if Chiang secured the cooperation of Soong, he might be able to construct a semi-Fascist regime, and, noting the growing influence of Italy in China, suggested that his country provide a more positive sign of friendship by implementing the tariff clauses of the Sino-French Convention of 1930. That suggestion, of course, stopped well short of taking over economic and military responsibilities in the northwest of China.

The French had scant interest in provoking the Japanese and even less in angering the Soviets. In face of the Nazi peril, they were now working to improve relations with the Soviet Union:

> ...in September 1933 Edourd Herriot and Pierre Cot visited Moscow to discuss the possibility of an entente. That prospect, however, alarmed the Asia-Oceania section at the Quai d'Orsay. In the view from this quarter, Japan was supposed to be preparing for war with the USSR, and France might find herself committed by treaty to a struggle with the Japanese rather than the Germans. Ghosts of French dilemmas during the Russo-Japanese War stalked the scene: French aid for Russia would provoke a Japanese threat to possessions in the Far East which France might not be able to defend successfully. Hence, it was suggested that "perhaps" it would be well to hold off on any arrangement with the Russians until they and the Japanese had come to an agreement over the Chinese Eastern Railway and concluded a Non-Aggression Pact.[22]

While the Japanese displayed some concern about the Franco-Soviet conversations in regard to Russia's entry into the League of Nations, the possibility of Western aid for China agitated them more strongly.[23] On April 18,

1934, the Japanese government issued a statement which bluntly warned the Chinese not to seek foreign aid and cautioned foreign powers that, in the present circumstances, cooperative efforts in China, "even under the name of technical or financial assistance." would be interpreted in political terms.[24] In the view of Fernand Pila, the newly arrived ambassador in Japan, the Japanese government had never before "so markedly defined the role it intends to play and reserves for itself in the Far East."[25] Seeing the document as a decisive step in the elaboration of a Japanese Monroe Doctrine, Pila interpreted it primarily as a call for direct negotiations with China which would end in Japanese hegemony over that country. Although Japanese diplomats soon challenged such an extreme interpretation, Louis Barthou, Minister of Foreign Affairs, thought that "the questions posed...would normally involve the consultative prescribed for the signatory powers of the Washington Treaty" and wanted to know how the Americans and British would respond to this latest indication of Japan's willingness to go it alone.[26] It turned out that the Americans had no interest in invoking the treaty: their ambassador to Tokyo, along with his British colleague, simply queried the Japanese premier as to the import of the statement. Delivering a written explanation of his government's attitudes and policies to the Quai d'Orsay, a Japanese diplomat would thank the French for not even pursuing the matter that far and would note that Japan had no cause to complain of French policy. The French responded by welcoming the assurances in regard to China and the foreign interests there, but went on to note that international cooperation, the forms of which had been outlined at the Washington Conference, provided the Japanese with the means of dealing with developments which appeared to threaten their interests. Having reaffirmed the sanctity of treaty obligations, Barthou comforted himself with the notion that the French had pleased both the Japanese and the Chinese.

Pila, in Tokyo, took a less sanguine view of the situation. Confronted with issues like the Russo-Japanese tension along the Manchurian border, the negotiations over the Chinese Eastern Railway, the upcoming naval talks, and the expansionist plans of the increasingly influential Japanese military, he tended to relate them all, in one fashion or another, to his obsession with the likelihood of a Japanese-sponsored Monroe Doctrine in East Asia which would entail the destruction of the Washington settlement and, by extension, of the Western interests which it buttressed.

A wide-ranging interview with premier Hirota allowed him to voice some of his concerns, but he could not have been satisfied with its tenor. Hirota made it clear that the Japanese would insist upon excluding from the initial naval discussions and from the conference itself those questions "which would affect directly the position of Japan in the Far East, for Japan is solely in charge of and responsible for that position; *therefore*, there would be no discussion of Manchukuo or the Nine Power Treaty."[27] As for Russo-Japanese relations, the premier thought that something less than "perfect cordiality" would continue for a long time along the frontiers and observed ambiguously that the Chinese Eastern Railway issue "which has sometimes appeared as a tragedy could very well end as something of a comedy."[28] He viewed Sino-Japanese relations more optimistically: some agreements had already been reached, and if they had not been announced, it was because the Japanese did "not wish to compromise the Nanking government or even to inconvenience it on the eve of the Fifth Kuomintang Congress."[29]

Hirota went on to dismiss rumours of a renewal of the Anglo-Japanese alliance and any need for a Pacific pact comparable to the Locarno treaty. He even more firmly rejected the notion of reestablishing ties with the League of Nations. Although dismissed by Hirota and, indeed, by the British themselves, the rumours of a renewed Anglo-Japanese alliance were taken seriously in some quarters.[30] When the section of the French Naval Staff concerned with armaments turned its attention to Japan, it readily envisioned a British recognition of Manchukuo and the eventual conclusion of a new entente. But this prediction was but a subordinate part of a larger analysis of the East Asian situation in which much turned on France's relations with the Soviet Union. The naval men expected the continuation of Russo-Japanese tension: the resolution of the Chinese Eastern Railway problem simply opened the way for new trouble, especially in regard to Outer Mongolia. Moreover, with their imperialist intrigues in northern China now apparently threatened by the Soviet Union's increasingly pro-Western attitudes, the Japanese had fallen back on blaming the French for this new situation. Here two different interpretations of the Soviet entry into the League of nations collided.

According to the Japanese, "the Soviets hope to find in the League of Nations support which can facilitate the realization of their political objectives and allow them to gain eventually moral and material aid against Japan."[31] The French, on the other hand, had sought to assure the Japanese that their policy "of rapprochement with the Soviets was dominated solely by European preoccupations and sought first of all to detach the USSR from Germany.[32] As the Japanese clung to their own point of view, the French officers turned their attention to the possibility of a deterioration in Franco-Japanese relations and, more concretely, to what "will happen to French interests in the Far East in case of an outbreak of conflict in the Pacific."[33] Nursing no illusions about the strength of the French position in the region, they posed a stark choice:

- Either to allow the violation of our neutrality, which scarcely seems worthy of a great power interested in maintaining its sovereignty;
- Or to declare ourselves in favour of one of the belligerents, either Japan or the USSR.[34]

Inevitably the officers rejected the first option and called for a strengthening of the defences of France's possessions in the Pacific, but they also made no secret of their misgivings:

> The entry of the Soviets into the League of Nations will lead us, in effect, more than ever before, to remain in the wake of the anti-Japanese policy which has been practised until now by the Geneva establishment and will thus lead us, inevitably, to take the side of the USSR against Japan.[35]

While fearing the intrigues of the British and others in regard to the naval issue, the French themselves did not pursue an especially straightforward policy. Still deeply resentful of the parity with Italy imposed at Washington and now deeply concerned about their European security, they looked forward to a Japanese denunciation of the Five Power Treaty. But they also feared the isolation which could result from angering the Americans and British by public support of the Japanese position. Hence, when pressed strongly by the Americans and the Japanese before and after the initial naval discussions, they did everything possible to remain non-committal. At the Naval Conference itself, recognizing that the Japanese were no more sympathetic to their specific concerns than the Americans, they tried not to intervene too directly in the debates. Still, it came as a relief when Admiral Robert could finally declare that France would not be bound henceforth by the parities adopted in 1922. In other words, having begun the decade with a commitment to the sanctity of all which they had signed, the French now gladly observed the destruction of one of them. If it was abandoned in keeping with its provisions, such would henceforth be less and less the case. More specifically, the Five Power Treaty had been an integral part of the more general Washington framework which at least paid lip service to the integrity of China.

The Asia-Oceania section at the Quai d'Orsay had had no difficulty in relating the Japanese denunciation of the Washington parities to the idea of a Japanese Monroe Doctrine for the Far East. Recognizing that the Japanese need for markets gave them a stake in good relations with other countries, it still warned against any illusions in this regard: "If Japan does not desire war, it is prepared to make it, and its military party supports it. It is only to the extent that the Nanking government shows itself willing to accept all the conditions, both political and economic, which Japan will impose upon it that it will be possible to avoid Far Eastern conflict."[36] The view from Peking, however, was more nuanced: "For two years, whereas the Japanese have known how to obtain from the Chinese, in factual terms, all the practical advantages desired, the Chinese can flatter themselves for not having abandoned an inch of the inaccessible terrain of principles. All the resources of the Chinese imagination, involved for centuries in the art of saving appearances, contribute to the display. It could still last for a long time."[37] But a new element came into play when Wang Ching-wei, the Chinese Foreign Minister, declared himself in favour of close Sino-Japanese friendship. That statement forced the French Minister to China to look further ahead and, in doing so, to return to an old theme: arguing that "the eventuality of a Sino-Japanese alliance could be full of menace in regard to the concerns of the white powers in the Far East," he warned that "it is necessary to accept it as quasi-inevitable and it would be wise to prepare for it."[38]

Wang had a chance to explain his position in an interview with the French Minister: "Comparing China to a man who, after submitting to an amputation (the secession of Manchuria), now saw his jugular vein being cut (the massive buying of silver by the American Treasury)," he now wanted "the reestablishment of normal and even cordial relations with Japan."[39] Seen from his perspective, China's real hope lay in an international loan participated in by the Japanese. As it appeared that some action might well have to be taken in face of China's deepening monetary crisis, the French Foreign Ministry consulted with the Finance Ministry and the Bank of Indochina before reaching a sobering conclusion:

> If from the economic point of view it seems expedient not to leave the Chinese government grappling with difficulties which could have repercussions throughout the world and especially in our Far Eastern colonies, if it seems equally necessary not to allow only the Japanese government the task of restoring the Chinese economy as that would lead to Japan's domination of China, it is also indispensable to approach the financial assistance of the Chinese government with the greatest prudence.[40]

Caution seemed all the more appropriate in that the British Treasury, which the French also consulted, saw major technical and political obstacles to the reorganization of Chinese finances. Still, after the British despatched Sir Frederick Leith-Ross to investigate the situation, his efforts helped to bring about the Chinese decree which forbade payment in silver and required foreign banks in China to turn over their silver reserves at a price fixed by the government. Although the British and the Americans financially backed the measure, the French chargé d'affaires in China very much doubted that it would work.

Japanese hostility to the decree soon over-shadowed French skepticism in regard to it. Whether or not the day was selected for its special connotations, on November 11, 1935, the Japanese Foreign and War Ministries issued statements sharply critical of it. As was only to be expected by now, the War Ministry's statement was the blunter of the two: "the decision of the Chinese government can lead China to a catastrophe in face of which Japan could not remain inactive."[41] In point of fact, the Japanese military had not been, nor would it be, "inactive," for it had extended its activities in north China and had continued to threaten an advance below the Great Wall. Faced with this threat, the Chinese asked the British and Americans, but not the French, to intervene diplomatically on their behalf, but only to be rebuffed. But having come to believe that the Japanese army aimed at bringing north China into closer economic bonds with Manchuria and the mother-country, a prospect which boded ill for Western interests in the region, the French became more active. The ambassador to Washington urged, in early November 1935, that the time had come for the powers with interests there consult about north China. But as the Americans still wished to avoid anything resembling an invocation of the Nine Power Treaty, the French had to settle for a press conference at which Cordell Hull, the Secretary of State, voiced a concern with the situation. Hardly impressed by such expressions of foreign opinion, on the night of February 25, 1936, young Japanese assassinated several cabinet ministers deemed opposed to further expansion on the Asian mainland.

Two days later the French Chamber of Deputies ratified the Franco-Soviet Pact. Rousing memories of the Russo-Japanese War, it made a bad impression in Japan where the Foreign Ministry noted that it "will only favour, with all the risks involved, Soviet policy in the Far East."[42] Insisting that the pact applied only to Europe and would become inoperative if either of the signatories attacked a third nation, the French assured Hirota that France aimed at being both an "influential friend of Japan and a quasi-ally of Russia."[43] He replied that, while he understood their position, the French must also understand that "the

Japanese people cannot forbid themselves from thinking that the pact, by reinforcing the security of the Soviets in Europe, will allow them to increase their military forces in the Far East and, thus, will facilitate their policy of expansion and even aggression."[44] Attempting to arrive at a more general appreciation of the matter, the Quai d'Orsay decided that "the peoples of the Far East are...little accessible to juridical reasoning; interest alone motivates them" and, therefore, would have to be catered to through diplomatic action.[45] This meant, concretely, that French diplomacy should work to lessen Russo-Japanese hostility by encouraging the demilitarization of the common frontier sought by the Japanese and the non-aggression pact aimed at by the Russians. Even if the chances of France serving as a successful mediator between Russia and Japan were scant, no consideration seems to have been given to the possibility that a genuine relaxation of tensions along the Manchurian and Mongolian borders, though it might increase Russian strength in Europe, would allow the Japanese to devote more attention to China and even to Indochina.

Still, despite the intense Japanese concern with the frontiers shared by the Russians, the French ambassador in Tokyo soon began to worry about the emergence of a southern orientation in their policy, an economic orientation backed by the navy. Such visions darkened when incidents in China brought Japanese warships into the South China Sea and gave rise to rumours of a coming Japanese occupation of the island of Hainan. While that did not occur, its very possibility prompted uneasy reflections on the part of the French:

> Because of its geographical position...Hainan is a strategic position of the first order, for it commands the Gulf of Tonkin, our ports of Haiphong and Tourane, and the Singapore-Hongkong route. In the hands of the Japanese, the island would surely rapidly become a well-organized naval, air and military base and would constitute a permanent menace to the security of Indochina and the freedom of communications with the Far East.[46]

Compounded by growing evidence of Siamese sympathy for Japan, this unease gave way to gloom with the reflection that protests in regard to the occupation of Hainan would most likely be ineffectual: having failed to invoke their 1907 accord with Japan in relation to Manchuria, the French would find it difficult to make use of it in regard to Hainan.

To make matters worse, on November 25, 1936, Germany and Japan came together in the anti-Comintern Pact. Although the French ambassador in Tokyo did not believe that it would actually change much in the Far East, he soon found himself having to insist repeatedly, much to the annoyance of his Soviet colleague, that France's ties with Russia, being limited to European considerations, involved no danger for Japan. Yet when the military attaché in Tokyo tried to account for the decline of French influence there he placed the blame squarely on the Franco-Soviet Pact. In the covering letter with which he forwarded the report, the ambassador went further in noting that the attaché had not considered "the serious damage done to our authority in this country, where one fears communism like the plague, by certain domestic disorders magnified, I hope, by a hostile international press."[47] In brief, the politics of the French Popular Front had intruded into Franco-Japanese relations or at least into the diplomatic reporting of them. Be that as it may, the ambassador was on surer ground in arguing that the shift in Japanese opinion had also been brought about "by the prodigious success of Germany in achieving repudiations without sanctions."[48]

If Japan had to be courted further, China could not be wholly ignored. On December 12, 1936, the troops of General Chang Hsueh-liang staged the kidnapping of Chiang Kai-shek at Sian in a murky affair which rouses some sympathy for the analysts at the Quai d'Orsay who concluded: "Chinese politics are too complex for it to be possible to follow all the detours and to foresee the results."[49] As it took time for these results to become clearer, the French ambassador to China could still envision, as late as March 11, 1937, the possibility of a Sino-Japanese settlement, brought about by the Germans and Italians, which would allow the Chinese to turn their attention to the campaign against extraterritoriality. But as early as February 2, 1937, his colleague in Moscow had caught the possible implications of the changing attitudes toward each other on the part of the Nationalists and Communists. By April 28, 1937, the ambassador to Japan could refer to "a phenomenon which, if it became well established, would be the most important event—perhaps the only event having genuine importance in the whole Far East...the awakening of China to the consciousness of its unity and the birth of a Chinese patriotism."[50] In his view, the new Chinese nationalism would force the Japanese to moderation, but in order to secure a settlement, the Chinese themselves would have to become more moderate. Confronted with this scenario, Foreign Minister Yvon Delbos scribbled on the margin of the despatch: "From there it is only one step to a novel."[51]

The French military attaché in Tokyo perhaps took that step when he suggested that, if met by Chinese moderation, that forced upon the Japanese by Chinese national sentiment would "mark a check in the constant ascension of this country during the last half century."[52] Seeing war as "an eventuality to envision very seriously," his colleague in China was much less sanguine.[53] Prepared to think in terms of a Japanese war against both China and Russia, he deemed it unlikely that the Japanese would be in a position to invade Indochina, though they would be able to cut the maritime link between France and its colony. Still, in his view, the possibility of a Japanese invasion could not be completely discounted. He made two points in regard to that possibility: first, the Japanese would move initially to secure Hainan and, second, though he knew it "will cause smiles," he urged that "it would be expedient not to neglect the aid that China could bring us."[54]

A week later, on July 7, 1937, Chinese and Japanese troops clashed at the Marco Polo Bridge outside Peking. As the fighting began to spread, Delbos sought for "a method of action which obliges the United States to assume immediately its share of the common responsibilities of the states which signed the Nine Power Treaty."[55] While American participation would have been necessary for any effective action, this interest in involving the United States also sprang from a desire to prevent the Chinese from carrying their case to the League where the French posited two unpalatable courses of action for its Council:

Either the Council, giving into considerations of expediency, will delay and seek to cover its weakness by subterfuges, and it is unnecessary to emphasize the risks which this will entail for the prestige of the institution. Or it will enter resolutely upon the path opened by Article 16 and consequently will move towards sanctions, and it is equally easy to measure the dangers, especially in the current circumstances, of such a policy.[56]

In the latter case, sanctions would have only "a relative effectiveness," and France, "very vulnerable in Indochina, will be the first to feel the consequences."[57]

With the Americans displaying no interest in French representations, the situation worsened, on September 11, when premier Hirota drew the French ambassador's attention to press reports of their backing a Chinese appeal to the League and pointed to "the bad effect" of such support on France "whose interests in the Far East are not at all opposed to those of Japan."[58] Learning shortly thereafter that Hirota had complained to his British colleague about the French supplying China with war material via the Hanoi-Yunnan-fu railway, the ambassador began to wonder whether the groundwork might not be being laid for the bombing of the railway on the Chinese side of the frontier or a move directed against Hainan or the southern Chinese city of Pakhoi. In other words, only slightly more than two months after the incident in north China, the undeclared war had expanded to the extent that French interests in south China might be threatened.

Fears in regard to Indochina itself came from Governor General Brevié who, in September, drew the government's attention to the inadequacy of the arms at his disposal: "If Indochina one day finds itself in face of a Hainan occupied by the Japanese and before a Siamese army equipped and officered by them, it will be an even more dangerous situation than at present when we have a 150 day supply of Lebel cartridges, a 75 day supply of grenades, and a 80 day supply of light artillery munitions."[59] Two months later he returned to the same theme: "The fact that Indochina is practically lacking all means of maritime defence and has only an inadequate aviation can lead to an aggression or even a blockade of our coasts."[60]

Although they paid some attention to other French interests in East Asia, the analysts at the Quai d'Orsay focussed their concern upon the stakes in Indochina and the Chinese provinces which bordered it. In their view, the security of Indochina dictated special alertness in regard to Hainan and the Paracels archipelago. The attention of the Japanese government had already been called to France's "special interest" in Hainan, "an interest recognized in 1898 by the Chinese government under the form of an engagement not to cede it to a third party" and to the sovereignty claimed over the Paracels by France and China "which could not be weakened in regard to a third party."[61] If the initial Japanese reactions to this message had been favourable, they had reversed themselves in light of a concern with "the role...played by Indochina in supplying war material to China."[62] As for the neighbouring Chinese provinces, the analysts noted, along with the importance of the Hanoi-Yunnan-ful railway, that a French banking consortium had been approached by the Chinese government in regard to a line from Langson to Nanning with then a further extension to the Canton-Hankow line. But the Councillor of the Japanese embassy in Paris had warned recently that war material moving along the Yunnan line would provoke bombing raids against both it and the projected new line. The Quai d'Orsay thought that the results of such raids would be catastrophic: "In the first case there will result for a French company considerable material damage for which it surely will never be compensated. In the second case, the realization of a work of vital importance to French economic influence in south China will be retarded for a long time."[63] The French, all in all, faced a choice between "efficacious support for China and the risks which this support poses for our Asian possessions."[64] The solution recommended was that the government should allow the export of arms to China on the part of both national and private manufacturers, but it should also forbid their transit across Indochina.

Such contortions were matched in Geneva where a French delegate to the League's Consultative Committee on the Far East expressed sympathy for China, but pointed to the constraints imposed by the European situation and the reluctance of Washington to take a strong stand. But Chinese persistence in arguing their case soon dissipated such verbal good-will, and the delegate ended in congratulating himself that, in the deliberations of the committee, "conscious of the dangers for our possessions, which a hostile attitude towards Japan would entail, conscious also of the weakness of our means against so resolute an adversary, conscious finally of our need for free hands in Europe, England and ourselves are constantly found in strict accord with the Netherlands and Australia in preferring a sense of realities and responsibilities to a blind, perilous and sterile dogmatism."[65] Such dogmatism, of course, had to do with the provisions of the League's Charter. Not surprisingly, then, the decision to hold a Nine Power Conference in Brussels provoked sighs of relief in Geneva.

Recognizing that the Brussels Conference might lead to a reversal of policy, the French government still banned the transit of war materials across Indochina with the hope that "Japan will respond to our attitude with an equal consideration of our situation."[66] Implying for the French an unspoken bargain with the Japanese, the ban was a crippling enough blow to China for Washington to intervene. Speaking through Under-Secretary of State Sumner Welles and off the record, as well as disclaiming any intention of interfering in French affairs, the American President voiced his concern. Although he did not respond immediately to this intervention, Delbos began to worry about whether the French had gone too far in favouring the Japanese. Confronted with these qualms, the ambassador in Tokyo swiftly brought him back to the reigning interpretation of reality: with the security of Indochina being the matter of primary importance, "our situation in the Far East is of extremely vulnerable in relation to a country as militarily powerful and ferociously egotistic as Japan."[67] Noting the virulent anti-British campaign being conducted in Japan, he went on to warn that "if the Japanese navy fabricates or lets circulate the rumour that it would be advantageous to attack Hongkong, it could just as well turn its attention to Haiphong if we abandon the ban on the transit of war material through Indochina."[68]

Delbos carried the French dilemma to Brussels in early November: "Since the transit can scarcely take place except through Indochina, we risk either, by refusing it, paralysing China or, by reopening it, provoking Japanese reprisals which in that case we do not wish to face alone."[69] Hence, he suggested a coordination of the activities of the British, American, and French fleets. If Antony Eden liked that idea, the American delegate, Norman Davies did not. According to Delbos, Davis declared that "America would be prepared to renounce the Philippines if that could contribute to peace" and suggested "very discreetly that France might perhaps manifest similar sentiments by not being inflexible on the subject of Indo-china."[70] Whatever the exact nature of that proposal, Davis further offended Delbos by also proposing a working committee composed of Great Britain, the United States, and a smaller state, either Belgium or Holland. Delbos found it incredible that his country, "the country most interested int the Far East," should be excluded from this committee.[71] Suspicion in regard to the American position was not really alleviated after the Chargé d'affaires in Washington and a former Minister of Colonies, Jacques Stern, met the president who, after returning to his distaste for the transit ban, assured his guests that *a Japanese attack against Hongkong, Indochina, or the Dutch Indies would also constitute an attack on the Phillippines.*"[72]

Despite this verbal assurance, the French still suspected that they had been selected to go it alone on behalf of the other Western powers, and, in replying to the president's earlier intervention, they stressed that "the dangers which could menace Indochina are neither imaginary nor distant" before concluding that this made it impossible "to modify our present position as long as we remain in uncertainty in regard to the degree of international cooperation" which might be achieved in Brussels.[73] The Brussels meeting, however, failed to produce either compromise or cooperation.

If the American pressure on the French in regard to the transit issue had mounted, so too had that of the Japanese. Their General Staff complained to the French military attaché that intelligence sources had reported the Chinese to be buying arms in Hanoi and Haiphong which were to be conveyed across the border in trucks and noted that, if such reports were proven true, then the Japanese would intervene to stop the arms flow. Several days later the complaints and the threat were repeated.

The attaché believed that the Japanese were seeking an excuse for action in south China where the ambassador now feared a move against Canton which "could involve a landing on Hainan and even portend an analogous move against Pakhoi if the Japanese persuade themselves that Indochina is...a centre of arms provisioning."[74] Delbos assured the ambassador that, with the exceptions provided for in the initial decree, the ban had been "scrupulously observed" and urged that no chance be missed in emphasizing to the Japanese "the perfect correctness of our attitude."[75] They, however, did not relent: when the military attaché insisted upon the correctness of the French stance, he was met with the suggestion of "the sending to Indochina of a Japanese officer to whom our authorities could provide proof of the reality of the closing of the frontier."[76]

This suggestion raised, if still only indirectly, the issue of sovereignty. That issue was posed more immediately in another area after a visit by a French naval vessel to the Spatlly Islands, in the South China Sea, revealed the presence of Japanese who had installed a radio transmitter, raised their national flag, and destroyed a marker set up in 1933 as a sign of French sovereignty. On December

9, 1937 the French protested officially to Tokyo. The Japanese, however, refused to back down. Indeed, Hirota followed his rejection of the French contentions with what could be interpreted as a threat: "If the authorities of Indochina are disposed to interfere with the industry of subjects of the Empire found there or to create problems for their installations, the Imperial Government will find itself forced to take measures for the protection of those under its jurisdiction."[77] He would reaffirm this stand in a note of February 23, 1938.

By then another island issue had assumed greater importance in French eyes, for news had arrived that, though repulsed by local resistance, a small party of Japanese had tried to land on Hainan. Believing that Hirota had promised that the Japanese would abstain from such an action, Delbos expressed his shock. Referring vaguely but accurately enough to services which France had rendered Japan since the start of the conflict with China, he worked himself up to what could also be construed as a threat: "We can only persevere in this attitude as long as the Imperial Government responds with equal consideration for our interests in the Pacific and abstains from all action which hurts them."[78]

Disingenuously invoking "the spirit" of the Franco-Japanese treaty of 1907 as the cause of France's refusal to allow "Indochina to serve as a base for the military provisioning of China," he now threatened that "any action of the Japanese government which tends to break the balance which this treaty has the goal of preserving in the Gulf of Tonkin will force us to reconsider the actions we have taken in this regard."[79] The French ambassador carried this message to the Vice Minister for Foreign Affairs, and the naval attaché took it to the Admiralty, only to be met with denials that any such landing had taken place. The French could then conclude that their informal bargain with the Japanese still held.

Islands continued to bedevil Franco-Japanese relations. In February 1938 a French gunboat reported the presence in the Paracels of Japanese who, just as in the case of the Spratlies, had raised their national flag. Perhaps as a result of the strong Japanese stand in regard to the other islands, Delbos rejected the suggestion of the Governor General of Indochina that the occupants be given a choice between acknowledging French authority or being expelled. Delbos' fears were shared by the naval commander in Indochina who, though he insisted upon the need for a response in light of the strategic importance of the islands, recognized that "if we act alone, we risk encountering an energetic reaction on the part of the Japanese government, and if we are obliged to retreat in face of this reaction, our moral situation in the Far East, especially in the eyes of our Indochinese, will suffer greatly."[80] But by now Governor General Brevié not only favoured a stronger stand in regard to the Paracels, but generally a tougher line. Considering the improvement in the Chinese military situation and the necessity of dispelling Chinese complaints about the ban, he thought that the time had come "to revise it, either in law or in fact, and to enlarge the scope of the exemptions."[81] Needless to say, such sentiments encountered a chilly reception in Paris where it was believed that little had changed since the Governor General's pessimistic reports of the previous autumn. When the Japanese ambassador discussed the Far East with Alexis Léger on May 20, the Secretary General of the Quai d'Orsay protested against various Japanese activities and attitudes which made it difficult for the French to follow "the policy of balance" which they had hitherto pursued "in the Gulf of Tonkin and south China," but he also assured the diplomat that his government did not intend "to modify the position it had taken in regard to transit across Indochina of war material destined for China."[82]

The notion of balance required that the French do everything possible to keep the Chinese at a distance. In early May General Georges had been approached by Rachjmann, now Director of the League's Hygiene Services, who suggested a plan for Franco-Chinese cooperation which would involve:

- *On the part of China*: The guarantee of the Indochinese border with the participation of Chinese troops in its defence; in case of world war the placing of Chinese effectives (soldiers and workers) at the disposition of France.

- *In return on the part of France*: Authorization for the transit of war material across Indochina; the placing at the disposition of China of French personnel for the equipping of arsenals and especially *the despatch of a military mission*.[83]

The ambassador to China, however, warned that any effort on the part of the Chinese to replace their departing German military advisers with French officers should be greeted with extreme caution. And when the president of the Union Franco-Chinoise of Peking and Shanghai tried to follow up Rachjmann's overture, his attention was drawn to the constraints on French policy dictated by both the European and the Far Eastern situations. In the view of Foreign Minister Bonnet, "the support that France can lend to China will be all the more efficacious as long as it remains discrete and we are careful not to compromise our moral authority and political position in the Far East by imprudent demonstrations."[84]

Still, the possibility of closer Franco-Chinese ties fuelled a virulent anti-French campaign in a Japanese press which now urged the occupation of Hainan. Faced with this barrage, the French insisted that the ban on the transit of war material was still in effect, that the few French aviators who worked for the Chinese government did so on their own account, and that the plans for the Longson-Nanning railway went back decades and the signing of the contract had taken place before the outbreak of hostilities. But the continuing vilification in the press, the diplomatic complaints, and the growing insistence on the despatch of a Japanese military mission to Indochina also prompted a stiffening of French policy in the summer of 1938. Not only did they protest the bombing of open cities in China, but they even threatened to end the ban on the transit of war material. If the projection of preemptive Anglo-French landings on Hainan partook of fantasy, a decision was made to occupy the Paracel and Spratly islands. Moreover, with the energetic Georges Mandel, now installed as Minister of Colonies, the French worked to strengthen the defences of Indochina on the basis of a 400 million franc loan.

Events quickly underscored the weakness of their position. The mission sent to occupy the Paracels encountered a 10,000 ton Japanese cruiser there. Its captain did not interfere with the landing, but he explained that, as Japan did not recognize the French claim to the islands, he might receive orders to expel them. More ominously, before departing he warned that the Japanese would probably return in force to occupy the islands. At the same time the French had moved ahead with plans to occupy the Spratlies. Wishing to avoid provoking the

Japanese, they first settled some Vietnamese fishermen there. When informed of this, the Japanese ambassador in Paris repeated his government's rejection of the French claim to sovereignty. But already, with the arrival of a Japanese naval vessel, the Vietnamese had been compelled to lower the French flag and evacuate the islands. Then, on August 13, the Japanese placed their own marker on the main island in the group. Although the diplomats would continue to argue about the matter, superior Japanese naval power had carried the day.

The Far East, with all its problems, must have seemed infinitely far from Paris as the Czech crisis unfolded in September. But with their capture of Canton on October 21, the Japanese became blunter in their dealings with the French:

> ...the situation in south China no longer allows delay in discussions: if arms or munitions continue to pass through Indochinese territory, the Japanese government will have to take efficacious measures to oppose the entry of this material into China. That will result in a state of affairs infinitely regrettable for the maintenance of the amicable relations which have existed for years between France and Japan.[85]

In face of such pressure, the French took what comfort they could in Premier Konoye's statement of December 22 which seemed to some observers to indicate a shift in Japanese attention from south China to Siberia. Indeed, relief at the possibility of such a diversion seems to have driven thoughts of the Franco-Soviet pact from the minds of the French, a reaction all the more understandable in light of the *débâcle* at Munich.

Entanglement with the Soviets in East Asia, in any event, promised less than the cooperation with the British and Americans longed for during the summer of 1938. But the French were still not prepared to follow them in supplying aid to a China which had rejected the terms of the Konoye statement. Despite Chinese entreaties, they refused to consider any major relaxation of the transit ban. Still, the hardening of the British and American positions forced the QAuai d'Orsay to reexamine its policy. Despite a plethora of qualms and qualifications, a new note of firmness entered Japanese policy when Foreign Minister Bonnet had the Japanese informed:

> ...the recent official declaration of the Imperial Government in regard to the policy which it intends to follow in the Far East has received close attention by the government of the Republic. It appears to the government of the Republic that this policy would be little compatible with the provisions of the Nine Power Treaty.
>
> The government of the Republic holds that it could not accept or recognize any modification of the order of things established in China by the treaties in force which did not issue from an initial consultation with the interested powers and which said powers accepted.[86]

Once again, however, actions would speak louder than words.

Japanese troops landed on Hainan in early February 1939. Instructing his ambassador to see the Japanese Foreign Minister as quickly as possible, Bonnet rehearsed all the old arguments: "The Japanese government knows that the measures taken to prevent the transit of war material across Indochina, despite the entire freedom in this matter provided by international law and the particular prescriptions which would have resulted morally for France from its membership in the League of Nations, constitute...from the French point of view, the counterpart of Japanese abstention in the Gulf of Tonkin in general and at Hainan in particular."[87] When the ambassador met with Foreign Minister Arita, on February 14, an effort was made to assure him that the occupation "will not go beyond military necessities, either in regard to its duration or even in regard to its character."[88]

But the French now had to consider other options. Thus, when Wellington Koo, the Chinese ambassador, approached the Quai d'Orsay to inquire about how the occupation of Hainan might affect the transit issue, he was told that "an easing of the régime in effect appeared possible."[89] Shortly thereafter the chargé d'affaires in Shanghai was informed that, "without fundamentally changing the position of the French government in regard to the furnishing of arms to China and, more specifically, the transit of war material across Indochina, it has been decided to interpret henceforth, in practice, in a less rigorous manner," the current policy.[90]

The French received another shock when, after rejecting a proposal of international arbitration, the Japanese the subjection of the Spratly Islands to their authorities on Formosa. The Quai d'Orsay's *Direction politique* now decided that "to the systematic disregard of its interests, the French government can only respond by opening without restrictions the transit of arms through Indochina."[91] Bonnet, however, refused to move beyond the informal easing of the ban. Moreover, while recognizing that "the Japanese seizure of China is obviously contrary to French, American and British interests," he maintained that this in itself did not "suffice to convince the French government to open to the Chinese government prospects of assistance which, in the present state of things in China, would be unilateral."[92] The Chinese, however, continued to press for aid. They wanted French capital for "a programme of construction in the southwest aimed at linking Yunnan-fu...and Chengtu...with the Indochinese railroads on the one hand and with those of the Burma frontier on the other...and the establishing of industrial factories for the fabrication of chemical and other products with the goal of accelerating economic development in the southwest of China."[93] Aside from the reference to Burma, this projection appeared to be an old French imperialist dream come true. The world of the late 1930s, however, was not that of the late 1890s.

While they complained about a decision to forbid the export of iron ore from Indochina, the Japanese reacted more strongly in the late spring of 1939 when the British and French moved towards their ill-fated discussions with the Russians. As one possible response to these negotiations lay in the transformation of the Anti-Comintern Pact into a military alliance, the French government again wished to reassure Tokyo:

> It has...constantly refused to take into consideration the hypothesis of a Far Eastern conflict pitting France against Japan. That is why the Franco-Soviet Pact does not include a guarantee for the Far East and why the French have never sought nor accepted for a single moment in any circumstance, an extension in this sense.[94]

But Bonnet also thought that "a transformation of the Anti-Comintern Pact into a military alliance would justify a reexamination of our current ideas."[95] By now European and East Asian problems had become tightly enough interlocked for the French to believe that both China and Japan had become less interested in a Far Eastern settlement than in the roles they might play in a European war. More strikingly, faced with the possibility of war in Europe, Bonnet himself lost interest in a Sino-Japanese peace which would allow Japan "the free disposition of all its forces against the USSR and against our own establishments."[96] He also worried that, "in giving the impression of considering China as a negligible factor, we risk encouraging an arrangement whereby Japan could be tempted, on the eve of a generalized conflict, to relax its terms at the expense of foreign interests."[97] But before doing anything decisive, the French still wanted to mobilize American support.

That consideration became all the more important when, on June 12, the Japanese announced a blockade of the British and French concessions at Tientsin. Although the affair arose initially out of an Anglo-Japanese dispute over police powers, the French had to be brought into it to make the blockade effective. In face of the situation, Bonnet thought it "essential to avoid taking measures likely to exasperate Japanese sentiment before being assured of being able to maintain them and give them complete efficacy."[98] This stance, however, brought him back to an old problem: "measures taken in concert by Paris and London will probably not gain the desired result if the government of the United States...refuses to associate itself with them."[99] As the French perceived the matter, the Americans voiced lofty sentiments and urged action upon others rather than acting of these sentiments themselves.

At least the British and French came together in late June for a military conference at Singapore where they discussed cooperation in the event of war. The first part of the talks had to do with a European war in which Japan did not intervene directly, the second, with the case of Japanese intervention. In the first instance, the danger did not reside in any real German or Italian threat in the area, but rather in the advantages which the Japanese might seek to acquire without actually going to war. While they agreed upon the need to strengthen the defences of Indochina, the instructions of the two delegations differed when it came to the concessions in China: if the British favoured evacuating the garrisons, the French had firmer orders: "to resist by force any attempt which the Japanese might make to occupy the concessions in time of either war or peace."[100]

Considering the possibility of the Japanese entering the war, the military men first defined their essential and non-essential concerns.[101] But even this division could not obscure a sobering conclusion: "Our weakness gives such a superiority to the Japanese that it will be impossible to maintain our essential lines of communication and to forbid the enemy to seize bases for advanced operations from which it could directly menace our interests."[102] In face of this grim prospect, the conference urged aid for China in the event of war. But not all that much had changed, for it also opposed any talks with the Chinese short of the outbreak of war.

Another appreciation of East Asian conditions came from René Cassin, a scholar who had travelled in Indochina and China during the spring. He urged that *"the danger of a Japanese victory is incomparably more immediate and more grave*...than that of a Chinese victory."[103] While that point might have been taken as self-evident, he felt that he had to make it in opposition to "certain businessmen in the concessions" who believed that a Japanese victory would buttress "order and the European preponderance."[104] More strikingly, he pointed out that "the Japanese army is now *less of a menace to Chungking and the non-occupied regions of China than the to the Chinese south and French Indochina.*"[105] Sketching the situation in larger terms, he postulated:

> Japanese victory would imply the loss of all the European positions in the Far East; it would entail the renewal of the Siamese danger...It will give our Annamese subjects and protegés the idea that France has not known how to defend its positions and, hence, that it is weak. A stimulus to Pan-Asianism and all sorts of baseness or internal rebellion.[106]

Hence, he thought that "in its own interest, France must undertake a policy of support for China, which has the sympathy of all the Annamese."[107] Yet even Cassin drew the line when it came to offers of Chinese troops for the defence of Indochina.

Reflecting upon the Chinese problem, the French ambassador returned to the depressingly familiar: with strong American support, the French and British could act firmly, but without it, they would run grave risks. While he believed that in the latter case France had "every interest in making up with Japan," he was worried.[108] France had pursued a"a policy of suppleness and neutrality " in regard to both China and Japan, but he feared that "the Japanese army will not lend itself for long to the courtenous transactions it had accepted until now and...will shortly compel us to choose between Chungking and Tokyo."[109]

The unrelenting pressure in regard to the transit issue, the expanding demands at Tientsin, and the evasiveness of the Americans in face of proposals for action in common, all fuelled a sense of time running out in the summer of 1939. So too did the rumours of a coming military pact uniting Germany, Italy and Japan and, to a lesser extent, the reports of heavy fighting between Russian and Japanese units along the Mongolian border. Devoting surprisingly little attention to this last development, the French were even less prepared for a far more serious move on the part of the Soviet Union.

The German-Soviet Pact of August 23 altered everything in Europe and, or so it appeared for a time, in the Far East. Released from the obligations of the Anti-Comintern Pact, Japan could move in several directions: into isolation, into some sort of combination with Germany and Russia, or even into an alignment with Great Britain and France. Initial disarray and anti-German sentiment in Japan provided the French with the scant comfort they could find in the aftermath of the Nazi-Soviet agreement, but they had to consider all three possibilities. As they rejected the viability of isolation, the question became whether they and the British could court the Japanese more successfully than the Germans and the Russians. The British willingness to make concessions to the Japanese could only have pleased the French ambassador in Berlin who throughout late August urged upon his own government "the primordial importance, in the present circumstances, of assuring, even at a high price, the support of Japan and taking the lead in this before being outdistanced by Germany."[110] With France agreeing to the establishment of a Japanese consulate at Noumea, accepting without objection the naming of a Japanese ambassador to Paris, and lifting the ban on the export of iron ore from Indochina to Japan, Bonnet needed no urging along these lines. The way was being opened for an East Asian settlement, arranged fundamentally at the expense of China, which would align Japan with France and Great Britain.

China and the United States, however, stood in the way of such a course of action. At a disadvantage in lacking instructions from their government, both the Chinese ambassador and the First Secretary in Paris welcomed the possibility of mediation, but warned against any "hasty decision" aimed at rallying Japan to the Anglo-French side.[111] The ambassador, moreover, stressed the need for American involvement in any mediation effort. Washington, however, remained cool to the notion of mediation at this point. Discussing the matter with the French ambassador, Sumner Welles remarked that, with the Japanese definitely alienated from Germany and seeking better relations with the Western powers, "it would as little opportune to pressure them as to court them with too much solicitude."[112]

Appealing to national self-interest, the French diplomat replied that "the American government, if it wants to maintain its position in China and still supports the independence of that country, would be wise not to wait until France and England have been obliged to disinterest themselves in China's fate."[113] Having failed to move Welles with that threat, the Frenchman left the State Department with the impression that the Americans "counted on Russian military assistance to China holding Japan in check without the relations of this last power with the United States being compromised."[114]

Two days later German tanks rolled into Poland. But even the dawn of the cataclysm did not completely drive the Far East from the mind of the French Foreign Minister. Although the formation of Wang Ching-wei's puppet government had led him to doubt that "a mediating action can be undertaken at this moment with any chance of success," Bonnet still hoped for "a quick and concerted action, profiting from the psychological shock of the German-Soviet Pact, to entice Tokyo to an exchange of views on the Chinese question."[115] That hope, however, was to prove as fruitless as his efforts to prevent a French declaration of war on Nazi Germany. Like those efforts, its realization would surely have involved further appeasement of the aggressor. As matters turned out, France went to war in Europe on September 3, 1939, and, with the outbreak of that conflict, the *Documents diplomatiques français, 1932-1939* ends. Given France's primary stake in European affairs, that ending makes perfect sense. But when viewed from the Far Eastern perspective, the massive documentary collection ends very much in the middle of things.

Ultimately involving the very losses which the French so feared, the East Asian conflict would continue and eventually expand. If that story cannot be pursued on the basis of these documents, they do shed light on the motives and manoeuvres of French Far Eastern policy, if such it can be called, during the 1930s.

Two phases can be detected in that policy. Pessimistic passivity characterized it in the period lasting from the Manchurian crisis to the eruption of undeclared war in China in mid-1937. The French began this phase by seeking to affirm the sanctity of international treaties without offending the Japanese. Later, despite their fears of a Japanese-sponsored Monroe Doctrine for East Asia, they would tacitly approve the Japanese denunciation of the Five Power Treaty, a bulwark of the post-war Far Eastern settlement. Unable to reach any accord with the other Western powers interested in East Asia and unwilling to strengthen China, they did little more than respond ineffectually to the actions of others. Action on their own clearly entailed risks which the French were unwilling to take. Indeed, their most energetic action in Europe during this period, the conclusion of the Franco-Soviet Pact, provoked a hostile reaction in Japan which the French, at their most active and abject, tried to assuage.

With the outbreak of hostilities in China, the French had to become more active in their pursuit of what was in effect inaction. Thus, they worked against strong support for China at Geneva and, less clearly, at Brussels. Moreover, having recently acquired expertise about such matters with the Spanish Civil War, they forbade the transit across Indochina of war material destined for China. This ban rested upon the assumption of a trade-off with the Japanese who, in return for it, were expected to refrain from occupying the island of Hainan and intruding into the Gulf of Tonkin. Refusing to play by the rules of the game, the Japanese challenged French claims to sovereignty over the Spratly Islands and the Paracel Islands and eventually occupied Hainan. Increasing the threat to Indochina, this last move led the French towards an easing of the transit ban and a more serious consideration of relations with China. The worsening European situation also entered into the picture in that it led Foreign Minister Bonnet to conclude that France had a stake, not in ending the Far Eastern conflict, but in prolonging it. However, despite the prospect of securing gains in south China which have delighted imperialists of an earlier generation, the French continued to keep the Chinese at arm's length in the military domain.

Although several factors were invoked in justification of this stance, the primary motive was the desire to avoid getting sucked into the East Asian conflict on the side of China. That desire, like so much else, sprang from the weakness of the French position in the Far East. Consequently, they looked to the British and especially the Americans to take the lead in checking Japanese expansion. But if the French could point to their vulnerability, as well as to more pressing concerns, so too could the others. The German-Soviet Pact only exposed all the weaknesses intrinsic to French policy in Europe and the Far East. But the new degree of vulnerability in Europe encouraged efforts to take advantage of Japan's sudden isolation in order to end the East Asian conflict. Although it might well have entailed major concessions on the part of the French and British, a successful conclusion of those efforts would even more likely been at the expense of China, for what was aimed at was less peace itself than the rallying of Japan to the Anglo-French side in a new world war. On the very eve of that war, the active appeasement of Japan had come to eclipse the more passive appeasement characteristic of French Far East policy during the earlier years of the 1930s.

Notes

1. *Modern Asian Studies*, 23, 1 (1989), pp. 117-49.

2. J.B. Duroselle's *La Décadence, 1932-1939* (Paris: Imprimerie Nationale, 1979) concentrates, quite rightly, upon the European scene. But given the increasingly interlocked power relations of the 1930s, his scant number of references to East Asia, as well as any mention of the Brussels Conference (November, 1937), is baffling. The problem appears to spring from his conviction that Indochina simply could not be defended. Taken in itself, that opinion is very probably correct. Certain it was voiced at the time, as Doroselle indicates (p. 267), by Admiral Raoul Castex. But while others might well have shared such a view, nobody in a position of power dared voice it, let alone act upon it.

   Castex's notion of falling back upon a bloc composed solely of France and her Afcrican possessions can be traced at least as far back as Onésime Relus' *Lâchons l'Asie, Prenons l'Afrique* (1904) which produced a violent reaction on the part of French imperialists committed to endeavors in the Far East. See John F. Laffey, "Imperialists Divided: The Views of Tonkin's Colons Before 1914," *Histoire sociale / Social History*, IX, 19 (May, 1977), pp. 92-113, p. 103. Other continuities reaching back to the turn of the century will appear later in this article.

3. For the French stake in East Asia on the eve of World War II, see Roger Levy and Andrew Roth, *French Interests and Politics in the Far East* (Mew York: Institute of Pacific Relations, 1941). For the decline of the ability of one of the major forces behind economic imperialism to influence policy, see John F. Laffey, "Lyonnais Imperialism in the Far East, 1900-1938," *Modern Asian Studies*, 10, 2 (1976), pp. 225-48, 240-8. As for public opinion, the ambassadors in Tokyo did not take it into account. It proved more difficult to do so in the case of China.

4. Account of a Meeting, of Sept. 6, 1932, Ministère des Affaires Etrangères, Commission de publication des documents relatifs aux origines de la guerre 1939-1945, *Documents diplomatiques français, 1932-1939*, 1re série (1932-1935), I (9 juillet-l4 novembre 1932) (Paris: Imprimerie Nationale, 1964), pp. 275-90, p. 277. Henceforth these works will be cited as *DDF* with the date of publication.

5. Report of the French Delegation to Geneva, July 9, 1932, *Ibid.*, pp. 7-9, p. 9.

6. René Massigli, Associate Delegate at the Disarmament Conference, to Edouard Herriot, Minister of Foreign Affairs, Sept. 22, 1932, *Ibid.*, p. 360.

7. Note of the Chinese Legation in Paris, Sept. 19, 1932, *Ibid.*, pp. 348-9, p. 348.

8. Massigli to Herriot, Sept. 23, 1932, *Ibid.*, pp. 376-7, p. 377.

9. Note of the Department (French Service of the League of Nations), Nov. 18, 1932, *DDF*, Ire s., II (15 novembre 1932-17 mars 1933) (1966), pp. 22-6, p. 23.

10. Note of the Asia-Oceania Sub-Division; "Japan, China and the French Interests Involved in the Sino-Japanese Conflict," June l5, 1933, *Ibid.*, pp. 444-9, p. 444. For the roots of this kind of thinking, see John F. Laffey, "Racism and Imperialism: French Views of the 'Yellow Peril,' 1894-1914," *Third Republic / Troisième République*, I, 1 (Spring, 1977), pp. 4-52.

11. *DDF*, 1re s., II, p. 145.

12. *Ibid.*

13. *Ibid.*

14. *Ibid.*, p. 449.

15. *Ibid.*

16. Damien de Martel, Ambassador to Japan, to Joseph Paul-Boncour, Minister of Foreign Affairs, March 13, 1933, *Ibid.*, p. 800.

17. Auguste Wilden, Minister to Peking, to Paul-Boncour, April 21, 1933, *DDF*, Ire s., III (17 mars 15 juilllet 1933) (1967), pp. 274-5, p. 275.

18. Paul-Boncour to the Diplomatic Representatives of France in Peking, Tokyo, London and Washington, April 29, 1933, *Ibid.*, p. 375.

19. Leaving an interview with the despairing Soong, the French Minister noted the number of police, with drawn revolvers, who surrounded him and reflected that "in the disorder and jostling which, on these occasions, are inevitable, the least incident can provoke a killing." Wilden to Paul-Boncour, May 3, 1933, *Ibid.*, pp. 413-4, p. 414.

20. Philippe Baudet, chargé d'affaires at Nanking, to Wilden, July 17, 1933, *DDF*, 1re s., IV (16 juillet-12 novembre 1933) (1968), pp.112-4, p. 12.

21. *Ibid.*, p. 13.

22. Note of the Asia-Oceania Sub-Division, Oct. 2, 1933, *Ibid.*, pp. 470-1, p. 471.

23. Japanese concern at this pointed tended to focus upon the activities of Dr. Ludwig Rachjmann, the League's representative in China. But their suspicion of him was easily matched by that of the French Chargé d'affaires in Peking who believed, realistically enough, that the plans of Rachjmann and his associate, Jean Monnet, for a banking consortium which would draw upon Chinese and foreign capital to finance the projects of the National Economic Council, faced enormous obstacles. A nastier note sounded when the serious social failings of Rachjmann and his wife entered into the balance: they had refused to join the circles in Shanghai and Nanking closed to Chinese, had adopted the Chinese view of the unequal treaties, had expressed shock at the troops in the foreign concessions, "and when they saw at Nanking the war flags of the various powers floating over the Yangtze, four hundred million Chinese almost came to appear, in their eyes, as an oppressed minority." Henri Hoppenot, Chargé d'affaires at Peking, to Louis Bathou, Minister of Foreign Affairs, April 19, 1934, *DDF*, 1re s., VI (13 mars-26 juillet 1934 (1972), pp. 297-301, p. 301. Although marked by affection for Rachjmann, Jean Monnet's *Memoirs* (Garden City: Doubleday and Co., 1978) reveal next to nothing about his own activities in China.

24. Declaration of the Japanese Government, April 17, 1934, *DDF*, 1re s., VI, pp. 274-5, p. 275.

25. Fernand Pila, Ambassador to Japan, to Barthou, April 23, 1934, *Ibid.*, pp. 330-2, p. 331. Pila was a member of Lyonnais family concerned with East Asia since the nineteenth century. For the activities of his father, see John F. Laffey, "Les racines de l'impérialisme français en Extrême Orient," Jean Bouvier and René Girault (eds.), *L'impérialisme français d'avant 1914* (Paris: Mouton, 1976), pp. 15-37.

26. Barthou to André Lefebvre de Laboulaye, Ambassador to the United States, April 28, 1934, *DDF*, 1re s., VI, pp. 375-6, p. 376.

27. Pila to Barthou, Sept. 17, 1934, *DDR* 1re s., VII (27 juillet 1934-31 octobre 1934) (1979), pp. 479-81, p. 480.

28. *Ibid.*

29. *Ibid.*

30. In a discussion with the French ambassador, Sir Victor Wellesley, the head of the Foreign Office's Far Eastern section, noted that, while there were those who looked back to the Anglo-Japanese alliance with nostalgia and sought its renewal, "this suggestion has no chance of being accepted, as much because of the opposition of liberal opinion, as because of the consequences it would have in relation to the United States." Charles Corbin, Ambassador to Great Britain, to Gaston Doumergue, President of the Council, Oct. 12, 1934, *Ibid.*, pp. 723-5, p. 725.

31. Note of the Naval Staff (Naval Armaments Study Section), Oct. 11, 1934, *Ibid.*, pp. 710-15, p. 712.

32. *Ibid.*, p. 713.

33. *Ibid.*

34. *Ibid.*, p. 714.

35. *Ibid.*

36. Note of the Asia-Oceania Sub-Division, Jan. 28, 1935, *DDF*, 1re s., IX (16 janvier-23 mars 1935) (1980), pp. 148-9, p. 149.

37. Wilden to Pierre Laval, Minister of Foreign Affairs, Feb. 6, 1935, *Ibid.*, pp. 273-4, p. 274.

38. Wilden to Laval, Feb. 21, 1935, *Ibid.*, p. 392.

39. Wilden to Laval, March 7, 1935, *Ibid.*, pp. 514-5, p. 514.

40. Note of the Asia-Oceania Sub-Division, March 16, 1935, *Ibid.*, pp. 553-4, p. 554.

41. J. B. Barbier, Chargé d'affaires in Tokyo, to Laval, Nov. 12, 1935, *DDF*, Ire s., XIII (16 octobre-31 décembre 1935) (1984), pp. 319-20, p. 319.

42. Pila to Pierre Etienne Flandin, Minister of Foreign Affairs, March 6, 1936, *DDF*, 2e série (1936-1939), I (1er janvier-31 mars 1936) (1963), p. 473.

43. Flandin to Pila, March 10, 1936, *Ibid.*, pp. 486-7, p. 486.

44. Pila to Flandin, March 14, 1936, *Ibid.*, pp. 553-4, p. 553.

45. Note of the Department, March 30, 1936, *Ibid.*, pp. 708-10, p. 709.

46. Note of the Asia-Oceania Sub-Division, Sept. 28, 1936, *DDF*, 2e s., III (19 juillet-19 novembre 1936) (1966), pp. 428-30, p. 429.

47. Albert Krammrer, Ambassador to Japan, to Yvon Delbos, Minister of Foreign Affairs, Dec. 14, 1936, *DDF*, 2 e s., IV (20 novembre 1936-19 janvier 1937) (1967), pp. 234-5, p. 234.

48. *Ibid.*

49. Note of the Asia-Oceania Sub-Division, Dec. 21, 1936, *Ibid*, pp. 302-3, p. 303.

50. C.-A. Henry, Ambassador to Japan, to Delbos, April 28, 1937, *DDF*, 2e s., V (20 février-31 mars 1937) (1968), pp. 604-10, p. 607.

51. *Ibid.*, n. 1, p. 610.

52. Lieutenant Colonel Ch. E. Mast to Edouard Daladier, Minister of National Defense and War, June 16, 1937, *DDF*, 2e s., VI (1er juin-29 septembre 1937) (1970), pp. 133-9, p. 138.

53. Lieutenant Colonel G. Sabbatier to Daladier, June 30, 1937, *Ibid.*, pp. 251-5, p. 252.

54. *Ibid*, p. 255.

55. Delbos to Corbin, July 13, 1937, *Ibid.*, pp. 370-1.

56. Note of the League of Nations Sub-Division, June 30, 1937, *Ibid.*, pp. 381-3, p. 381.

57. *Ibid.*, p. 383.

58. C.-A. Henry to Delbos, Sept. 12, 1937, *Ibid.*, pp. 761-2.

59. Note of the Asia-Oceania Sub-Division, April 21, 1938, *DDF*, 2e s., IX (21 mars-9 juin 1938) (1974), pp. 450-4, p. 451.

60. *Ibid.*

61. With the "tacit assent" of a China which had been assured by France that "its rights remained reserved." plans were being for the gunboat *Marne* to land a civilian mission in the Paracels to construct signal and navigation works. Note of the Asia-Oceania Sub-Division, Oct. 5, 1938, *DDF*, 2e s., VII (29 septembre 1937-16 janvier 1938) (1972), pp. 38-41, p. 38.

62. *Ibid.*

63. *Ibid*, p. 39.

64. *Ibid*, p. 40.

65. Ernst Lagarde, Member of the French Delegation to the Consultative Committee on the Far East, to Delbos, Oct. 7, 1937, *Ibid.*, pp. 55-9, p. 57.

66. Delbos to C.-A. Henry, Oct. 25, 1937, *Ibid.*, p. 226. The ban did not apply to materials ordered by the Chinese before July 15, 1937 nor to French and foreign materials which had left their ports of loading before Oct. 13, 1937.

67. C.-A. Henry to Delbos, Oct. 30, 1937, *Ibid.*, pp. 284-5, p. 284.

68. C.-A. Henry to Delbos, Nov. 1, 1937, *Ibid.*, pp. 298-9, p. 299.

69. Note of the Minister (Delbos), Nov. 6, 1937, *Ibid.*, pp. 346-50, p. 348.

70. *Ibid.*

71. *Ibid.*, p. 346.

72. Jules Henry, Chargé d'affaires in Washington, to Delbos, Nov. 7, 1937, *Ibid.*, pp. 355-7, p. 355.

73. Jules Henry to Delbos, Nov. 11, 1937, *Ibid*, pp. 390-2, 390, 391.

74. C.-A. Henry to Delbos, Nov. 13, 1937, *Ibid.*, p. 416.

75. Delbos to C.-A. Henry, Nov. 13, 1937, *Ibid.*, pp. 418-19, p. 419; Delbos to C.-A. Henry, Nov. 18, 1937, *Ibid.*, p. 449.

76. C.-A. Henry to Camille Chautemps, Minister of Foreign Affairs *par interim*, Dec. 3, 1937, *Ibid.*, p. 594.

77. C.-A. Henry to Delbos, Jan. 13, 1938, *Ibid.*, pp. 901-3, p. 903.

78. Delbos to the Diplomatic Representatives of France in Tokyo and London, Jan. 21, 1938, *DDF*, 2e s., VII (17 janvier-30 mars 1938) (1973), pp. 32-3. p. 33.

79. *Ibid.*

80. Admiral Petit, Commander in Indochina, to César Campinchi, Minister of Marine, May 6, 1938, *DDF*, 2e s., IX, pp. 653-5. p. 654.

81. Note of the Asia-Oceanian Sub-Division, April 21, 1938, *Ibid.*, pp. 450-4. p. 453.

82. An Interview of the Secretary General, May 20, 1938, *Ibid.*, pp. 806-7. p. 807.

83. Edouard Daladier, Minister of War, to Georges Bonnet, Minister of Foreign Affairs, May 23, 1938, *Ibid.*, pp. 863-5, 863-4.

84. Bonnet to Emile Naggier, Ambassador to China, June 3, 1938, *Ibid.*, pp. 1009-10, p. 1010.

85. Communication of the Japanese Embassy in Paris, Oct. 26, 1938, *DDF*, 2e s., XII (3 octobre-30 novembre 1938) (1978), p. 387.

86. Bonnet to C.-A. Henry, Jan. 14, 1939, *DDF*, 2e s., XIII (ler décembre 1938-31 janvier 1939) (1979), pp. 650-1, p. 650. 87. Bonnet to C.-A. Henry, Feb. 10, 1939, *DDF*, 2e s., XIV (ler février-15 mars 1939) (1980), p. 163.

88. C.-A. Henry to Bonnet, Feb. 14, 1939, *Ibid.*, pp. 195-6, p. 195.

89. Note of the Asia-Oceania Sub-Division, Feb. 17, 1939, *Ibid.*, pp. 239-40.

90. Bonnet to Frédéric Knobel, Charegé d'affaires at Shanghai, Feb. 20, 1939, *Ibid.*, pp. 239-40. Alexandre Varenne, a former Governor General of Indochina, wanted to go considerably farther. In his view, it was necessary to finish once and for all with these methods of "perpetual evasions and subterfuges which have not succeeded...in attracting to us...the consideration of Japan, and which, on the other hand, begin to merit for us on the part of China an attitude if not hostile, at least reserved, which is only too justified." Having no illusions about the strength of the French forces in Indochina, he recommended looking north: "Reservoir of men, immense resources in materials, such can be this south China to which we are bound tightly by interests which have become common, and which only asks to show this community of interests by closer and closer accords, even by military cooperation." The Quai d'Orsay showed no interest in this kind of thinking. Note of Alexandre Varenne, Feb. 25, 1939, *Ibid.*, pp. 380-5, 380-1, 383.

91. Note of the Direction politique, March 31, 1939, *DDF*, 2e s., XV (l6 mars-20 avril 1939), pp. 338-40, 339-40.

92. Bonnet to Corbin, April 7, 1939, *Ibid.*, pp.500-1, p. 501.

93. Communication of the Embassy of China, April 13, 1939, *Ibid.*, pp. 604-7, p. 605. Plans for Franco-Chinese economic cooperation were elaborated in the spring of 1939. Industrial centres producing war materials, fertilizers and chemical products were to be founded in south China, especially in Yunnan, with the understanding that China "will engage itself not to create, in the southern provinces, industries capable of competing with our own without first coming to an accord with them." Indochina itself, especially Tonkin, was to be further industrialized. While the ports of Tonkin were to be improved, the rail and road networks there were to developed in such a fashion as "to

drain toward Indochina" a part of the trade of south China. Finally, "economic advantages," most notably in regard to wolfram, tungsten and tin, were to be reserved to France "in return for the facilities which she will provide the Chinese government." The French, however, still drew the line at military cooperation: "As long as there is a chance of Japan remaining neutral in the case of a generalized conflict, we cannot conduct military conversations, to which the Chinese government will doubtlessly give publicity and which will provoke immediately the sharpest reactions on the part of the Tokyo government." Note of the Asia-Oceania Sub-Division, May 25, 1939, *DDF*, 2e s., XVI (ler mai-24 juin 1939) (1983), pp. 554-5; Note of the Asia-Oceania Sub-Division, June 6, 1939, *Ibid.*, p. 681.

94. Bonnet to C.-A. Henry, May 12, 1939, *Ibid.*, pp. 328-9, p. 329.

95. *Ibid.*

96. Bonnet to Henri Cosme, Ambassador to China, May 2, 1939, *Ibid.*, pp. 6-7, p. 7.

97. Bonnet to René Doynel de Saint-Quentin, Ambassador to the United States, May 13, 1939, *Ibid.*, pp. 353-4, p. 354.

98. Bonnet to Corbin, June 17, 1939, *Ibid.*, p. 880.

99. *Ibid.*

100. Final Report of the Franco-British Conference at Singapore, June 27, 1939, *DDF*, 2e s., XVII (23 juin-l2 août 1939) (1984), pp. 42-55, p. 44.

101. With the concessions in China and the maritime traffic in the South China Sea relegated to non-essential status, the military men defined their essential concerns as Singapore, Penang, the communications between Singapore and southern Indochina, the entire Indochinese coast, and Hongkong. Just how the withdrawal from the South China Sea might be squared with the defense of Hongkong was left unexplained.

102. *Ibid.*, p. 54.

103. Note of René Cassin, July 13, 1939, *Ibid.*, pp. 338-41, p. 338.

104. *Ibid.*

105. *Ibid.*

106. *Ibid.*

107. *Ibid.*

108. Cosme to Alexis Léger, Aug. 5, 1939, *Ibid.*, 734-6, p. 736.

109. *Ibid.*

110. Robert Coulondre, Ambassador to Germany, to Bonnet, Aug. 28, 1939, *DDF*, 2e s., XIX (26 août-3 septembre 1939) (1986), p. 178.

111. Note of the Asia-Oceania Sub-Division, Aug. 26, 1939, *Ibid.*, pp. 48-50, 49, 50.

112. Saint-Quentin to Bonnet, Aug. 30, 1939, *Ibid.*, pp. 222-3, p. 223.

113. *Ibid.*

114. *Ibid.*

115. Bonnet to Corbin, Sept. 2, 1939, *Ibid.*, p. 365; Bonnet to Saint-Quentin, Sept. 2, 1939, *Ibid.*, pp. 361-2, p. 361.

5

RACISM AND IMPERIALISM: FRENCH VIEWS OF THE "YELLOW PERIL": 1894-1914[1]

Visions of a "yellow peril" haunted some Westerners during the period between the Sino-Japanese War and the outbreak of World War I.[2] The more or less well-focused fears clustered around this specter sprang from several sources. The very size of the East Asian populations, along with their migratory propensities, roused unease. The potential economic and military might of countries like China and Japan provided serious commentators, as well as professional prophets of doom, with much to agonize about. Upheavals like the Boxer Rebellion and the Russo-Japanese War lent themselves to interpretation as either confirmations of dire predictions or dark portents of coming cataclysms. But Western perceptions of and reactions to the "yellow peril" tended to differ. Not all of the specter's features roused the same degree of concern everywhere. Americans, Australians, and Canadians primarily worried about migration from East Asia. If significant segments of the labor force in these countries fumed over the challenge to their wage standards posed by the immigrants, even those who willingly used the East Asians in backbreaking work proved none too happy with the notion of permanent settlement. The economic and military dimensions of the alleged threat roused more interest in Europe where two quite different reactions took place.

On the whole, the German *gelbe gefahr*, elaborated in characteristically imaginative detail by Wilhelm II, could be used to justify energetic action in the Far East, while the French *péril jaune* served as an argument against further expansion of formal and informal empire in that area of the globe. Like some of the arguments put forward after the Spanish-American War, the twist given to the "yellow peril" thesis in France underlines the extent to which racist prejudice could on occasion be mobilized in opposition to imperial expansion. But most of the French proponents of the thesis did not call for the repudiation of imperial endeavors outside of East Asia, and the debate between those who accepted and those who rejected the notion of a "yellow peril" took place largely within the ranks of the imperialist movement. Far from being a mere storm in an ideological teapot, this debate, coupled with changes in East Asia beyond the control of that movement, forced a clarification of the attitudes and goals of the internally divided, numerically small, but influential majority of Frenchmen concerned with Far Eastern affairs during the two decades before World War I.

If anxiety about the economic might of an industrialized East Asia appeared elsewhere in the West, it made its deepest inroads in a nation where industrial development lagged far behind the growth already experience by Great Britain, Germany and the United States. The *péril jaune* was seen primarily as an economic threat. Other French worries, however, complemented the economic nightmare. All the powers possessing colonies in Southeast Asia had to cope with the problems posed by substantial Chinese minorities. But France alone, in the part of the Indochinese empire made up of Tonkin, Annam and Cochinchina, had to deal, not only with Chinese migrants, but with an indigenous population which in many respects had been integrated into the traditional East Asian order built around China. The alliance with Russia, moreover, created special difficulties for the French. Other Westerners worried about the repercussions of the Russo-Japanese War in their colonies, but the Japanese appeared to present the French alone with immediate, external and internal, threats to an important imperial possession. Economic considerations had to give way, at least momentarily, to more concern with political and military affairs. But in the end the Russo-Japanese War, rather than fulfilling the prophecies of disaster initially provoked in France, brought a shift in colonial thinking and, more important, paved the way for the incorporation of Japan into the ranks of the imperialist powers on terms acceptable to the French. The Russo-Japanese struggle, however, did not wholly discredit the notion of a "yellow peril," for France continued to suffer from industrial backwardness and change continued to accelerate in the Far East.

Fear of the "yellow peril" came to encompass all of the East Asian peoples, but distinctions were made among them. The Japanese gave the French the most immediate cause for alarm on occasion, but the Chinese, whether acting alone or in tandem with the Japanese, roused the greatest fear. Such fear only took root in the last decade of the nineteenth century. By then French commentators, having long ago abandoned the Sinophilia of the eighteenth century *philosophies*, had embraced attitudes more congenial to nineteenth century imperialists. Nineteenth-century French views ran along much the same lines in business and intellectual circles: Philippe Testenore, the president of Lyon's Union des Marchands de soie, read the Chinese out of the ranks of civilized nations, while Ernest Renan contended that the nature of the Chinese language precluded "all philosophy, all science, all religion."[3] As late as the 1880s even the isolated observer who worried about China coming to constitute "a true social danger" in the "commercial and industrial" arena remained mesmerized by the size of the Chinese market, as well as by the purported commercial advantages offered by France's hold over Indochina, and hence did not challenge France's imperialist role in East Asia.[4] Despite the part played by the French in the military and cultural life of Japan during the early years of the Meiji Restoration, as well as the changes which had taken place there subsequently, the Japanese hardly fare better: in 1889 Jean-Louis de Lanessan, who would soon become Governor General of Indochina, described them as racially inferior to the Chinese.[5]

If East Asians might create difficulties on occasion for Westerners resident in their lands, they did not appear to threaten the West itself. Frenchmen concerned with East Asia, often drawing upon latent or overt racist sentiments, could afford a relaxed self-confidence.

The Sino-Japanese War introduced the catalytic agent of fear. During the period between its conclusion and the crushing of the Boxer Rebellion in 1900, a variety of ideologues, politicians and business spokesmen came to believe that grave dangers confronted France in the Far East. Paul d'Estournelles de Constant, a former diplomat who now held a seat in the Chamber of Deputies, played the most important role in spreading the new message of the "yellow peril." Lecturing in cities like Nantes, Marseille, Bordeaux and Nancy, as well as contributing to journals which helped shape bourgeois opinion, he elaborated the basic arguments of those convinced of the existence of this danger. "The Japanese victory over China," in his opinion, opened "a new chapter in the history of the world." The "yellow peril" lay in economic competition. The threat of Chinese and Japanese industrial production demanded the attention of all Europeans and, indeed, of all peoples of European origin. But the Europeans, motivated by "the most blind calculations and the most barbarous egoism," preferred to built factories in China which, as the German diplomat, Max von Brandt, had predicted, would end in competing with their own industries. Estournelles de Constant pictured a world of "universal, growing, unlimited surplus production, higher and higher tariffs, more and more economical, rapid, perfected transport, more and more skillful and widely spread copying," with all of these factors leading to lower returns for the labor expended by Frenchmen. Although he saw dangers in the American and Japanese economic competition, he worried most about China, the economic threat of the future. Chinese competition would lead to "unemployment, general distress, the closing of workshops, strikes, revolts, revolution, civil war and chaos." The Boxer Rebellion provided him with the striking demonstration of another aspect of the East Asian peril, but he did not really expect the Western powers to draw the proper lessons from it. He feared that its suppression might lead to a foolish division of China among the powers or, more likely, to increased foreign investment and factory building in a still united China. The sane course of action, in his view, would be for the Western nations to think of the consequences of their activities, curb their appetites, and unite in face of the common peril.[6]

The former diplomat carried his case into the Palais Bourbon. In 1898 he attempted to persuade his fellow deputies of the folly of thinking of the dismemberment of China in terms of the division in Africa: a divided China, aided by an influx of European capital, would develop far more rapidly than Africa and pose a far more serious danger to Europe. French participation in the division of China would be suicidal, for China would prosper at the cost of "bankruptcies, unemployment, misery in Europe, and, consequently, strikes, revolts, social upheavals."[7]

The following year, reflecting on the confrontation with Great Britain at Fashoda, he launched a more general call for an end to "colonial megalomania."[8] Later in 1899, during the discussion of the colonial budget, Estournelles de Constant returned to the Chinese question: where others saw four hundred million customers he detected four hundred million producers. Once again he argued that investment in China, mobilizing "a formidable army of merchants, workers, producers and surplus producers," would only harm French industrialists and workers.[9]

Estournelle de Constant's apocalyptic views could not be dismissed as those of an isolated eccentric. Others shared them.

The possibility of a Sino-Japanese combination, constructed around the notion of "Asia for the Asians," sparked genuine alarm.[10] If some worried about the military threat posed a revitalized East Asia, most commentators defined the "yellow peril" in economic terms.[11] A former military attaché in Peking predicted that the industrialization of China would force the French to extend the working day to sixteen hours and to reduce wages to twenty centimes a day, that only the socialists would profit from such conditions, and that the situation would lead, through "economic upheaval," to the end of "our civilization and our social order."[12] But such grim prophecies did not produce immediate despair for even some of those inclined to accept the existence of a "yellow peril" hoped that catastrophe still could be averted. Internal upheavals in China, in the opinion of one pundit, might prevent the militarization and industrialization of that gigantic nation.[13] Another believed that the positions secured by Russia and France to the north and south of China, respectively, would allow the two allies to play major roles in a gradual and pacific transformation of the Middle Kingdom.[14] But the call for a recognition of a common "Occidentalité" transcended such arguments in appeal. Entailing unity among the Western powers, such a recognition purportedly opened the way to effective defensive action against the common peril.[15] The emphasis here, just as in the preaching of Estournelles de Constant, fell upon the idea of cooperative restraint, but this recommendation never quite sealed off the possibility that defense might take preemptive, essentially offensive, forms.

The "yellow peril" thesis inevitably attracted attention in the French business community. The Sino-Japanese War allowed Castonnet des Fosses, in an address to the Parisian Société de géographie commerciale, to return to the dangers of Chinese migration into France and to stress that upheavals in East Asia would ultimately affect the Western world.[16] Relying heavily on Max von Brandt's *Die Zukunft Ostasiens*, J. Hout explained to the readers of the *Journal des Chambres de commerce françaises* the very limited potential of the China market and the danger that the Sino-Japanese War had initiated the age of economic struggle between East and West by reinforcing Japan's industrial power.[17]

Charles Gachet painted a picture of a coming Sino-Japanese alliance, with Japan providing the leadership and organization, while China supplied manpower and raw materials.[18] He saw on the horizon "an unprecedented economic revolution": Asia would be closed to Western trade and then the East Asians would flood Western markets with their products.[19] At the very least, in the opinion of another commentator, the provisions of the Treaty of Shiminoseki would allow the Japanese to unleash a major commercial drive in the East Asian markets traditionally dominated by Westerners.[20] The editors of the *Journal des Chambres de commerce françaises* saw fit to carry the analysis of a Belgian observer: Asia posed no military threat to the West, but Europe would lose its Asian markets as that area of the globe became itself a major center of industrial production.[21] An anonymous contributor to the *Bulletin de Société de géographie de Marseille*, an organ which usually favored expansion of Western trade and influence in China, argued that, once the powers had crushed the Boxers, they would be wise to recognize that "there was no urgency at all in making the Celestial Empire enter on the path of European progress."[22] The Boxer uprising, however, did not lend itself to easy use by the proponents of the "yellow peril," for, not only did Japan cooperate with the Western powers in crushing it, but the Chinese appeared to have acted in a manner which tended to confirm the nineteenth-century stereotype rather than to ratify the new fears.

Periodicals which disseminated "yellow peril" notions seldom completely endorsed them, for the lure of profits in China usually ensured the publication of contrary views, But the *Biulletom de la Société géographie de Lille*, given the nature of the constituency it served, provided the exception to the rule. This journal, like the other organs of the French geographical societies, reflected the interests of local capitalists who provided it with support.[23] The Lille business community, dominated by cotton manufacturers, shared the commitment of other French business groups to imperialism, and, indeed, in 1895 the local Chamber of Commerce agreed to cooperate with the Chambers of Commerce of Lyon, Marseille, Bordeaux, Roanne and Roubaix in sending a mission to explore the possibilities of profit in China.[24]

But unlike the business communities of Lyon, Marseille and Bordeaux which inclined toward free trade, that of Lille had espoused a fiercely protectionist position in regard to the French domestic and colonial markets. If any business community in France was likely to worry seriously about the prospect of an economic "yellow peril," the Lillois manufacturers constituted a group especially liable to be disturbed by the prospects of an alliance between the two East Asian nations, in which the Japanese would provide leadership and the Chinese manpower and raw materials, and a consequent loss of Western markets in the Far East.[25]

The possible results of the construction of the Trans-Siberian railway, a favorite project of French financiers, particularly attracted their attention: they envisioned all too clearly cheap East Asian products rolling along the completed railroad to swamp European markets.[26] To the cotton goods producers of Lille, East Asian competition could not be ignored: The Japanese presented the threat of the moment, the Chinese that of tomorrow.[27] In short, for the Lillois manufacturers, if not for the financiers of Paris, an East Asian threat really existed, and Max von Brandt's pleas for European unity in face of the East Asian threat had to be endorsed.[28] The Lillois also found it advantageous, to make use of the "yellow peril" to score points against those whose view of the ideal tariff structure for France differed from their own: their geographical journal suggested, for instance, that Japanese fabrics had begun to compete with those produced in Lyon.[29]

Far more significantly, while recognizing the importance of East Asia to France in terms of the competition between Russia and Great Britain during the struggle for concessions in China, the Lillois assigned primacy of place to France's role in Africa rather than in Asia: colonial African markets, ideally tied in a neo-mercantilism fashion to French industry, provided a much more satisfying prospect than the economic peril which appeared to be rising in the Far East.[30]

The "yellow peril" thesis provoked heated responses from those imperialists who, unlike the Lillois, thought either in more global terms or in specifically East Asian terms. According to Denys Cochin, whose commitment to the missions matched his devotion to imperialist profit, if views like Estournelles de Constant's had prevailed in the past, Columbus would never have left Europe.[31] Eugène Etienne, the leader of the *parti coloniale* in the Chamber of Deputies, also decisively rejected Estournelles de Constant's opinions.[32] Such imperialists preferred the views of the Belgian consul who dismissed the whole idea of a "yellow peril."[33] They shared the opinion of the commentator who argued that the "yellow peril" was "much more apparent than real": China might possess immense resources, but the Chinese lacked "the spirit of enterprise and initiative" which would allow them to make use of their resources.[34]

The Europeans, of course, came into the picture here. The flow of capital towards China could hardly be reversed: a China being transformed by banks, railways and mining endeavors offered European financiers a greater return than the modest three per cent found at home in State bonds.[35] French financiers in particular would benefit from China's need for capital.[36] And the fabulous market of four hundred million could not be overlooked at a time when European industry needed outlets for its products.[37]

Vistas of opportunity, in short, countered apparitions of disaster. But quick dismissals of the possible dangers posed by investment in China did not satisfy the need for more closely reasoned arguments in answer to the cries of alarm voiced by the "yellow peril" theorists. Some of those entranced by the visions of the Chinese Eldorado may have found comfort in the arguments advanced by Alfred Fouillée and J. Novicow. Fouillée believed that, though China was on the eve of an economic revolution which would allow four hundred million producers to challenge the Westerners, they white race, as long as its leveling democrats did not get out of hand, would remain "the durable elite of humanity, invincible and respected."[38] The Chinese threat, in his opinion, would actually produce benefits, for it would force the Western powers to forget their minor quarrels with each other and to unite in face of "the common peril."[39] The biologist Novicow, after providing a sensitive sketch of the relationship between the "yellow peril" thesis and the more widely diffused cultural pessimism of the *fin de siècle*, offered a more effective rebuttal to the idea of an East Asian threat: the Chinese, once launched upon industrialization, would not remain content with low wages; the Europeans possessed better machinery than the Asians; and sheer numbers hardly guaranteed economic progress.[40]

But Novicow dismissed easy assumptions of Caucasian superiority and dared to suggest that "the yellows have as much to fear from the whites as the whites do from the yellows."[41] Nocicow, like Fouillée, gave too much away. The intellectual balance, achieved by the two in very different fashions, hardly recommended itself to most of those involved in the East Asian wing of the imperialist movement.

Louis Vignon provided these imperialists with a far more congenial treatment of the "yellow peril" in the same year that Novicow's book appeared. Vignon detected three dimensions in his opponents' case. He ruled out the military and migration threats, neither of which had been taken that seriously by the French "yellow peril" theorists and devoted his closest attention to the economic danger which E. Faguet had reduced to the competitive struggle between "the five franc worker" and "the five *sous* worker." Vignon first reviewed the arguments of the "pessimists": the harm done to Manchester by the development of the Indian cotton industry, the ability, self-confidence and resources of the Japanese, the coming industrialization of China, and even the signs of industrial development in Indochina. He then asked what practical measures the pessimists would take to banish the peril. He wanted to know which Western powers were prepared to restrain themselves in East Asia. He himself could find no "efficacious remedies" for the threat. But he did not see catastrophe in it, for economic competition among the peoples of the word hardly constituted novelty. The coming of industry to India, China and Japan would give rise to "some passing crises but not to "an irreparable upset."

After touching upon the differentials in wages, the disparity in the productivity of yellow and white workers, the role which taxes, strikes and socialist agitation would play in raising Asian wages, the Western edge in "the spirit of invention," the profits to be found in Western investment in East Asian industrialization, the part which such industrialization would play in creating a new mass of consumers in the world, and the obstacles to such industrialization, Vignon concluded that "the prodigious energy of the European peoples, their considerable lead in everything, permits confidence in their future; thus, one should not confuse an economic evolution, a new development of human industry, with a 'peril' menacing Europe with ruin and death."[42]

Vignon's views parallel those of the two groups most dedicated to expansion in East Asia. The Lyonnais silk merchants, once pebrine had ravaged French sericulture in the 1850s, took the lead in promoting the French thrust into the Far East. Parisian financiers, on the other hand, only began to develop a major interest in the region late in the nineteenth century. The aims of the two groups differed in important respects. The Lyonnais primarily desired markets and raw materials in China, while the financiers looked for investment opportunities there. The Lyonnais wanted France to play a predominant role in the south and west of China, while the financiers sought returns on investments throughout the Middle Kingdom.[43] But whatever their differences, the silk and financial magnates stood united in their interest in the possibility of a "yellow peril" and, more important, in their eventual rejection of the notion.

The Chicago Exposition of 1893 alerted the Lyonnais to the possible competitive threat posed by Japan in the area of silk production, and two years later the Lyon Chamber of Commerce devoted attention to the report made by a local missionary who had investigated the Japanese silk industry on its behalf.[44] But Lyon's businessmen did not take the Japanese peril that seriously: they expected that the defeat of China would galvanize that country into life and that Japan would be the chief victim of Chinese competition.[45] The Lyon Chamber of Commerce wanted to know more about China itself, and even before the end of the Sino-Japanese War it embarked upon the organization of a major exploratory mission to that country. Immediately before the mission's departure, the Chamber's president emphasized one of its major goals: "We do not know if the yellow race is the enemy of the white race as some maintain. But if it is really so, it is better to know one's enemy than to be ignorant of him."[46]

Lending no credence to the existence of a "yellow peril," the voluminous report issued after the return of the mission took a line congenial to both commercial and financial imperialists:

It is of this Chinese, enriched by a rational exploitation of the resources of his soil, under the *inevitable* direction and with the equally *indispensable* capital of the old countries—and not the Chinese of the present who lives on thirty-five centimes a day—that European industry had need.[47]

Ulysse Pila, the Lyonnais capitalist most interested in the East Asia and the chief organizer of the mission, not only went on to paint an optimistic picture of the commercial outlets offered by the Chinese to the French, but backed his views with concrete business undertakings.[48] Henri Brenier, a leader of the mission who had already dismissed an Asian peril in a long analysis of the purported challenges posed to Lancashire by the rise of cotton manufacturing in India, supported Pila's opinions before concluding that the "yellow peril" was really the "yellow illusion."[49] Given such perspectives, the Boxer Rebellion could only come as a major disappointment, and the Lyon Chamber concluded that the treaty of Shiminoseki, "which theoretically opened China to the commerce and industry of the West," had not led to that country's becoming one of the "great nations which prosper under the influence of our Western civilization."[50] China, in the Lyon Chamber's opinion, stood revealed once again as a country where "respect for the truth has never existed."[51]

Such sentiments harked back to the earlier attitudes of the nineteenth century, and neither the high hopes nor the subsequent disappointment had anything to do with "yellow peril" theories.

Although they disagreed with the Lyonnais reading of the Chinese situation in some important respects, the Leroy-Beaulieu family, the chief spokesmen for the world of finance, arrived at much the same conclusions in regard to the "yellow peril." If Paul Leroy-Beaulieu initially worried about such a threat and made use of the notion to counsel European cooperation and the curbing of the demands of the workers, he succumbed to the lure of the profits offered by investment in China.[52] Pierre Leroy-Beaulieu, who traveled to the Far East in order to investigate conditions more closely, certainly presented French financiers with an exciting prospect of the investment opportunities arising from the coming construction of railways and the development of industry.[53] His survey of the situation allowed him to arrive at a comfortable conclusion: "If Europe must one day share the markets of the Far East with the yellow races, she is not close to being driven from them and not at all near to seeing these races come to struggle with her on her own territory. Let her show some wisdom and she will not have to worry about this famous yellow peril."[54] The Boxer Rebellion did not lead to a radical modification of this view, but it did force the introduction of a note of caution: the real investment opportunities would come when the Chinese, after having been left in some peace, discovered "the advantages of European innovations," and in the meantime it would be an error to seek more railway concessions and an even more serious mistake to demand territorial concessions.[55] Faced with the Boxer rising, Pierre Leroy-Beaulieu, without accepting their arguments, arrived at a point familiar to the proponents of the "yellow peril" thesis: restraint necessitated unity among the powers.[56]

Frenchmen living in Indochina found it as difficult to accept the benign view of East Asian conditions favored by the Parisian financiers and Lyonnais merchants as to embrace the pessimistic conclusions of the "yellow peril" theorists. Morbidly aware of the dangers encountered in the Far East and yet not prepared to acquiesce in the dark vision which called into account their role in the area, they were caught in a genuine dilemma when they attempted to balance "peril" against "illusion." If the *Avenir du Tonkin* noted on occasion the dire possibilities of a general economic threat and a more specific Sino-Japanese combination, its contributors more usually tried to draw distinctions among the East Asian peoples so as to avoid the terrifying image of a gigantic *bloc*.[57] The portrayal of the Vietnamese as "a bastardy race" of "monkeys" who managed to fuse "pride with servility" tended, on the whole, to mitigate concern with an internal threat.[58] The Chinese, however, posed internal and external problems. A Ligue Anti-Chinoise, founded in 1895 with the goal of ending their immigration, proclaimed: "*Le céleste, voilà l'ennemi.*"[59] The Tonkinese *colons*, moreover, could not discount the possibility that unrest in China would boil over into Indochina.[60] The Japanese roused yet another kind of concern, and a *colon* publicist found no sense in the authorities exposing the defenseless of Indochina to a visiting Japanese military mission.[61]

The *Revue Indo-Chinoise*, representing a broader spectrum of opinion than the *Avenir du Tonkin*, found in the Japanese "a striking example of the intellectual robustness of the races of the Far East" and hoped that the Vietnamese, under the proper French guidance, would do as well as their brothers to the north.[62] But the darkening international situation after the Boxer Rebellion discredited such views and drove the French of Indochina to a more comprehensive vision of the "yellow peril." The Anglo-Japanese alliance, interpreted as a British betrayal of Europe and Christian civilization, appeared to pave the way for Japanese mastery in the Far East.[63] The image of the "yellow peril" filled out as worries spread about increasing Japanese influence in Siam and China.[64] A Japanese desire for Indochina could be assumed, but the more immediate danger lay in the prospect of a Russo-Japanese clash.[65] If some commentators tried to exorcize this peril by indicating the advantages Japan would find in cooperation with the French and the Russians, such whistling in the dark did not provide much reassurance.[66] The Japanese need for outlets for their excessive population and production might be acknowledged, but real sympathy lay with Russia's role as "the advanced sentinel of Europe" in an East Asia where the "yellow peril" threatened to take the form of China, "with the aid of Japan," making in fifteen years the military progress accomplished by the Japanese in twenty years. According to some observers, the Japanese, motivated by envy and pride, hated the white race and aimed at spreading their "hegemony over all the peoples of the yellow race."[67] The greatest peril, in the opinion of one commentator,[68] came from their desire "to *Japanize*" the Chinese empire, and, hence, it was all the more fortunate that the Japanese could not defeat the Russians.[69]

Metropolitan opinion tended to fall into line with these views. Having once argued that Estournelles de Constant's stress on the dangers of international competition actually buttressed the case for imperialism and having dismissed the notion of an economic "yellow peril," the powerful Union coloniale turned its attention early in the twentieth century to the Japanese threat to Indochina entailed by France's ties with Russia and to the internal threat posed by the readiness of the colony's French inhabitants to express their virulently racist sentiments.[70]

Seizing upon the latter issue, the Comité de l'Asie française took the view that the French had to put their Indochinese house in order if they wished to counter the Japanese dream of dominating "the economic development of all of yellow Asia."[71]

Given the concern about Japan, the Anglo-Japanese alliance inevitably appeared as a betrayal of Western civilization.[72]

Metropolitan commentators certainly perceived the danger of a Russo-Japanese clash as real enough, though once again whistling in the dark, some observers tended to discount it.[73] Prepared to write off Korea as either already a Japanese colony or destined to become one, imperialist pundits fretted about alleged Japanese intrigues in Siam.[74] China provoked even more concern.

One could still view that country in terms of Guizot's old slogan. "*Enrichissez-vous*," but one also had to fear a Sino-Japanese combination constructed around an anti-Western slogan of "Asia for the Asians."[75] Unfortunately from the French perspective, the Japanese aspired to be "the educators of the yellow race."[76] The metropolitan imperialists, forced by circumstances to confront the geo-political and economic dimensions of the Japanese problem, moved away from the easy assumptions dominant before the turn of the century.

The now more widely spread currents of unease coalesced into stark fear with the outbreak of the Russo-Japanese War.[77] If that conflict provided Jean Jaurès with an opportunity to ridicule the notion of a "yellow peril," neither the economic nor the moral arguments of the Socialist leader appealed to convinced imperialists.[78] They were far more likely to be swayed by the reasoning of Paul Doumer, a former Governor General of Indochina who had returned to the Chamber of Deputies. Doumer confidently expected a Russian victory, but he also feared the consequences if a Japanese triumph: Japanese hegemony throughout the Far East, the expulsion of Europeans from China, and, most important, the Japanese mobilization of China against Europe. The war, therefore, appeared to him as "an episode, the possibly decisive phase in the struggle of our race with the yellow race." The situation, in his view, called for Western unity. The focus of cooperative action on the part of France, Russia, Germany, Great Britain and the United States, should be on China rather than Japan, for China, with its talented population and immense resources, could not be allowed to enjoy a "complete independence."[79]

Henri Moreau, in an apocalyptic work, dropped Great Britain and the United States from the pleas for cooperation and called instead for a European defensive entente linking Paris, Saint Petersburg, Rome, Vienna and Berlin.[80] European unity, from Brest to the Urals, would be the best response, in his opinion, to the "yellow peril" and the sinister Anglo-American-Japanese-Siamese combination which aimed at the destruction of the French empire.[81] Few observers possessed imaginations as rich as Moreau's, and some still went so far as to recognize Japan's more or less legitimate need to expand.[82] Pierre Leroy-Beaulieu even had the grace to admit that, if the Japanese had shown little respect for the right of each country to an independent existence, neither the French, the English nor the Russians had distinguished themselves in that respect.[83] Such realism, however, did little to assuage the anxieties of those who now perceived Russia as the defender of the entire white race.[84]

The vacillations of René Pinon, writing in the *Revue des deux mondes*, perhaps best reflected the uncertainties which sprang from the rapid unfolding of events in the Far East. He disavowed any intent to conjure up "the phantom of the mongol ogre," but he argued that, if the "yellow peril" was hardly imminent, neither was it wholly imaginary. Reflecting upon past external threats to Western civilization, he initially hoped that the new menace would force Westerners into greater unity. But after the fall of Port Arthur he came to a much more sober conclusion: future historians would see that date as marking the watershed between the nineteenth and twentieth centuries and, much more important, the divide between the ages of European expansion and contraction.[85]

French fears did not focus solely on Japan. Take country, taken alone, might be contained. But China, seen as the real prize in the struggle between Russia and Japan, introduced another element into the calculus of power.[86] Some worried that China would abandon neutrality and go to the aid of Japan.[87]

Others feared an eventual Sino-Japanese combination, a prospect even supposed to worry the British.[88] A fundamental threat seemed to lie in "an armed, productive, exporting China" led onto new paths "by the audacious ambition of victorious Japan."[89] If a triumphant Japan succeeded in mobilizing the immense labor power of China, then East Asian markets would be closed to Europeans, Far Eastern goods would inundate Europe, and European wages would fall.[90] It could be presumed that Japan wished to secure control over the massive Chinese population and to use it "as an instrument which will assure her hegemony over the entire Far East and make her mistress of the Pacific, this other Mediterranean, towards which the axis of world politics seems to be shifting."[91]

Whatever the future menace of China, the Russo-Japanese War posed a far more immediate danger to Indochina. In France, for instance, it encouraged the spread of ideas like those expressed in Onésime Reclus' *Lâchons l'Asie, Prenons l'Afrique*. After surveying the strength of the other Western powers in East Asia, the difficulties encountered by the French in their dealings with the Vietnamese, and the Japanese threat, Reclus proposed an exchange of France's Asian possessions for new territories in Africa and concentration on the development of empire in the western Mediterranean region.[92] Those devoted to the cause of empire in East Asia, of course, could hardly tolerate such opinions. Confronted with Reclus' "strange, baroque work," one observer simply denied that Indochina faced any serious external threat.[93] After describing the "yellow peril" thesis as marked by "the most fantastic hypotheses," another commentator argued that, while Reclus might be right theoretically, his position made no sense in terms of real life which destined white men to remain in Asia "at least until a revivified Asia eliminates them."[94] Here again China constituted the crux of the problem.[95]

Those who believed that they would soon confront the Japanese in Indochina found less time to worry about the Chinese menace of a more or less distant future. Often elaborated in terms of an all-encompassing "yellow peril," a Japanese threat to Indochina tended to be taken for granted in the colony: one did not have to accept the authenticity of the "Kodama Report," an alleged Japanese plan of conquest published in the *Echo de Paris*, to agree that in general it revealed the nature of Japanese designs.[96] Manias about the operations of Japanese spies in Indochina and Japanese intrigues in Siam developed.[97] The real horror sprang from the belated discovery that the Vietnamese could not be relief upon in the event of a Japanese attack.[98]

Given the weakness of its garrison and distance from France, the colony could not be defended unless its rulers enjoyed the support of support or at the very least the "benevolent neutrality" of the subject population.[99] The Vietnamese, however, revealed a disquieting propensity to identify with the Japanese and even looked to them as potential liberators.[100]

Now confronted with a pressing need "to win the hearts and minds of the people," French imperialists had to consider the prospects of reforms within Indochina.[101]

The colonial theory of Association, presented as the antithesis of the hitherto dominant theory of Assimilation, appeared to offer the means through which the French situation might be remedied.[102] The Associationist school of colonial theorists argued that the various peoples of the world profoundly differed from each other and demanded that these dissimilarities be taken into account in the government of the empire. But the associationist perspective lay open to conflicting interpretations. It could be expounded, in the most general terms, either as a call to enlightened toleration of the customs of the diverse peoples subjected to the sway of French power or as the logical conclusion of viciously racist postulates. The ambiguities did not end there. In the case of Indochina, Association could be presented by Albert de Pourvourville as entailing the preservation of traditional institutions and beliefs, as well as the indigenous elite, and by Jean Barnère as implying the transformation of the Vietnamese into "a *people*" and bringing them into the modern world. Such ambiguities allowed various groups to define Association in terms of their own interests. The Tonkinese *colons*, for instance, after having championed Associationist ideas for years, attacked Etienne Clémentel, the first Colonial Minister to espouse them officially, as the "partisan of association and the victim of disassociation."[103] The *colons* complained that "under the coloring of Association, we raise the Yellows, we lower the Whites."[104] Here the *colons* gave too much credit to the metropolitan politicians wh, lacking ideas of their own but in need of a response to the dangers revealed by the Russo-Japanese War, rallied to Association as a convenient slogan. Colonial administrators, who usually paid lip-service to the imperial theory most influential in Paris at any given time but who coped with immediate problems in a largely pragmatic fashion, proved no more adept than the politicians when it came to resolving the ambiguities at the heart of the Associationist position.

The very notion of a "yellow peril" introduced a note of discord into Associationist theory. Gustave Le Bon, the first major theorist of this colonial school, devoted an entire chapter to "the economic struggles between East and West" in his *Psychologie du socialisme* where he used "yellow peril" arguments in an effort to discredit socialism.[105] Leopold de Saussure shared Le Bon's worries about the emergence of Japan as an industrial power and, equally important, his view that the acquisition of Western industrial skills by the Japanese had not modified values and customs which, for essentially racial reasons, not only differed from but decisively conflicted with those of the West.[106] But Jules Harmand, another proponent of Association and a former Minister to Tokyo, took a significantly more nuanced stand. He emphasized the existence of a "hierarchy of races and civilizations," the distinction between the material and moral components of a civilization, and the success of the Japanese in taking over the former, but not the latter, from the West.[107] Harmand still did not accept the idea of an inevitable conflict. A year after the conclusion of the Russo-Japanese War, without once mentioning the "yellow peril" thesis, he denied propositions central to it, the desire of the Japanese to mobilize the population and resources of China and the affinities of the Chinese and Japanese.[108]

Harmand's ideas struck a responsive chord among those who believed, despite misgivings, that France or, in larger terms, the West, could still play a significant role in East Asia, especially in China. During the Russo-Japanese War Pierre Leroy-Beaulieu arrived at the tepid conclusion that, whatever the results of the struggle, Westerners would henceforth have to pay closer attention to "the yellows."[109] According to Paul Pelliot, the eminent Sinologist, the "renovation of China" threatened the West, but, as the clock could not be turned back, it would be wise to reach an acceptable *modus vivendi* with the forces of change, while seeking to prevent the Japanese from dominating the education of the Chinese.[110] René Pinon certainly worried about "the birth of a Monroe doctrine of use to the yellow world," but, after a painstaking effort at evaluating the Chinese situation, he concluded that the "Japanization" of China might work to the detriment of Japan.[111] Louis Aubert also feared "Japanese Monroes," with their calls of "Asia for the Asians" and their goal of the "Japanization" of China, but he emphasized the "slow and pacific" route which the Japanese would take to achieve their aims, the obstacles created by the very scope of their ambitions, and the advantages which their possession of capital gave to the Americans and Europeans over the Japanese when it came to assisting in the development of China.[112]

Others proved less inclined to make any concessions to the possibility of a "yellow peril." As early as October 28, 1905, Ulysse Pila, speaking on behalf of the Lyon Chamber of Commerce, at a meeting with Paul Beau, the Governor General of Indochina, stressed that their ties with Great Britain allowed the

French to benefit from the Anglo-Japanese alliance, denied a Japanese threat to the French possessions in Asia, noted signs of change in China, and called for the maintenance of the "open door" policy there. Although uneasy about the prospects for French trade in China, Pila believed that the transformation of that country required capital and that the French, working in cooperation with foreign financiers, would supply it. The Chamber of Commerce's president, Auguste Isaac, used the same occasion to deny any external or internal threats to Indochina. In the congenial setting provided by the Lyonnais imperialists, the Governor General felt free to elaborate on plans for higher education in Indochina which were designed to shape "an indigenous elite" and to attract to the colony those Chinese students who now flocked to Japan for their education. Beau justified his educational projects in terms of the current talisman of Association which, in this case, allowed for change as long as it remained confined to channels sanctioned by and of benefit to the colonial masters.[113]

The idea that Europeans still had a major role to play in East Asia also dominated another response to the disquiet created by the Russo-Japanese War. The French of Indochina, despite their worries about a Japanese threat, still could not accept arguments which cast doubts upon the permanence of what they regarded as their acquired rights. A critic for the *Revue Indo-Chinoise*, consequently, forcefully rejected the visions, presented in Raoul Castex's *Jaunes contre Blancs*, of a "yellow invasion" and "humanity...doomed to racial struggles." This review, acknowledging that Asia stood on the eve of a "grandiose revolution," argued that opposition to sweeping and inevitable change would fuse madness with criminality. But believing that the white race still had a major role to play in directing the course of the Asian transformation, the critic went on to challenge the "yellow peril" thesis by insisting that the nations of Asia were as divided among themselves as those of Europe. In his view, aristocratic England, aware of the differences among the East Asian nations, had had the good sense to align itself with Japan, while democratic France, swayed by racist prejudices, had hesitated to seek such ties. France's mistakes, however, could be made good by a sound native policy in Indochina and more sophisticated diplomacy.[114]

Leaving aside the question of the sophistication of French diplomacy, the new pattern of international relations established after the Russo-Japanese War favored this perspective at the expense of "yellow peril" alarums. Lecturing at the prestigious Ecole des Sciences Politiques, Robert de Caix, the chief spokesman for the Comité de l'Asie française, reviewed the evolution of events since the Russo-Japanese struggle. He noted the "yellow peril" fears focussed on Japan at the conclusion of the conflict, but argued that subsequent developments had revealed their hollowness. It now appeared to him that in 1904 the Japanese had undertaken "the most legitimate war in the national defence." Subsequent difficulties with the United States had helped to introduce a note of caution into Japanese policy. In any event, the Japanese, turning back to internal development, needed Western capital. They did not threaten Indochina. Caix took comfort in all the diplomatic arrangements, the Anglo-Japanese alliance, the Franco-Japanese accord of 1907, the Russo-Japanese settlement of the same year, the Root-Takahira agreement of 1908, which tended to stabilize conditions in East Asia by guaranteeing the integrity of

China. These accords were especially important, for it had become clear, in Caix's opinion, that "the enormous problem that the reform of China poses for our generation" dominated the Far Eastern situation. Unfortunately, in his view, "the future of the Chinese reform" remained "absolutely uncertain," and this very uncertainty prompted him to argue that the French should concentrate on Indochina rather than China. But Caix did not make the mistake of neatly separating the Indochinese and Chinese situations. Not only did he call for better treatment of France's subjects, but he warned against opposing reform in China, for, in his opinion, such opposition would surely give rise to difficulties in Indochina.[115]

Caix's insistence on the folly of opposing reform in China because of the inevitable repercussions in Indochina underlined the real and potential connections between developments throughout the Far East during the period between the end of the Russo-Japanese War and the outbreak of World War I. If the appeal of apocalyptic visions of a comprehensive "yellow peril" tended to contract during these years, such connections still served to keep alive varying versions of the racist thesis. Japan's recent victories and current strength, as well as the impressions these made in Indochina and China, continued to provoke concern in some quarters.[116] The spread of nationalism, the Manchu reforms and the 1911 revolution in China also roused considerable uneasiness.[117] The Tonkinese *colons*, on the frontier of empire, naturally enough proved most susceptible to fears of the Japanese and/or Chinese.[118] But even the *colons* comforted themselves on occasion with the idea that, despite developments like the Chinese revolution, relatively little had really changed in East Asia.[119] Others, more generally secure than the *colons* and hence less given to hysteria, could afford cooler visions of the changing situation in the Far East.

Imperialist opinion largely came to accept and, in some instances, to welcome Japan's admission to the divided ranks of the imperial powers which had hitherto made up a white-man's club in East Asia. Sober calculations replaced racist fears. Imperialists now found it possible to believe that neither a Sino-Japanese combination nor a Japanese threat to Indochina had to be taken seriously.[120] By the spring of 1913 it could even be suggested that, in exchange for French capital, Japan "could, with us and for us, police the Far East."[121] The Chinese revolution stalked behind this proposition: an essentially conservative Japan stood in attractive contrast to a revolutionary China which had become "the propagandist of disorder and anarchy."[122] This view, however, emerged from a welter of conflicting opinions. The colder appraisals, though freed from the burden of racist fantasy, did not necessarily end in either clarity or general agreement. French commentators squabbled over the inevitability and desirability of change in China. Even those who accepted both elements disagreed among themselves over the coming transformation's proper limits. Confronted with efforts at change in China, observers divided over prospects for success. Jules Harmand emphasized the long time required for truly significant change.[123] General Négrier, whose view of China harked back to the prejudices dominant in the nineteenth century, simply ruled out the possibility of China representing any "yellow peril."[124] The more cautious found it impossible to predict, even after careful efforts at analysis, the results of either reform or revolution.[125] Others believed that the acceptance of the idea of change among the Chinese opened the way for an increase of French influence in areas like education.[126] Yet others, with their eyes fixed on the investment opportunities to be secured through international consortia, welcomed the changes which promised to produce financial benefits.[127] Eugène Etienne, still the leading colonialist politician, drew imperialist hopes together in a vision of the French providing "our capital, our engineers, our teachers" to China in an effort aimed at "the common profit of China, France, humanity."[128]

Whatever the balance struck in the differing appraisals of the Chinese situation, the prospect of a "yellow peril" had been excluded from them. Despite varying emphases in the different analyzes, the conclusions tended, on the whole, to reinforce imperialist appetites: China appeared to be incapable of major change and, hence, still open to old-fashioned imperialist exploitation, or willing to embark on massive change and, therefore, in desperate need of foreign capital. Such conclusions, along with the acceptance of Japan as a "respectable" imperial power, made it possible for contributors to the influential *Revue des deux mondes* to explore the economic, political, and ideological dimensions of the changing East Asian situation without having to burden the readers with the racist specter.[129] The majority of French imperialists interested in East Asia, despite signs of panic during the Russo-Japanese War, much preferred this approach to an East Asian world in which opportunities for profit could still be detected.

The thrust of imperialist sentiment, along with that of the diplomatic arrangements worked out in East Asia after the Russo-Japanese War, led some to welcome Japan's entrance into World War I on the side of France. Early in the global struggle Robert de Caix found it perfectly natural to end a lecture with a rousing "banzai."[130] But visions of the yellow peril had not wholly vanished. In Tonkin a *colon* publicist greeted the news of Japan's entry into the war in an entirely different fashion: "I seem to hear from here the 'banzai' of the entire Japanese empire on the day of the fall of Tsingtao. And I will not be the only one to hear it. All yellow ears, from now on, strain and listen."[131] The following year Japan's presentation to China of the Twenty-One Demands seemed to confirm the prophetic powers of those who two decades earlier had feared Japan taking the lead in the modernization of China. But to exalt the prescience of the "yellow peril" theorists would be to misconstrue the history of the twenty years between the Sino-Japanese War and World War I. The real peril in East Asia, as Anatole France remarked, was "white" rather than "yellow."[132]

Anatole France's reading of the situation, like those of Novicow and Jaurès, went some way to save French honour. But the motives of most of those who opposed the "yellow peril" thesis had little to do with humanitarian sentiments. The debate, on the whole, did not pit humanitarians against racists. Nor did the main line of fracture between the waring camps run between an anti-imperialist, racist, defensive and pessimistic body of sentiment an imperialist anti-racist, aggressive and optimistic current of opinion. Onésime Reclus and the Lillois manufacturers, who fixed their optimistic gaze on Africa rather than the Far East, hardly fit into an anti-imperialist pattern. Neither do the Tonkinese *colons* who, whatever their racist fears of the peoples surrounding them, refused to accept the idea of dismantling the French empire in Asia. The Parisian financiers and Lyonnais merchants and manufacturers, who focused their attention on East Asia, certainly spurned the "yellow peril" variant of racism and even modified their views of the East Asians somewhat when it became apparent that the cooperation of the indigenous populations might be necessary in order to achieve their imperialist goals in China and Indochina, but they never quite abandoned convictions of racial superiority which antedated the rise of the "yellow peril" theories. The heated dispute essentially involved questions of whether or not East Asians menaced domestic prosperity and/or the French position in Indochina, and it took place largely within the confines of the imperialist movement.

The chasm lay between Social Imperialists and Liberal Imperialists. Proponents and opponents of the "yellow peril" thesis accepted the notion of the benefits to be derived from empire. But the Social Imperialists concentrated their attention upon the profits to be garnered—for themselves and, by extension, for French society—within the framework of a neo-mercantilism colonial structure.[133] This structure allowed relatively backward French industries to reap rewards which otherwise would have been denied them in the international market and, consequently, the Social Imperialists could only feel directly threatened when confronted with prophecies of an overwhelming economic danger. Liberal Imperialists, like the Lyonnais manufacturers, whose silken commodities dominated the international market, and the Parisian financiers, who sought returns outside France and the French empire, were much more open to the notion of informal empire knit together by trade and investment. The Liberal Imperialists did not scorn the colonies—Ulysse Pila possessed substantial holdings in Indochina and the Russo-Japanese War gave the financiers some bad moments—but they differed from the Social Imperialists in their acceptance of an international division of labour and their willingness to contemplate passing crises within the French and global economies. Their readiness to cooperate with others abroad and to accept stresses and strains within French society did not prevent them from also claiming that their undertakings served the general interests of France: what proved of benefit to them would, on the whole and in the long run, benefit the nation. Putting the matter more crudely, the clash took place between those who did and those who did not possess stakes in East Asia.

Members of the former group tended to discriminate among the East Asian peoples. This readiness to make distinctions curbed any inclination to accept the vision of the menace posed by an undifferentiated "yellow horde." If concern with the Far East did not wholly free them from confusion, it gave them some grasp of the significance of specific events and larger developments. But an excessive optimism, an almost inevitable failing of proponents of imperialist *Realpolitik* vitiated much of their analyzes of long-term trends.

The very lack of concrete or fancied interests in the Far East allowed Social Imperialists to perceive more accurately some of the possible implications of accelerating change in the area and to make certain predictions which could seem to be confirmed during the course of subsequent decades. Not only the Twenty-One Demands of 1915, but the Lyon Chamber of Commerce's eventual retreat into protectionism and the Japanese aggression against China during the

1930s could be related back to the apprehensions expressed by "yellow peril" theorists before 1914. Fragments of predictions confirmed, however, do not necessarily justify prophets. The scientific racism of these theorists may have lent their notions an aura of ideological respectability, but meta-historical vagueness, an integral part of the larger pessimism which Novicow quite rightly detected in the *fin-de-siècle*, did not equip them to deal with the events of their time in a very meaningful fashion. Those who elaborated or accepted the "yellow peril" thesis never found a satisfactory answer to the hard question of how the alleged threat might be vanquished.

Counseling cooperation and restraint among the imperial powers was one thing, but achieving it was quite another. In fact, the opponents of the "yellow peril" thesis came to share the interest in unity and forbearance and, during the years after the Russo-Japanese War, found enough cooperation and restraint, within the confines of a fragile international order in East Asia, to allow them to continue to pursue imperialist goals.

It was by no means accidental that Jules Harmand, who had served as Minister in Tokyo, broke with the other theorists of Association, not by abandoning their racist postulates, but by stressing Japan's lack of aggressive designs and the difficulties standing in the way of rapid change in China. Harmand, like others, reached the comfortable conclusion that French imperialists still had room in which to manoeuver in the Far East.

Although destined in a variety of permutations to enjoy a long life in France, as well as elsewhere in the West, the notion of a "yellow peril" had by 1914 reached a momentary impasse in France. Too many discredited predictions littered the ideological landscape, and, always weak when it came to prescription, the prophets of the "yellow peril" had not persuaded their countrymen to act upon their gloomy views. Indeed, their repetitious arguments had produced results quite different from those they desired.

The "yellow peril" thesis, far from undermining the dedication of some Frenchmen to imperialist activity in the Far East, sharpened the perception of their interests, alerted them to possible dangers, and strengthened their resolve to reap the benefits of expansion. The "yellow peril" theorists' doubts about these benefits reinforced the commitment to securing them. The French variant of the "yellow peril" vision, though less directly than the German version, also ended in buttressing imperialism in East Asia.

Notes

1. *Third Republic / Troisème République* I (Spring, 1976).

2. Heinz Gollwitzer, *Die Gelbe Gefahr. Geschichte eine Schlagrworts, Studien zum imperialistischen Denken* (Gottinggen, 1962). Gollwitzedr provides the only survey of the ways in which different nationalities viewed the "yellow peril," but he made little effort to relate these variant visions to the aims of different groups, especially imperialist groups, within particular national contexts.

3. Chambre de commerce de Lyon, *Révision du traité de Tientsin avec la Chine: Lettres à S. Exc. le Ministre de l'Agriculture et du Commerce* (Lyon, 1870), 8; Ernst Renan, *De l'origine du language* (Paris, 1864), 194 cited in Gilbert Gadoffre, *Claudel et l'univers chinois* (Paris, 1968), 35.

4. Castonnet des Fosses, "La Chine industrielle et commerciale," *Bulletin de la Société de géographie de Lyon*, April-June, 1888, 331-65.

5. J.-L. de Lanessan, *L'Indo-Chine français, étude politique, économique et administrative sur la Cochinchine, le Cambodge, l'Annam et le Tonkin* (Paris, 1889), 38.

6. Paul d'Estournelles de Constant, "Le Péril prochain—L'Europe et ses rivaux," Revue *des deux mondes*, April l, 1896, 651-86, 667, 686; Paul d'Estournelles de Constant, "Concurrence et chomage—Nos rivaux, nos charges, notre routine," *Ibid.*, July 15, 1897, 407-46; M. Estournelles de Constant, "Préface," Edmond Théry, *Le Péril jaune* (Paris, 1901), 5-27. For Von Brandt's views, see his *Die Zukunft Ostasiens* (Stuttgart, 1895).

7. February 7, 1898, *Journal Officiel*, 231-7.

8. January 23, 1899, *Ibid*, 34-40.

9. December 8, 1899, *Ibid.*, 544-9.

10. "Europe et Japon," *La Revue de Paris*, May 15, 1895, 293-303; Jean de Bloch, "Les illusions de la conquête chinoise," *La Revue des Revues*, August1l5, 1900, 341-6.

11. F. Schrader, "Le Monde jaune," *La Revue de Paris*, July 1, 1896, 127-48; Le Père Colore, "Ly-Hong-Tchang," *Ibid.*, 1896, 491-522; Deluns-Montaud, "La Guerre et la Paix," *Questions diplomatiques et coloniales*, June 1, 1897, 385-96; Jean de Bloch, *La Revue des Revues*, August 15, 1900, 344.

12. G. de Contenson, "Chine et Japon: notes et souvenirs," *Questions diplomatiques et coloniales*, January 15, 1898, 92-8.

13. Le Pére Colore, *La Revue de Paris*, August 1, 1896, 521.

14. F. Schrader, *La Revue de Paris*, July 1, 1896, 146.

15. Deluns-Montaud, *Questionas diplomatiques et coloniales*, June 1, 1897, 391-3.

16. Castonnet des Fosses, "Discours, 5 novembre 1894," *Bulletin de la Société de géographie commerciale de Paris*, XVI (1894), 695-6.

17. J. Huot, "Conséquences économiques de la guerre sino-Japonaise," *Journal des Chambres de commerce françaises*, May 10, 1895, 141-2.

18. Ch. Gachet, "Les Conséquences possibles du conflict sino-japonaise," *Bulletin de la Société géographie commerciale de Paris*, XVII (1895), 57-9.

19. *Ibid.*

20. H. Br., "Le Traité de Simonosaki, ses clauses commerciales et la concurrence japonaise," *ibid.*, XVIII (1895-1896), 742-8.

21. H.T., "Le péril asiatique," *Journal des Chambres de commerce françaises*, September 1l, 1899, 279-80.

22. "Chine," *Bulletin de la Société de géographie de Marseille*, 2me trimestre 1900, 216-9.

23. For the role played by the geographical societies and their organs, see John F. Laffey, "Municipal Imperialism in Nineteenth Century France," *Historical Reflections / Réfflexions historiques*, I (June, 1974), 81-114.

24. For the mission launched by the Lyon Chamber of Commerce, see below.

25. A. Merchier, "Choses d'Asie—Le Japon et la Chine," Bulletin *de la Société géographique de Lille*, May, 1895, 285-308.

26. "La lutte économique des deux Mondes," *ibid.*, January 1898, 107-8; L.T., "La situation militaire des puissances européennes en Extrême-Orient en 1898 (suite)," *ibid.*, July, 1899, 5-34.

27. "La Chine et le Japon au point de vue économique," *ibid.*, May, 1895, 343-5.

28. L.F. Lambert, "La situation économique en Chine et au Japon," *ibid.*, October, 1895, 212-5.

29. "Les soieries du Japon," *ibid.*, March, 1897, 216.

30. L.T., "La situation militaire des puissances européenes en Extrême-Orient en 1898," *ibid.*, June, 1899, 401-10.

31. December 8, 1898, *Journal Officiel*, 547.

32. "Budget des Colonies—Discours prononce à la Chambre des Députés le 6 mars 1899," *Eugène Etienne, Son oeuvre coloniale—algégienne et politique. Discours et écrits divers réunis et édités par la "Dépêche Coloniale"* (Paris, 1907), 272-306; "Budget des Colonies, Discours prononce à la Chambre des Députés, le 8 décembre 1899," *ibid.*, 307-25.

33. "La péril jaune,"*Journal des Débats*, February 21, 1896,1.

34. Marcel Monnier, "La Chine d'aujourd'hui et la Chine de demain,"*Bulletin de la Société géographie commerciale de Paris*, XXI (1899), 294-304.

35. René Pinon et Jean de Marcillac, *La Chine qui s'ouvre* (Paris, 1900), 4.

36. Anon., *La Chine. Expansion des grandes puissances en Extrême-Orient (1895-1898)* (Paris, 1899), 126.

37. E. Frandon, "Du développment possible du commerce entre France et la Chine," *Bulletin de Société de géographie commerciale de Paris*, XXII (1900), 572-620; Henri Blancheville, "L'Europe et l'avenir du marché chinois," *Journal des Chambres de commerce françaises*, December 25, 1900, 510-2.

38. Alfred Fouillée, "Le caractere des races humaines et l'avenir de la race blanche," *Revue des deux mondes*, July 1, 1894, 76-107.

39. *Ibid.*

40. J. Novicow, *L'Avenie de la race blanche, critique du pessisimisme contemporain* (Paris, 1897), 11-2, 18, 20-1, 64, 69-70.

41. *Ibid.*, 149.

42. Louis Vignon, "Le Péil Jaune," *Revue politique et parle-mentaire*, December, 1897, 560-92.

43. Laffey, *historical Reflections*, I (1974), 108-10. For the role of the Lyonnais in East Asia during the nineteenth century, see John F. Laffey, "Les racines de l'impérialisme français en Extême-Orient," *Revue d'histoire moderne et contemporaine*, XVI (April-June, 1969), 282-99.

44. Auguste Chabrières et Joseph Guinet, *Les soies et les soieries à l'Exposition de Chicago, Rapports présantées à la Chambre de commerce de Lyon* (Lyon, 1894), 18, 119; "Rapport de M. Marnas sur la fabrique de soieries japonaise," *Compte rendu des travaux de la Chambre de commmerce de Lyon, Année 1896* (Lyon, 1897), 85-98.

45. "Une revanche de la Chine," *Bulletin des soies et soieries*, June 8, 1895, 3-4.

46. Edouard Aynard, "Mission de exploration commerciale en Chine," *Compte rendu des travaux de la Chambre de commerce de Lyon, Année 1895* (Lyon, 1896), 297-326.

47. Henri Brenier, "Conclusions," in Chambre de commerce de Lyon, *La Mission Lyonnaise d'exploration commerciale en Chine, 1895-1897, 2e partie, Rapports commerciaux et notes diverses* (Lyon, 1898), 431-51. Ehphasis in original.

48. Ulysse Pila, "Necessité de l'expansion française en Chine, le Marché chinois," *Questions diplomatiques et coloniales*, June 15, 1897, 449-57; Ulysse Pila, "La Mission lyonnaise d'exploration en Chine et le développment de notre commerce exteieur," *ibid.*, September 1, 1897, 129-93. For Pila's career, see Laffey, *Revue d'histoire moderne et contemporaine*. XVI (1969), 295, fn. 7.

49. Henri Brenier, "L'évolution industrielle de l'Inde. Contribution à l'étude du développment de la grande industrie dans lExtrême-Orient," *Annales de l'Ecole libre des sciences politiques*,

July, 1894; September, 1894, 614-37; January 15, 1895, 77-94; H. Brenier, "L'illusion jaune," *La nouvelle*, I, (1899), 427-44.

50. "Revisions des traités de commerce avec la Chine," *Compte rendu des travaux de la Chambre de commerce de Lyon, Annee 1902* (Lyon, 1903), 256-61.

51. *Ibid.*, 258.

52. Paul Leroy-Beaulieu, "L'Extrême-Orient et la civilisation européenne," *L'Economiste français*, May 4, 1895, 557-9; Paul Leroy-Beaulieu, "De nouvelles perspectives financières et commerciales pour le monde civilisé," *ibid.*, August 31, 1895, 269-71.

53. Pierre Leroy-Beaulieu, "Lettres d'Extrême-Orient: Pekin; les chemins de fer en Chine,' *ibid.*, December 25, 1897, 829-31; Pierre Leroy-Beaulieu, "L'Avenir de la France en Chine: le rapport de la mission lyonnaise," *ibid.*, December 24, 1898, 857-9; Perre Leroy-Beaulieu, "Le Problème chinois, *revue des deux mondes*, January 1, 1899, 43-73; Pierre Leroy-Beaulieu, *La Rénovation de l'Asie: Siberie—Chine—Japon* (Paris, 1900), 482.

54. Pierre Leroy-Beaulieu, "Lettres d'Extrême-Orient: Shanghai, les concessions; la monnaie; l'industrie euro-péenne et les salaires en Chine," *L'Economiste français* Junauary 8, 1898, 38-40.

55. Pierre Leroy-Beaulieu, "Les Emprunts chinois et l'avenir financier de la Chine," *ibid.*, July 21, 1900, 85-7; Perre Leroy-Beaulieu, "La Chine et le monde civilisé," *ibid.*, September 29, 1900, 425-7.

56. *Ibid.*, 427.

57. "Caveant Consules," *Avenir du Tonkin*, January 20, 1900. i; A.G., "Le Péril jaune," *ibid.*, Febrary 10, 1900, 1; "Bulletin," *ibid.*, July 29, 1900, 1; B., "Le Japon et la Chine," *ibid.*, August 24, 1900, 1. 58. G., "Appréciations Subjectives," *ibid.*, December 29, 1900, 1; M.N., "Le Serment," *ibid.*, June 9, 1897, 1; Michael du Breil, "Mentalité Française, Mentalité Annamite (3e article)," *ibid.*, April 30, 1905, 1. Such citations could be easily multiplied.

59. "Ligue Anti-Chinoise," *Supplement de l'Avenir du Tonkin*, May 4, 1895, n.p.

60. Paul de Vareilles, "Concessions nouvelles," *Avenir du Tonkin*, June 12, 1897, 1; George Marx, "La Chine et les Grandes Puissances," *ibid.*, February 5, 1898, 3. Marx invoked memories of the Black Flags in discussing the chances of a Chinese eruption across the frontier. For the Black Flags, see Ella S. Laffey, "La formation d'un rbelle: Liu Yong-fu et la création d'armée des Pavillions Noires," in Jean Chesnaux *et al, Mouvements populaires et sociétés secrètes en Chine au XIXe et XXe siècles* (Paris, 1970), 248-66.

61. M.N., "Les Japonais en mission," *Avenir du Tonkin*, April 24, 1897, 1.

62. "Revue des journaux," *Revue Indo-Chinoise*, April 22, 1901, 344-5.

63. Madele, "Angleterre et Japon," *Avenir du Tonkin*, March 22, 1902, 1; "Hebo-Revue," *Revue Indo-Chinoise*, March 10, 1902, 209-10.

64. "Hebo-Revue," *ibid.*, March 17, 1902, 233-4; A. de Pourvourville, "Le traité Anglo-Japonais et ses menaces (Suite et fin)," *Avenir du Tonkin*, March 29, 1902, 1; A. Raquez, "Hebo-Revue," *Revue Indo-Chinoise*, June 9, 1902, 513-4; "Expansion Japonaise," *Avenir du Tonkin*, September 4, 1902, 1; H.R., "Les Japonais au Siam," *ibid.*, September 17, 1902, 1; A. Raquez, "Hebo-Revue," *Revue Indo-Chinoise*, February 23, 1903, l6l-2; A. Raquex, "Japon et Siam," *ibid.*, March 2, 1903, 190-1; A.V., "L'Infiltration des Japonais en Chine," *Avenir du Tonkin*, September 21-2, 1903, 1.

65. A. Raquez, "Hebo-Revue," *Revue Indo-Chinoise*, July 7, 1902, 609-10; "L'infiltration des Japonais en Chine," *ibid.*, October 12, 1903, 935-6.

66. A. Raquez, "Hebo-Revue," *ibid.*, May 4, 1903, 385-6; Rising Sun, "Consequences d'un conflit russo-japonaise," *ibid.*, August 31, 1903, 786-97; September, 14, 1903. 840-6. The latter article first appeared in the metropolitan *Questions diplomatiques et coloniales.*

67. René Moraux, "L'Expansion Japonaise," *Revue Indo-Choise*, January 5, 1903, 8-9; J.A., "La Russie en Chine," *ibid.*, December 7, 1903, 1081-83.

68. A. Racquez, "Les dindons de la farce," *ibid.*, July 27. 1903, 666-8; Moriack, "Russes et Japonais," *ibid.*, December 21, 1903, 1115-19.

69. *Ibid.*, 1118.

70. "Chronicle coloniale," *Quinzaine coloniale*, August 10, 1897, 73-9; "Le péril jaune et la relèvement des prix et des salaires en Chine," *ibid.*, May 25, 1900, 311; "Le péril jaune," *ibid.*, June 10, 1901, 326-7; Alcide Ebray, "La Russie et la Manchourie," *ibid.*, April 25, 1902, 225-6; "Annamitophiles et Annamitophobes," *ibid.*, November 25, 1903, 746-7.

71. "La politique japonaise en Chine," *Bulletin du Comité de l'Asie française*, October, 1901, 300-2.

72. Robert de Caix, "L'Alliance Anglo-Japonaise," *ibid.* February, 1902, 51-7.

73. Robert de Caix, "Alliances franco-russe et anglo-japonaise," *ibid.*, March 19, 1902, 100-1; R.C., "La Russie et le Japon," *ibid.*, October, 1903, 424-6; Paul Labbé, "L'Oeuvre du Comité—La réunion générale annuelle," *ibid.*, November, 1903, 462-71; R.C., "Russie et Japon," *ibid.*, January, 1904, 20-2.

74. Robert de Caix, "Corée," *ibid.*, June, 1903, 232-40; "La Russie et le Japon," *ibid.*, December 1903, 565-6; R.C., "Questions siamoises," *ibid.*, May, 1902, 195-8; J.I.T., "Affaires du Siam," *ibid.*, June, 1902, 244-6; René Moreaux, "L'expansion japonaise," *ibid.*, October 1902, 434-5; "Le traité franco-siamois," *ibid.*, Movember, 1902, 475-7.

75. Robert de Caix, "Les intérêts français en Chine," *ibid.*, May, 1903, 182-8.

76. "Les Japonais, éducateurs de la race jaune," *ibid*, February, 1903, 83-4.

77. The intensity of the reaction to the supposed Japanese threat misled even so scrupulously careful a scholar as Virginia Thompson into the conclusion that the Russo-Japanese War "marked the beginning of the yellow peril psychology in France." Virginia Thompson, *French Indochina* (New York, 1968 [1937]), 103.

78. Jean Jaurès, "La Guerre russo-japonaise et l'Alliance franco-russe," *La Revue socialiste*, March, 1904, 305-16.

79. Paul Doumer, "La Crise d'Extrême-Orient," *Revue économique internationale*, May, 1904, 573-97.

80. Henri Moreau, *L'Alliance anglo-yankee-japonaise, maîtresse de l'Indo-Chine* (Paris, 1904), 65.

81. *Ibid.*, 79, 116, 174.

82. René Pinon, "La lutte pour le Pacifique," *Revue des deux mondes*, February 15, 1904, 772-807; Pierre Leroy-Beaulieu, "Le Japon et ses resources dans la guerre actuelle," *ibid.*, March 15, 1904, 389-419; Captaine Jacquet, "La Guerre Russo-Japonaise," *Revue Indo-Chinoise*, July 15, 1904, 117-38.

83. Pierre Leroy-Beaulieu, *Revue des deux mondes*, March 15, 1904, 398.

84. "Le Japon et la Chine," *Bulletin du Comité de l'Asie française*, October, 1904, 456-7.

85. René Pinon, "La guerre russo-japonaise et l'opinion européene," *Revue des deux mondes*, May 1, 1904, 186-219; René Pinon, "Le péril jaune au XIIIe sièle," *ibid.*, March 1, 1905, 143-75; René Pinon, "Après la chute de Port Arthur," *ibid.*, 545-6.

86. René Pinon, "La Chine et les puissances européennes (1894-1904)," *ibid.*, August 1, 1904, 627-66.

87. R.C., "La Guerre," *Bulletin du Comité de l'Asie française*, March, 1904, 124-31.

88. "La Guerre," *ibid.*, April, 1904, 186-92.

89. Pinon, *Revue des deux mondes*, August 1, 1904, 566.

90. Pinon, *ibid.*, May 1, 1904, 195.

91. Ch. Depincé, "Blancs contre jaunes," *Quinzaine coloniales*, January 25, 1905, 49-51.

92. Onésime Reclus, *Lâchons l'Asie, Prenons l'Afrique* (Paris, 1904), 66, 285.

93. A. Raquez, "Lâchons l'Asie—prenons l'Afrique," *Revue Indo-Chinoise*, October 30, 1904, 563-77.

94. Alfred Schreiner, "Extrême-Orient nouveau," *ibid.*, December 15, 1904.

95. *Ibid.*

96. A. Raquez, "La Guerre," *Avenir du Tonkin*, February 10, 1904, 1; Xieng La, "La Défense de l'Indo-Chine," *Bulletin du Comité de l'Asie française*, February, 1904, 85-9; Jean Barnère, "L'Evolution de l'Asie et la question indigène en Indo-Chine," *ibid.*, 89-92; "La Japon et la Chine," *ibid.*, October 190, 456; Eugène Etienne, Discours, "Le Comité—Le dîner de l'Asie

française," *ibid.*, December, 1904, 547-51; Moreau, *L'Alliance*, 8, 16, 116; "La Guerre,"*Bulletin du Comité de de l'Asie française*, January, 1905, 8-17; Depincé, *Quinzaine coloniale*, January 25, 1905, 50; "Les relations franco-japonaises," *Bulletin du Comité de l'asie française*, February, 1905, 67-8; Captaine d'Ollone, "Dîner de l'Union coloniale française et du Comité de Madagascar," *Quinzaine coloniale*, February 25, 1905, 128-33; Alf. Meynard, "Courrier Hanoi," *Avenir du Tonkin*, February 26, 1905, 1; Ba, "Discussion du 'Rapport Kodama,'" *ibid.*, March 10, 1905, 1; March 11, 1905, 1; March 13-14, 1-2; "La défense de l'"Indo-Chine," *Quinzaine coloniale*, June 10, 1905, 338-9; François Deloncle, "Préface," to Raoul Castex, *Jaunes contre Blancs, le problème militaire indo-chinois* (Paris, n.d. [1905]) 5-9; Castex, *Jaunes contre Blancs*, 19-20, 25, 29; Lt-Colonel Péroz, *France et Japon en Indo-Chine* ([Paris], 1906, 52, 75, 77-8, 97, 99, 131; Le Captaine Paul Cassou, *Etude sur la situation militaie de l'Indo-Chine* (Paris, 1906), 3,51, 66.

97. A. Raquez, "Espionnage (II)," *Avenir du Tonkin*, Jully 31, 1904, 1; Castex. *Jaunes contre Blancs*, 48-9; Péroz, *France et Japon*, 97; Cassu, *Etude*, 67-8; Louis Albert, *Paix Japonaise* (Paris, 1906), 95.

98. Barnère, *Bulletin du Comité de l'Asie française*, February, 1904, 90; Le N., "Confiance et Trahison," *Avenir du Tonkin*, April 9, 1905, 1; Henri Lamônier, "Aures Habent...," *ibid.*, April 10-1, 1905, 1; Louis Bonafont, "Lettre Ouverte à M. Clémentel, Ministre des Colonies," *ibid.*, May 4, 1905, 1; Albert de Pourvourville (Matgioi), *Les défenses de l'Indo-Chine et politque d'association (Paris, 1905)*, 63-4; Castex, *Jaunes contre Blancs*, 43-5; Cassou, *Etude*, 70, 101-6, 177; Jean Ajalbert, *L'Indo-Chine en péril* (Paris, 1906), 14-5.

99. "La Guerre," *Bulletin du Comité de l'Asie française*, February, 1904, 68-76; Pourvourville, *Les défenses*, 111, 125.

100. Henri Maître, "Ferments Dangereux," *Avenir du Tonkin*, March 30, 1905, 1; Cassou, *Etude*, 107; Ajalbert, *L'Indo-Chine*, 17.

101. "La Guerre," *Bulletin du Comité de l'Asie française*,February, 1904, 75; Castex, *Jaunes contre Blancs*, 100-1; Cassou, *Etude*, 344; Edouard Payen, "L'Année 1905 en Indo-Chine," *Bulletin du Comité de l'Asie française*, January, 1906, 7-9.

102. Barnère, *ibid.*, February, 1904, 92; Pourvourville, *Les défenses*, 112-3, 127-8, 135-6, 139, 196, 200; Ajalbert, *L'Indo-Chine*, 30, 79; Aubert, *Paix*, 244. As Raymond Betts quite rightly argued, the official sanctioning of Association resulted from "a growing fear of the supposed 'yellow peril.' " Raymond Betts, *Assimilation and Association in French Colonial Theory, 1890-1914* (New York, 1961), 156.

103. G.M., "Psychologie et Assimilation," *Avenir du Tonkin*, May 15-6, 1899, 1-2; "Esprit de Association, *ibid.*, September 15, 1900, 1; G., "Assimilation à outrance," *ibid.*, December 17-8, 1900,11; Edgi, "Un factum," *ibid.*, February 19-20, 1906, 1.

104. Henri Laumônier, "Hola! Doucement donc!," *ibid.*, November 24, 1905, 1.

105. Gustave Le Bon, *Psychologie du socialisme* (5th ed., Paris,1907), 234-52. The first edition appeared in 1898. For earlier expressions of his fear of an Asian economic peril, see Gustave Le Bon, *Les Civilisations de l'Inde* (Paris, 1887), 716 and Gustave Le Bon, *Psychologie des foules* (Paris, 1963 [1895]), 99-100, 226.

106. Leopold de Saussure, *Psychologie de la colonisation française* (Paris, 1899), 277-9. For Le Bon's view of the Japanese, see *Psychologie des foules*, 38-9, 273. Years later, after a Japanese diplomat challenged Le Bon's interpretation in an introduction to a translation of his works, Le Bon reasserted his belief that "European ideas have simply entered the ancestral armature of the Japanese soul, without modifying its essential parts." Gustave Le Bon, *Les Opinions et les croyances, genèse— évolution* (Paris, 1911), 69.

107. Jules Harmand, *Domination et colonisation* (Paris, 1919), 156, 7;-2, 271. The first edition appeared in 1910.

108. Jules Harmand, Discourse, "Union Coloniale Française, Dîner du 28 Novembre," *Quinzaine coloniale*, December 10, 1906, 703-10.

109. Pierre Leroy-Beaulieu, "La Situation et les perspectives économiques de la Chine," *Revue des deux mondes*, April 1, 1905, 559-90.

110. Le Comité—Conference de M. Paul Pelliot," *Bulletin du Comité de l'Asie française*, April, 1905, 130-7.

111. René Pinon, "La Japonisation de la Chine," *Revue des deux mondes*, August 15, 1905, 786-824.

112. Aubert, *Paix*, 37, 53, 85, 94, 96, 214.

113. "La colonisation en Indo-Chine—Réception de M. Beau, gouverneur général de l'Indo-Chine (Rapport de M. Ulysse Pila)," *Compte rendu des travaux de la Chambre de commerce de Lyon, Année 1905* (Lyon, 1906), 204-53.

114. "Bibliographie: *Jaunes contre Blancs* par R. Castex," *Revue Indo-Chinoise*, 2e semestre, 1905, l506-8.

115. Robert de Caix, "L'Extrême-Orient," *Ibid.*, March, 1910, 193-212. He delivered this lecture on December 11, 1909.

116. "Communication de M. Bons d'Anty, Consul de France, "Le Comité—Assemblée générale annuelle," *Bulletin du Comité de l'Asie française*, April, 1906, 137-4l; "L'Evolution de l'esprit annamite," *ibid.*, August, 1906, 297-306; Aspirations annamites ("Gardons l'Asie!)," *ibid.*, October, 1906, 378-88; Noel Peri,"L'education nouvelle en Chine," *Revue Indo-Chinoise*, 2e semestre, 1907, 1287-1301 (This article first appeared in the *Revue de Paris*); Z., "L'évolution des idées en Indochine et en Extrême-Orient et M. de Lanessan," *ibid.*, 1366-81; "Lettre du Tonkin," *Quinzaine coloniale*, June 10, 1907, 456-7; "Les menées japonais en Indo-Chine," *ibid.*, November 10, 1908, 95-8; "Un complot en Cochinchine," *ibid.*, December l0, 1908, 1072-5; Négrier, "Les forces japonaises en 1908," *Revue de deux mondes*, July 15, 1909, 338-75; Félix Klein, "Japonais et Américains," les vraies difficultés," *ibid.*, October 1, 1909, 672-704.

117. Peri, *Revue Indo-Chinoise*, 2e semestre, 1907, 1398; P. Ibos, "L'Armée jaune," *Asie française*, August, 1911, 355-63; "Variétés: Misère et deché de l'"Annam," *ibid.*, September, 1911, 414-8; Emile Lutz, "Origine et développement des idées réformistes en Chine," *ibid.*, November, 1911, 488-91; "La Révolution chinoise," *Quinzaine coloniale*, January 10, 1912, 1-2; P.B., "Le danger ch inois en Indochine," *ibid.*, January 25, 1913, 61-2.

118. For represenative views, see L. de Charmettes, "Propagande japonaise," *Avenir du Tonkin*, March 25, 1906, 1; Edgi, "Infiltration japonaise," *ibid.*, December 10-11, 1; Henri Lamônier, "Dangereux voisins," *ibid.*, August 7-8, 1911, 1; E. Ferrières, "Le régeneration financière du Japon," *ibid.*, September 29, 1912, 1; De pourvourville, "Les Complicités chinoises et l'agitation anti-française," *ibid.*, September 29-30, 1913, l.

119. Henri Laumônier, "N'Exagerons Pas," *ibid.*, March 1, 1914, 1.

120. "Un Accord franco-japonais," *bulletin du Comité de l'Asie française*, May, 1907, 169-70; "Le Japon et la Chine," *QuinzaIne coloniale*, May 25, 1908, 428-9; Robert de Caix, "La Chine, le Japon et les Etats-Unis," *Bulletin du Comité de l'Asie française*, December, 1908, 495-50l1 Robert de Caix, "Les Japonais au Foukien," *ibid.*, February, 1909, 298-301; "Coup d'oeil sur la situation de l'Indochine. Conférence de J. Harmand," *Quinzaine coloniale*, November 25, 1910, 285-94; Robert de Caix, "la modification et le renouvellement de l'alliance anglo-japonaise," *Asie française*, July, 1911, 307-9; Kataphronète, "L'Indochine et les négociations commerciales franco-japonaise," *ibid.*, March, 1911, 119-20.

121. Jean Thibaut, "Chronique de l'Extrême-Orient, I. Japon," *revue Indo-Chinoise*, April, 1913, 472-5.

122. *Ibid.*, 473.

123. Jules Harmand, "Le rôle politique des colonies et la défense de l'Indo-Chine," *Revue bleu*, November 2, 1907, 545-51.

124. Négrier, "Les forces chinoises en 19l0," *Revue des deux mondes*, August 1, 1910, 567-605.

125. Rouire, "La Transformation de la Chine, I. Les Origines du mouvement réformiste, les édits impériaux et leurs résultats," *ibid.*, March 1, 1910, 180-208; "II. L'Evolution des idés chinoises, l'avenir des réformes," *ibid.*, May 1, 1910, 204-28; Pierre Khorat, "Psychologie de la révolution chinoise," *ibid.*, March 15, 1912, 295-330.

126. J. Legendre, "L'Enseignement en Chine," *Revue Indo-Chinoise*, September, 1910, 207-17.

127. From 1909 to 1914 *Asie française* carried a steady stream of articles concerned with Chinese loans.

128. "Le Comité—Discours de M. Eug. Etienne à l"ecole libre des sciences politiques," *Asie francaise*, January, 1910, 7-l11

129. "La Défense de l'Indo-chine," *Revue des deux mondes*, April 15, 1906, 781-814; J. Harmand, "Le traité franco-siamois et le Cambodge," *ibid.*, July 1, 1907, 86-101; Vay de Vaya, "La fin d'un empire. La japonisation de la Corée," *ibid.*, January 1, 1908, 178-210; Vay de Vaya, "L'Evolution de l'éducation au Japon, I. La mentalité nipponne," *ibid.*, March 1, 1908, 191-215; "II. Les tendances socialistes et réactionnaires," *ibid.*, June 1, 1908, 676-708; René Pinon, "Le Boycottage," *ibid.*, May 1, 1909, 199-228; La Mazelière, "Les Institutions du Japon moderne," *ibid.*, March 1, 1911, 114-49; Pierre Khorat, "Le problème politique dans l'Inde anglaise et dans l'Indochine française," *ibid.*, June 15, 1914, 870-903.

130. "Variétés: Une Conferance sur le Japon," *Asie francaise*, July-December, 1914, 29-85.

131. Albert Lamblot, "Appréhensions," *Avenir du Tonkin*, August 21, 1914,1l.

132. Cited in Gollwitzer, *Die Gelbe Gefahr*, 159.

133. An excellent treatment of the French variant of Social Imperialism can be found in Sanford Elwitt, *The Making of the Third Republic: Class and Politics in France, 1868-1884* (Baton Rouge, 1975), 273-304. Professor Elwitt, however, does not fully articulate the distinction between Social and Liberal imperialists in his otherwise admirable discussion. His reasons are understandable, for while issues like colonial tariffs and the "yellow peril" brought the cleavage into the open, the general tendency of French imperialists was to band together in face of a public either interested in or hostile to formal and informal empire. It might be suggested that Eugène Etienne's success as a colonial politician derived in large part from his ability to get on well with Liberal Imperialists without abandoning his basic commitment to Social Imperialism.

IDEOLOGY

6

AUGUSTE COMTE:
PROPHET OF RECONCILIATION
AND REACTION[1]

France was scarred in the nineteenth century by social conflict arising from the unfolding of the implications of the revolution of 1789 and from the impact of the Industrial Revolution. In the first half of the nineteenth century the manifestations of this conflict, along with the specter of industrialization in Great Britain, provoked a "politics of reconciliation," a general reaction to social problems which comprehended quite divergent specific solutions. The differences among these solutions should not be underestimated, but they were all bound together by a horror of what was depicted as the disintegration of society into a chaos of struggling individuals and competing classes and by a common desire for the establishment of a new unity among these conflicting fragments. The French social thought of the early nineteenth century which consciously set itself in opposition to liberalism shared some common features: a desire for order, a concern with science, an interest in hierarchy, some recognition of the class struggle and a profound desire to end it, a willingness to see religion as an instrument of social cohesion, and a belief in the need for and the possibility of the good society in which all classes worked in harmony. All of these elements found a place in the system of Auguste Comte just as they had in the very divergent systems of the Catholic theocrats and the Utopian Socialists. While recognizing the common factors which relate the analyses and remedies of such disparate figures as Bonald and Saint-Simon, it is still necessary to point to factors which differentiate these systems in terms of conservatism and radicalism. This article seeks to establish the relationship of Auguste Comte to the broad intellectual pattern of the politics of reconciliation while also fixing his position in the reactionary-progressive spectrum within that pattern.

The revolution ignited in France in 1789 swept through Europe with the armies of the Republic and Napoleon, shattering the traditional framework of society, proclaiming "the rights of man," providing for the rapid advancement of some, decreeing the more rapid despatch of others, destroying the privileges of established churches, dissolving old pieties and more recent certitudes. Out of this political and social crisis came new ideas of social democracy. European society was deeply shaken and the final peace settlement appeared to some as too superficial to curb the forces of anarchy released by the revolution. The

Restoration restored little in France. The bourgeoisie had moved to the front rank of the French elite. But, satisfying neither the partisans of the *ancien régime* nor the more militant revolutionaries nor, in the end and decisively, its conservative liberal supporters, the Bourbon regime was overthrown. The July Monarchy, installed amid hopes for improvement, only aggravated the social crisis. A minority responded to Guizot's "Enrichissez-vous," and others suffered because of it. The July revolution and the monarchy it introduced failed to terminate a continuing social crisis.

Complicating the situation and increasing the misery of those unfortunate enough to be excluded from the prosperity of the bourgeois monarchy was the first impact of the Industrial Revolution. While it would be an error to exaggerate the amount of industrial development in France prior to 1848, significant changes did take place in the structure of the French economy. The number of spindles in the textile industry increased by fifty per cent between 1830 and 1848. Steam power was slowly coming to play a role in industry. Despite much confusion in the initial stages of financing and construction, the first efforts aimed at developing a railroad system stimulated the metal industries. The factory began to replace the small workshop in the larger cities, and the workers' idealization of the workshop became another indication of the misery caused by industrialization. In some industries, particularly at times of commercial crisis, wages declined drastically.[2] Justified by the liberal logic of Jean-Baptiste Say and Charles Dunoyer, the bourgeoisie opposed any attempt at remedying conditions, which they saw as partaking of a Malthusian permanency. In response to such developments, Lyon and Paris witnessed short-lived insurrections. The monument of the July Monarchy, Daumier's *La Rue Transonnain*, was left in the wake of one of these abortive revolts.

The men of reconciliation elaborated their analyzes and solutions in the face of one or both of the revolutionary currents. The politics of reconciliation which they developed looked forward to a time when the struggles among men had ceased. In the social sphere it sought the end of class conflict, but not the end of classes. Indeed, a vital element in the politics of reconciliation was the continued existence of classes although they position in the social structure—and this is usually the social hierarchy—might be altered. Several factors explain the emphasis on the continued existence of classes. One of these was the feeling that the violent class conflicts of the French Revolution had solved nothing. Allied to this was the deeply-rooted belief that love, a love which was essentially Christian *caritas*, could and should be the strongest bond among men, no matter what their social class. A third factor was the appeal of the message of companionship and association in a world still very much marked by existence of the small workshop and agricultural community and, perhaps more importantly, coloured by distorted images of how good life had been before the first impact of industry and the hardening of class barriers it brought with it. In some cases, yet another reason was the appeal of the revolutionary idea of "the career open to talent" and its corollary of the need for a social hierarchy with high position as the reward for ability. A somewhat more practical reason for the politics of reconciliation lay in the need of various reformers for capital in order to implement their schemes. While denouncing present abuses and threatening politicians and employers with the disastrous consequences of their policies, the men of reconciliation seldom renounced appealing to the ruling elite for support. Conservatives and radical utopians alike sought Fourier's "*la nouvelle Isabelle*," the patron who would finance the realization of their dreams. By a dialectical twist, this reliance on the existing elite for support and the consequent spurning of appeal to the masses often imparted an apolitical and even anti-political character to much of the politics of reconciliation.

Auguste Comte coined the term "sociology" in the forty-sixth lesson of his *Cours de philosophie positive* (1839). But the idea of the scientific study of society was hardly new with Comte. He himself recognized three prior efforts in this direction: political economy, the application of mathematics to the study of social phenomena, and Cabanis' attempt at the formulation of a physiology of the mind. Comte also praised what he regarded as the incomplete contributions of Montesquieu and Condorcet to the study of social phenomena.[3] Fragmentary elements from these sources appear scattered throughout Comte's work, but the major influences on Comte's intellectual development came from two other sources: the Catholic theocrats, Bonald and Maistre, and his former mentor, the utopian Saint-Simon. Comte's warm regard for "the immortal school which arose, at the beginning of the nineteenth century, under the noble leadership of De Maistre, worthily complemented by Bonald, with the poetic assistance of Chateaubriand" remained constant.[4] On the other hand, he came to dismiss his old friend and employer, Saint-Simon, as a "depraved juggler," "a vague and superficial writer," and a "charlatan" whose influence was "one of the characteristic symptoms" of the "mental and moral anarchy" of the times.[5]

The attraction of the thought of the Catholic reactionaries for Comte was not accidental. Saint-Simon had earlier praised the works of Bonald as "most estimable productions" of his time because of the theocrat's grasp of "the utility of systematic unity."[6] Comte's entire adult life stands as witness to the same concern with unity. More perceptive than many of their critics, Comte also realized that, however much they longed to an idealized medieval past, the theocrats were men of the nineteenth century and that this was nowhere more obvious than in their willingness to invoke the insights of science and the authority of reason.[7] Convinced that the only valid science was Catholic, Maistre described it as "a type of acid which dissolves all metals except gold."[8] Bonald proclaimed that it was necessary "to rise to the contemplation of the same order, and to consider society in general, by the same intellectual process and the same reasoning, which has existed in the exact sciences."[9] He believed that, once such a view was attained, one would be able to "deduce like algebraic formulas, the general maxims by which one resolves the events of society, past and even future."[10] While they differed on their definition of elements, Comte agree with Bonald's view that the proper functioning of the scientifically defined vital elements of society would constitute that "positive society" which order and conservation as its goal.[11] Again differing on the elements involved, both Saint-Simon and Comte agreed with Maistre, Bonald, and Chateaubriand upon the role religion would play in cementing the structure of the ideal society. Nor were the historical schema and evaluations of particular historical periods of these differing thinkers entirely dissimilar.

Saint-Simon was the young Comte's friend and employer between 1817 and 1824, and under his influence Comte took his first steps in the realm of system construction. Clearly Comte never understood Saint-Simon's most important contribution to social thought, the idea that the chief goal of politics should be the increase of production and the consequent amelioration of the condition of the poorest and most numerous class in society. But Comte derived much else from the magnificent chaos of ideas launched by Saint-Simon. The utopian socialist's juggling of various elites and classes in his numerous ideal schemes of society reflected his continuing concern with the selection of an elite capable of restoring and maintaining order in the nineteenth century. The former aristocrat, remained a revolutionary in his contempt for the elite of the *ancien régime*, his concern with "the career open to talent" which would prevent the new elite from becoming a closed corporation, his respect for the promise of the proletariat, and his ideas on the relationship between industrial production and the enrichment of life. Yet, he was a revolutionary interested in the termination of what he saw as an anarchical, that is, liberal, revolutionary process developing since 1789. This was to be one of the key functions of the new elite, a function which also greatly concerned Comte. Furthermore, although it manifested itself in a peculiar fashion, Comte never quite abandoned Saint-Simon's final view of the potentialities of the proletariat. There was, however, a more significant debt. One of the great problems with which Saint-Simon wrestled was the question of how to bind the new hierarchically conceived society together. Dissatisfied with his past answers based on Newtonian physics and then physiology, Saint-Simon finally turned to religion, to a "new Christianity," as the cement with which to replace the disruptive tendences of liberal society. His *nouveau Christianisme* provided his disciples and the heretic Comte with the vision of a secular religion having "a morality, a cult, a dogma, and an hierarchically organized clergy."[12] The principal object of such a religion would be "the fixing of the attention of all classes upon morality."[13]

Influenced by the theocrats and Saint-Simon, but also greatly aided by his own powerful intellect, Comte evolved a distinctive view of history and elaborated his own politics, sociology, and religion of reconciliation. Any attempt to locate Comte's particular system within the larger pattern of the politics of reconciliation must recognize his debt to the reactionaries and the utopian socialists and must also scrutinize the political and social implications of the distinctive elements of the Comtean system.

Comte believed that the nineteenth century would be "characterized by the predominance of history, in philosophy, in politics, and even in poetry."[14] In the enthusiasm of the nineteenth century for history, historical experience was pillaged for information supporting the differing world-views of reaction, liberalism, and radicalism. Not surprisingly, Comte found in it the verification of his theories concerning the stages leading to positivism. Science had foresight as its end, and, for the positivist, social science was the science of history.[15] In defining his attitude toward specific periods of history, Comte's thought parallelled in large part that of his intellectual forebears. Bonald and Maistre had needed no special impetus to hymn the praises of the ordered society of the Middle Ages, but the views of Saint-Simon and Comte, derived from more complex ideologies, were more subtle. Rejecting the Enlightenment's view of the medieval period, Saint-Simon praised it as an "organic" period of history.[16] But the great utopian's judgment of the period remained harsh: the feudal constitution was "essentially bad because entirely to the advantage of the governors and to the detriment of the governed."[17] Comte, also ratifying the past in terms of necessary development toward an ideal future, hailed the division of the governing powers of medieval society into the temporal and the spiritual. He saw the superior spiritual power of the Middle Ages as infusing morality into political affairs.[18] Here his ideas resembled those expressed in Maistre's *Du Pape*. Indeed, Comte claimed that his positivism rendered the medieval religion, Catholicism, "a more complete justice than any of its defenders, including the eminent De Maistre."[19] Yet, Comte, like his intellectual predecessors, then also had to come to terms with the revolutionary period, which he too perceived as originating in the disintegration of the medieval synthesis and especially in the Reformation.

We have seen that Maistre and Bonald, while rejecting the Enlightenment and Revolution, had yet been influenced by the emphasis placed on reason and science in these periods. Bonald in particular was impressed by the impersonal workings of the revolutionary mechanism:

A revolution has its laws, like a comet its orbit; and the first of all is that those who believe they direct it are instruments; some are destined to begin it, others to continue or finish it. The workers change as the work advances. Bonaparte was subjected to this law like all the others, more than the others.[20]

Saint-Simon and Comte, however, went further in ratifying by the logic of their systems the period dividing the world of the new synthesis in the nineteenth century from that of the old medieval synthesis. Saint-Simon described it as a "critical" period and portrayed the revolution as completing in the material sphere the destruction accomplished in the spiritual sphere by the *encyclo-pédistes*.[21] Comte was even less drawn by temperament than Saint-Simon to an appreciation of the era of metaphysics and revolution following the Middle Ages. Yet he also was forced to a canonization of the period as a necessary stage leading to his positivist synthesis. Comte admitted:

...passage from one social system to another can never be continuous and direct. There is always a transitional state of anarchy which lasts for some generations at least; and lasts the longer the more complete the restoration to be wrought.[22]

Physical and revolutionary period in the Comtean scheme performed the necessary function of discrediting the old organization of society; without the impetus provided by the radical criticisms of the old society would have remained stationary. The destruction of the old synthesis prepared the way for the founding of the positivist system.[23] Thus, the revolutionary period for Comte, as for Saint-Simon, was justified in terms of a further end and not in terms of the value of any of the revolutionary ideals.

Arguing that "the negative character of this great revolutionary operation naturally arouses a sort of philosophical repugnance," but convinced that "with all its errors and disorders" it was still a vital phase in the development culminating in the triumph of positivism, Comte elaborated his analysis of the French Revolution.[24] Typically, he isolated three schools of thought involved in it. Denying that either the "sceptical" and "frivolous" school of Voltaire or the "anarchic" school of Rousseau, the latter particularly dangerous due to its dedication to the ideal of equality, had contributed anything constructive to the revolution, Comte identified the cause of positivism with the "naturally organic, although necessarily vague" school of Diderot.[25] The leader of this revolutionary grouping, "the great Danton," was the only Western statesman worthy of honor since Frederick the Great.[26] Significantly, the revolutionary contribution of this school was the strengthening of traditions established earlier in the metaphysical epoch:

> The Dantonian school of Diderot, superior to demagogic illusions, alone developed the French traditions, by conceiving of the republican situation as destined to revive the necessary ascendency of the central power, instead of allowing local power triumph.[27]

This school's "admirable conception of revolutionary government" consisted of the institution of "a dictatorship similar to that of Louis XI, Richelieu, Cromwell and even Frederick."[28] Comte was quite willing to justify the revolutionary practice of this group: "while directing with an irresistible energy the defence of the republic, it compelled the abolition of royalty by the eliminating of diverse individuals attached to it."[29] For Comte, the reaction began with Danton's destruction, the result of the "suspicious rivalry of a bloodstained orator."[30] This "anarchic reaction" represented the temporary triumph of the school of Rousseau, whose disciples were the sinister "*docteurs en guillotine.*"[31] The period of reaction further "developed especially after the conquests of Bonaparte and was prolonged weakly under his successors."[32] The revolutionary crisis and the inadequate response to it created the political and social situation which Comte believed himself to be facing. As early as 1822 the remarkably consistent Comte began the formulation of his answer to the challenge of the revolution:

> The insufficiency of kings and peoples has proved the need of a new doctrine, alone capable of terminating the terrible crisis which torments society. The only way of ending this stormy situation, of halting the anarchy which daily invades society...of reducing the crisis to a simple moral movement, is to determine the civilized nations to quit the critical direction for the organic direction, to concentrate their energies of the formation of a new social system...It is nothing other than the formation and general adoption, by people and kings, of the organic doctrine which can alone make the kings quit the reactionary direction and the people the critical direction.[33]

In so far as his goal, like Saint-Simon's, was the termination of a continuing revolutionary crisis, that goal was only superficially counter-revolutionary. But, given the nature of the factors which were to accomplish that goal and his vision of the ideal positivist society, Comte's social and religious version of the politics of reconciliation, unlike Saint-Simon's, was profoundly reactionary.

The young Comte had been an anti-clerical liberal, professing equal distaste for Marat, Robespierre, Bonaparte, and Louis XVIII.[34] In 1817, however, a sentence appeared in what Comte would later dismiss as an otherwise useless pamphlet: "All is relative, there is the only absolute principle."[35] His use of relativism in analysis, along with a tendency to adapt his language to the beliefs of the diverse groups to which he appealed and his passion for synthesis, render it difficult to relate his political and social attitudes to the simpler standards of conservatism and radicalism. His most basic criticism of contemporary political life was that "two ideas are set up in radical opposition to each other—the retrograde spirit having directed all efforts in favour of order, and the anarchical doctrine having arrogated to itself the charge of Social Progress."[36] Only Comte's positivism could reconcile these conflicting concepts: "The fundamental reconciliation of, order and progress, constitutes...the privilege characteristic of positivism."[37] Positivism's immediate political task was to destroy the contemporary political parties by absorbing them "into the truly constructive party," and to accomplish this it sought "to rally all the worthy conservatives who are not true reactionaries and all the honest revolutionaries who are not really anarchic."[38] It could accomplish this because it spoke "to every class of society and to evey political party, the language best adapted to produce conviction, while maintaining the invincible originality of its fundamental character."[39]

Comte claimed to be "a constantly republican philosopher."[40] And he was—in a peculiarly Comtean fashion. He glorified the English revolution, "not the little and Anglican revolution of 1688...but the democratic and Presbyterian revolution" carried out under "the lofty genius" of Cromwell.[41] Nor, as we have seen, did he and shrink from justifying the treatment of royalty and its followers in the French Revolution.

The surest sign of Comte's revolutionary sentiment was his allowance for the right of rebellion—even in positivist society. Although carefully qualified and not altogether free from the hint of the medieval parallel, Comte did make use of the revolutionary and metaphysical idea of popular sovereignty:

> In revolutionary usage, its principal efficacy lies in directly justifying the
> right of insurrection. But positive politics represents such a right as an
> extreme recourse, indispensable to *all* society.[42]

Positivism was thus able to reconcile "habitual subordination with exceptional revolt."[43] Of course, the chances of conditions justifying this "extreme recourse" in the positvist society were minimal. Still, Comte claimed that he would not "hesitate either to approve it or to recommend it, if it really became indispensable."[44] Comte's willingness to consider the improbable danger of political evil in the positivist paradise and to provide a revolutionary answer for it perhaps more than anything else tends to justify his assertion that the positivist were "the true successors of the Jacobins."[45]

Such a claim, however, must be balanced against other elements of Comte's politics of reconciliation. Comte was perflectly capable of congratulating Nicholas I on the effectiveness of his censorship.[46] He also wrote to Raschid Pasha, the former grand vizier of the Ottoman empire, lauding the oriental leaders for "truly remaining at the head of their nations, always endeavouring to worthily fulfill the double function of government, to impel towards good and to resist evil" at a time when the contemporary Western leaders were "incapable of directing the social movement."[47] Comte argued that "however vicious the reactionary tendencies are, they are, in all respects, less contrary than the revolutionary disposition to the great construction which must characterize the nineteenth century."[48] He indicated personal reasons for his preference for a conservative regime in a letter to John Stuart Mill:

> I would be, I think, respected, or at least tolerated, as I was under Villèle and Polignac, when my attitude was exactly the same as today. It is hardly thus with the real revolutionary party...[in which] I would find more dangerous adversaries, accustomed to not stopping at any atrocity and who have deplorably systemised the use of the guillotine as a sort of uniform solution for all social dissidence.[49]

Not only was Comte's evaluation of the contemporary scene markedly conservative, but so were many of the ideas basic to the positivist system.

Comte believed the "fundamental principle of the human order" to be that "the living are essentially more and more governed by the dead."[50] Just as once truth has been established in a particular science there is no cause for dissent, so it would be with sociology: "To be always examining and never deciding would be regarded as something like madness in private conduct: and no dogmatic consecration of such conduct in all individuals could constitute any perfection of the social order."[51] Indeed, "true liberty is nothing else than a rational submission to the laws of nature," and, significantly, "the general laws of human nature, always existing before being known, have made most feel empirically how submission is morally superior to revolt."[52] Holding such views, Comte could propose a united front of conservatives and positivists.

Comprehending both his revolutionary strain and his conservatism, although more closely connected to the latter, was Comte's distaste for liberalism. To Comte the "bourgeois domination" of the July Monarchy was "more incapable than the legitimist regime of reconciling order and progress."[53] Comte saw the effects of parliamentary liberalism all around him, intellectual anarchy, corruption, the decline of morality, and the complete incompetence of political leaders.[54] He had particularly harsh words for the English parliamentary monarchy, "an exceptional institution, whose end cannot be very far off."[55] The much lauded English constitution was, for Comte, "as hostile as Jesuitism to human emancipation."[56] Comte's dislike of the constitutional processes of the liberal state led him to stand aside from the politics of parliamentary action. Nor was the positivist savant interested in doing anything but combatting the politics of the street, the vague socialist and communist sentiments of the proletariat. Believing that "ideas govern the world," he concentrated his efforts on persuasion and education.[57] His positivist spirit tended "to consolidate order, by the rational development of a wise resignation to incurable political evils."[58] But in abandoning "sterile political agitation," he abandoned any real effort in the direction of revolutionary change.[59] His politics of reconciliation, seeking to integrate order and progress, was essentially anti-political.[60] In terms of practical politics, positivism could only end in consolidating order.

In terms of positivist sociological theory and utopia, the result was largely the same. Bonald and Maistre had idealized the world of an agrarian aristocracy. Their solution to the problems issuing from the Revolution was a hierarchical structuring of society similar to the medieval organic model. Saint-Simon rearranged his favourite social classes almost as often as he changed his plans for the ideal society. But, neglected by the capitalist element of his industrial class, he finally turned his attention to the proletariat as the class capable of establishing stability in society. And for the positivist, "the most difficult problem of modern times" was "obviously the industrial proletariat."[61] Comte, living for years after the death of Saint-Simon, was perhaps even more acutely aware of class conflict in an increasingly industrialized society:

> A worse and wholly questionable mischief is the deeper hostility which has arisen between the interests of the employers and the employed...There is no doubt that the dissension has been aggravated by the arts of demagogues and sophists, who have alienated the working class from their *natural* industrial leaders; but I cannot but attribute this severance of the *head* and the *hands* much more to the political incapacity, the social indifference, and especially the blind selfishness of the employers than to the unreasonable demands of the workers.[62]

Comte could write scathingly of capitalists who

> ...have taken no pains to guard the workers from seduction by the organization of a broad popular education, the extension of which, on the contrary, they appear to dread; and they have evidently yielded to the old tendency to take the place of the feudal chiefs, whose fall they longed for, without inheriting their natural generosity toward inferiors. Unlike military superiors, who are bound to consider their humblest brother soldiers, the industrial employers abuse the power of capital to carry their points in opposition to the employed.[63]

He was especially contemptuous of the Classical Political Economy invoked by these which in face of industrial conflict hid "its organic helplessness under an irrational declaration of the necessity of delivering modern industry to its unregulated course."[64] Society was particularly threatened by "the evils inherent in the inequality of wealth, which affords the most dangerous theme to both agitators and dreamers."[65] This explosive social situation, however, was to be "the test of the positive philosophy, and at the same time the stimulus to its social ascendency."[66]

While he pilloried the capitalists and their errors, Comte still recognized them as the "natural" leaders of society and detected in them the promise of better things.[67] The "idle rich," whom Comte would place in a Dantean vestibule of hell, were tending to disappear.[68] The "active wealthy," "alone the temporal leaders of modern society," could solidify their position by "taking on a truly social character under the influence of the positivist religion."[69] Comte thought that the more perceptive among them had begun to realize that positivism was the only "weapon with which they can oppose the anarchic outbreak of communism."[70] In the ideal positivist society "the true supreme degree of practical abstraction institutes a *patriciat* destined naturally for the civil predominance."[71] Specially, the supreme temporal power of the positivist society was to be a triumvirate of bankers.[72] Checking any abuse of this temporal power would be the spiritual power of the Religion of Humanity and a code of industrial chivalry.[73] The *patriciat* would "bless" the positivist regime which bestowed on them "endless moral obligations," but which also enabled them to attain to "an entirely new civic grandeur" and allowed them to retain their wealth.[74]

Comte's view of the contemporary and future role of the proletariat was more complex. He thought that, just as the problem of the family was largely that of the role of woman in it, the problem of the country was essentially that of the proletariat. Comte believed that his course on the positive philosophy had given him ample opportunity to observe the various social classes, and he decided that "among the minds which are not professionally philosophical, it is among the true workers (clock-makers, mechanics, printers, etc.), that I have found until now the soundest appreciation...of the new philosophy."[75]

The proletariat was, for Comte, the class most emancipated from the theological point of view, though it was still unfortunately hampered by metaphysical biases.[76] Except for the philosophic class, "no other class of society is disposed to the general point of view as the proletariat."[77] The proletarians were "alone capable of becoming the decisive auxiliaries of the new philosophers."[78] Comte sympathized with many of their complaints: "true philosophers," i.e., positivists, "do not hesitate to sanction directly the instinctive protests of the proletarians against the vicious definition of property which attributes to it an absolute individuality, as the right to use and abuse."[79]

Comte warned Mill of the "advent of the proletarian masses on the political scene, where they have until now been only instruments."[80] All would be well if positivism could direct this intervention of the proletariat in history away from "utopias subversive of all society."[81] He was worried by what he considered the proletariat's "natural disposition to communism."[82] Particularly disturbing were the activities of "the truly undisciplined revolutionaries, the reds of London and Brussels."[83] Communism, however, like much else which circumstance forced Comte to consider, did have its place in his system. Its very existence compelled people to search for a better solution to the social problem.[84] And it had the advantage of tending to concern itself with moral rather than secondary political questions.[85] Unfortunately, it concerned itself with one aspect of the social problem, wealth, as if this were the only factor in a society "badly divided and badly administered."[86] Further, its "ignorance of sociability are manifested...in the dangerous tendency of communism to suppress all individuality."[87] Communism was an aberration which desired "to overturn society for abuses which are tending to disappear" or undergoing "the happiest moral transformation."[88] Fortunately, the increasing acceptance by the proletariat of the term "socialism" indicated the decreasing appeal of communism.[89] While the sentiment involved in socialism was genuinely altruistic, its ideal system had not yet been fully developed, that is, socialism had not led the proletariat to positivism.[90]

That accounted for the fact that "the rapid propagation of socialism inspires with just alarms the classes whose empirical resistance now constitutes the sole legal guarantee of the moral order."[91] It was clear, however, that, unless the positivist system was implemented, "the problem posed by the communists admits of no other solution than their own."[92]

Retaining some confidence in the French proletariat, Comte assigned it a decisive role in the transition to the final positivist society. As "the present entrepreneurs still remain under the tutelage of lawyers" and "are far from having acquired the generality of views and elevation of sentiments which their future requires," their social education had to take place under a dictatorship of proletarians.[93] Despite some signs of change for the better on their part, "the classes normally destined for the temporal supremacy" having "remained, in heart and mind, beneath their mission," it was among the proletarians that Comte found "types really worthy of political elevation by the generality of their views and the generosity of their sentiments."[94] The Comtean "dictatorship of the proletariat" would have to submit all its projects for discussion by the entire population, but its final decisions would be independent of all outside opinion. Even more revolutionary in terms of a nation of peasants and in light of their role in 1848, Comte decided that the election of the proletarian dictators would lie with Paris, with the departments having only the power of ratification.[95] Such an arrangement was supposed to accustom the people gradually to the disappearance of universal suffrage, not necessarily as reactionary a measure as it appears when one remembers the use made of it under the Second Empire and the hostility of the French countryside toward the revolutionary centre of Paris. Still, the proletarian dictatorship would remain only an interlude before the final positivist government of the bankers.

The position of the proletariat under the final positivist regime would be far from dictatorial. The chief service which positivism would perform for the proletariat then would be to incorporate this class into a society it had remained outside of since its birth in the Middle Ages.[96] The positivist state owed education to the proletarian, an positivist education which would give him "a true knowledge of our individual and collective nature" and would teach him to respect a social structure which benefited him.[97] The ruling elite was also obliged to provide the proletarian with work. Given the lack of any idea of constantly expanding production, how this was to be achieved was left rather value. Still, "the right to work" was a revolutionary demand in Comte's day as it is in any society with a permanent unemployment problem. And the nineteenth century lacked that sinister knowledge of how full employment could be achieved without threat to the social structure which the Third Reich imparted to the twentieth. Although far from gaining much material good from the positivist regime, the worker would be guaranteed the "principal material necessities."[98] But with Comte, as with the evangelist, the poor would always be with society: "It is the invariable lot of the majority of men to live on the more or less precarious fruits of daily labour."[99] The chief consolation of the workers would come from their role as "the indispensable auxiliaries of the spiritual power."[100] And the proletarians could comfort themselves with the thought that their domestic happiness was superior to that of the temporal and spiritual elites.[101] In the positivist scheme, they were to be satisfied with such benefits.

Faced with what appeared to be the complete disintegration of society in post-revolutionary France, many of the critics of this situation fell back on the social integration promised by religion. Their ideal societies were to be ruled by a spiritual power of a moral grandeur so great that it dominated, indeed even structured, the society. These systems then often betrayed a tendency to confuse the moral task of the religion with the establishment and maintenance of the ideal social hierarchy. Religion, for the theocrat and the utopian, often became an instrument of social control. In what he later called "the decisive pamphlet," published in 1826, Comte too stressed society's need for "a new spiritual order, as the first and principal means of ending the revolutionary period."[102] Like other new religions of the period, the Religion of Humanity constructed by Comte had roots in the religious cults of the French Revolution and was in part a response to the religious crisis involved in that upheaval. The role the Comtean religion assigned to science and class reconciliation also reveals the influence of Saint-Simon. But Comte's greatest debt in matters of religion was to the theocrats.

The deity of the theocrats, of course, was replaced by Humanity, "the whole of beings, past, present, and future.[103] The significance of this replacement cannot be underestimated. But the worship of the Comtean deity involved a spiritual hierarchy and a sacramental system. Comte's priesthood, like the Catholic, had both educational and sacramental functions.[104] The positivist priesthood counselled, consecrated, and regulated.[105] Its tasks included the reconciling of the proletariat to its inferior social status.[106] By means of its moral influence alone this priesthood would undertake the direction of Comte's good society. The positivist religion would there dominate and animate because "legitimate social supremacy belongs neither to force or reason, but to morality, governing alike the actions of the one and the counsels of the other."[107]

The Religion of Humanity would foster altruism, that Comtean neologism which he defined as "the necessary coincidence between duty and happiness which consists...in living for others."[108] This religion would motivate that essential reconciliation which was the goal of positivist society, for it rested upon "two connected dispositions: the devotion of the strong to the weak; and the veneration of the weak for the strong."[109] In the religiously sanctioned positivist social system, Auguste Comte could play the role of Maistre's pontiff.

Auguste Comte set out to construct a synthesis which would heal the wounds of the liberal society issuing from the French Revolution and tortured by the impact of industry. Because he was aiming at synthesis, Comte's system consecrated much that was revolutionary and reactionary. He came of a generation marked by the continued workings of the French Revolution and possessed some genuinely revolutionary sentiments. With some "repugnance," he sanctioned the Revolution. His evaluation of the capacity of the of the proletariat, in comparison with that of most of his peers, was generous. Whatever the distant echoes of John of Salisbury, he was prepared to admit the right of rebellion in the positivist society. However misdirected, his demand that society be studied scientifically look to the future rather than the past. Again, however mistaken in detail, his insistence that society be viewed as a totality was extraordinarily revolutionary in its implications when opposed to the fragmented world-view of nineteenth-century liberalism. The synthesis, however, remained weighted toward the Right. Comte was more at ease with the medieval period and its contemporary apologists than with the Enlightenment and its heirs. Humanity may have been a more progressive deity than the Christian God, but in Comte's system it was very much a deity with all the traditional trappings. The proletariat's place in the final positivist society was one of subservience, a subservience made more endurable by a religious opiate. Positivism attempted to offer something to everybody. It promised to "obviate or repress all the dangers which attended the institution of property, and correct popular tendencies by a wise analysis of social difficulties, and a salutary conversion of questions of right into questions of duty."[110] But the reconciliation of the bankers and the workers under the spiritual guidance of the priests of Humanity, in the context of Western European history, at least after 1848, was not only unrealistic, but profoundly reactionary. The theorists of reconciliation in this period were apt to find correspondence between the realm of the "the intellectual" and that of "the material." Following such a crude line of analysis and allowing for the requirements of a more practical politics than that of the theoretical systems of the politics of reconciliation, one could find a half-brother of Comte's in another deformed offspring of the revolutionary Saint-Simon: Louis Napoleon. The implementation under the Second Empire, not of Comte's system, but of his slogan, "order and progress," marked the triumph of order.

Notes

1. *Science & Society*, XXIX, 1 (Winter, 1965), pp. 44-65.

2. If one takes the wages of 1892 as a base figure of l00, in the French textile industry the wage scale during the first half of the century was as following: 1800......80   1820......80   1827......40 1850......45 Robert Schnerb, *Le XIX siècle, l'apogée de l'expansion européene (1815-1914)*, in Maurice Crouzet (ed.), *Histoire générale des civilisations* (Paris, 1955), p. 65.

3. Auguste Comte, "Opuscules relatifs à fondation de la science sociale," *La Revue occidentale* (May 1, 1882) pp. 386-99, cited in Henri Gohierr, *La Jeunesse d'Auguste Comte et la formation du positivisme*, t. *II, Saint-Simon jusqu'a la restauration* (Paris, 1936), pp. 43-7; Auguste Comte, *The Positive Philosophy of Auguste Comte*, freely translated and condensed by Harriet Martineau, II (London, 1896), pp. 194-203.

4. Comte, *Système de politique positive ou traité sociologie, instituant la religion de l'Humanité, contenant la dynamique sociale ou traité général du progrès humain (Philosophie d'histoire)* (Paris, 1853), p. 605.

5. Comte, *Système, III*, pp. xv-xvi.

6. Claude Henri de Saint-Simon, *Introduction aux travaux scientifiques du XIXe siècle*, pp. 211-12, quoted in Gouhier, *II*, p. 303.

7. Modern scholarship dealing with the theoccrats too often has neglected Comte's insihgt into the nature of the theocratic systems. He clearly recongnized that the great Catholic thinkers of the early nineteenth century had been affected by "the fundamental principle of the revolutionary doctrine, the supremacy of reason in regard to any question." Comte, *Appeal aux conservatives*, selection included in *Auguste Comte méconnu, Auguste Comte conservateur, extraits de son oeuvre finale (1851-57)* (Paris, 1898), p. 243. "The most zealous partisans of the theological polity are as apt as their adversaries to judge by their personal knowledge; and those who, in their writings, set up as defenders of spiritual government recognize, like the revolutionaries they attack, no other supreme authority than their own reason." Comte, *The Positive Philosophy, II*, p. 151. This analysis was the basis of Comte's appeal to the Catholics for a united front with the positivists.

8. Joseph de Maistre, *Du Pape*, in *Oeuvres, II* (Paris, 1875), p. 213

9. Louis Gabriel Ambrose Bonald, *Essai analytique sur lles lois naturelles de l'ordre social ou pouvoir du ministre et du subjet dans la société*, in *Oeuvres, I* (Paris, 1840), pp. 16-7.

10. Bonald, *Essai analytique*, p. 17.

11. *Ibid.*, p. 16.

12. Saint-Simon, *Nouveau Christianisme* (Paris, 1832), pp. 19-20.

13. *Ibid.*, p. 20.

14. Comte, *Système, III*, p. 1.

15. Emile Littré, *De la philosophie positive* (Paris, 1845), p. 26.

16. An admirable summary and critique of Saint-Simon's ideas about history may be found in Walter M. Simon, "History for Utopia: Saint-Simon and the Idea of Progress," *Journal of the History of Ideas*, XVII, 3 (June, 1956), pp. 311-31.

17. Saint-Simon, *De la reorganisation de la société eropéene*, p. 26, quoted in Simon, "History for Utopia," p. 316.

18. Comte, *The Positive Philosophy, III*, p. 88.

19. Comte, *Système de politique positive ou traité sociologie, instituant la religion de l'Humanité, I, contenant le discours preliminaire et l'introduction fondamentale* (Paris, 1851), p. 87.

20. Bonald, *Pensées sur divers sujets*, in *Oeuvres* (Paris, 1847), p. 282.

21. Saint-Simon, *Introduction aux travaux scientifiques du XIXe Siècle*, p. 57. cited by Gouhier, *II*, p. 289.

22. Comte, *The Positive Philosophy, II*, p. 148.

23. *Ibid., III* p. 137.

24. Comte, *Système, III*, p. 596.

25. *Loc. cit.*

26. *Loc. cit.*

27. *Ibid.*, p. 599.

28. *Loc. cit.*

29. *Ibid.*, 599-600. The last phrase might be considered one of the first expressions of the new language of sociologese, here as elsewhere directed toward the masking of an unpleasant reality.

30. *Ibid.*, p. 600.

31. *Loc. cit.*; also *Système, I*, p. 74.

32. Comte, *Système, I*, p. 67.

33. Comte, "Appendice gérérale," *Système de politque positive ou traité de sociologie, instituant le religion de l'Humanité, IV, contenant le tableau synthétique de l'avednir humain* (Paris, 1854), pp. 60 and 56.

34. Gohier, *La Jeunesse d'Auguste Comte et la formation du positivisme, I, Sous le signe de la liberté* (Paris, 1933), pp. 14-5, 238-9.

35. Comte, "Preface de l'Appendice générale," *Système, IV*, p., ii.

36. Comte, *The Positive Philosophy, II*, p. 141.

37. Comte, *Système, I*, p. 105.

38. Comte to M. Viellard, le 3 Aristote 64 (Feb. 28, 1852), *Système de politique positive ou traité de sociologie, instituant la religion de l'religion de l'Humanité, II, contenant la statique sociale ou le traité abstrait de l'ordre humain* (Paris, p. xxviii).

39. Comte, *The Positive Philosophy, II*, p. 184.

40. Comte to Nicolas I, le 10 Bichat 64 (Dec. 20, 1852), *Système, III*, p. xxix.

41. Comte, *The Positive Philosophy, III*, p. 175.

42. *Système, I*, p. 134. The emphasis is mine.

43. *Ibid.*, p. 135.

44. *Loc. cit.*

45. Comte to M. Hadery, Jan. 20, 1853, *Correspondance unédite d'Auguste Comte, II* (Paris, 1903), p. 246.

46. Comte to Nicholas I, le 10 Bichat 64 (Dec.20, 1952), *Système, III*, p. xxxi.

47. Comte to Raschid Pasha, 7 Homère (Feb. 4, 1853), *Système, III*, p. xlviii.

48. Comte, *Appeal aux consservatives*, in *Méconnu*, p. 234.

49. Comte to John Stuart Mill, June 27, 1845, *Lettres inédites de John Stuart Mill publiées avec les responses de Comte et une introduction par L. Levy-Bruhl* (Paris, 1899), p. 485. Incidently, the "definitive" biography of J.S. Mill by Michael St. John Packe, sanctified by the imprimatur of F.A. Hayek in the form of a preface, is marred by a complete misunderstanding, apparently based on a major error of translation, of Mill's use of the term, "Pedantocracy," in his correspondence with Comte and an inadequate understanding of Saint-Simon.

50. Comte to Nicholas I, le 10 Bichat 64 (Dec. 20, 1852) *Système, III*, p. xxxiv.

51. Comte, *The Positive Philosophy, II*, p. 153.

52. *Ibid.*, p. 188; see also *Système, II*, p. 400.

53. Comte, *Appeal aux conservatives*, in *Méconnu*, p. 212.

54. Comte, *The Positive Philosophy, II*, p. 167-81.

55. *Ibid.*, p. 165.

56. *Ibid.*, p. 341.

57. *Ibid., I*, p. 15.

58. *Ibid., II*, p. 186.

59. Comte to Clotilde de Vaux, June 2, 1845, *Système, I*, p. xxxviii.

60. Here an interesting comparison, part of a larger study of the politics of reconciliation, might be made between the ideas of Comte and Proudhon. It is not altogether accidental that the *Action française* should both invoke positivism and found a "Cercle Proudhon."

61. Littré, *De Philosophie positive*, p. 48.

62. Comte, *The Positive Philosophie, III*, p. 298. The emphasis is mine.

63. *Ibid*, pp. 298-99.

64. *Ibid.*, p. 299.

65. *Ibid.*, p. 318.

66. *Ibid.*, pp. 411-12.

67. *Ibid.*, p. 298.

68. Comte, *Système, II*, p. 403.

69. *Loc. cit.*

70. Comte to Mill, June 27, 1847, *Lettres inédites de John Stuart Mill*, p. 436.

71. Comte, *Système, IV*, p. 80.

72. *Ibid.*, p. 346.

73. Comte's interest in a system of industrial chivalry is not without some curious parallels today. See A.A. Berle, Jr., *New Directions in the New World* and *The Twentieth Century Capitalist Revolution* (particularly the chapters, "The Conscience of the King and the Corporation" and "Corporate Capitalism and 'The City of God' ").

74. Comte, *Système, II*, p. 415.

75. Comte to Mill, May l, 1844, *Lettres inédites de John Stuart Mill*, p. 313.

76. *Ibid.*, pp. 313-14.

77. Comte, *Système, I*, p. 137.

78. *Ibid*, p. 130.

79. *Ibid.*, p. 154.

80. Comte to Mill, Jan. 17, 1842, *Lettres inédites de John Stuart Mill*, p. 23.

81. *Loc. cit.*

82. Comte, *Appeal aux conservatives*, in *Méconnu*, p. 248.

83. Comte, *Système, I*, p. 153.

84. *Loc. cit.*

85. *Ibid*, p. 152.

86. *Ibid.*, p. 165.

87. *Ibid.*, p. 158.

88. *Ibid.*, p. 165.

89. *Ibid.*, p. 153.

90. *Ibid.*, p. 154.

91. *Loc. cit.*

92. *Loc. cit.*

93. Comte, "Note écrie le 17 juin 1852," sent in a letter of Dec. 20, 1852 to Nicholas II, *Système III*, xli.

94. Comte, *Système, IV*, p. 452.

95. Comte, "Note écrite le 17 juin 1852," *Système, III*, pp. xii-xiii.

96. Comte, *Système, I*, p. 150.

97. *Système, I*, p. 181; *II*, p. 415; *The Positive Philosophy, III*, p. 329.

98. Comte, *Système, II*, p. 415.

99. Comte, *The Positive Philosophy, II*, p. 189.

100. Comte, *Système, I*, p. 189.

101. *Ibid.*, *IV*, p. 83. The Comtean proletarian shares this benefit, of course, with his counterpart in Orwell's *1984*.

102. Comte, "Appendice générale," *Système, IV*, p. 192.

103. *Ibid*, p. 30.

104. *Ibid.*, p. 123.

105. *Ibid.*, *II*, p. 306; *IV*, p. 9.

106. *Ibid.*

107. Comte, *The Positive Philosophy, III*, p. 317.

108. Comte, *Système, IV*, p. 49.

109. *Ibid.*, p. 329.

110. Comte, *The Positive Philosophy, III*, p. 334.

7

"PSYCHOLOGICAL MAN" AND SOME PREDECESSORS

In his remarkable *Fin-de siècle Vienna: Politics and Culture* (1980), Carl E. Schorske proposed that "in our century, rational man has had to give way to that richer but more dangerous and mercurial creature, psychological man."[1] Demonstrating how "in Vienna...political frustration...spurred the discovery of this now all-pervasive psychological man," he argued, more generally, that increasingly "the search for an understanding of the ills that plague mankind tended to be translated from the public and sociological domain to the private and psychological one" and interpreted this shift in light of "a revolution of falling political expectations."[2] Obviously angered by more recent consequences of Schorske's "civic failure," Christopher Lasch had already devoted attention to the problem of "psychological man" in "an age of diminishing expectations."[3] Lasch had been greatly influenced by the conservative sociologist, Philip Rieff. In wresting with the question of how Freud's quest for "not more happiness but less misery" had been transformed into "the triumph of the therapeutic," Rieff had discovered "psychological man—the latest and perhaps the supreme individualist—opposed in depth to earlier modes of self-salvation: through identification with common purpose."[4]

Recognizing that it could only be built upon "monographic bits and pieces," Rieff disavowed providing "a history of our cultural revolution."[5] While monographic treatments of specific figures and problems in the history of psychology have appeared, the psychologizing of experience during the last century transcends narrowly defined disciplinary boundaries.[6] Although his most important work focussed on Freud, Rieff himself indicated as much when he placed "psychological man" at the end of a series of somewhat overlapping models of man: "Three character ideals have successively dominated Western civilization: the ideal of political man, formed and handed down to us from classical antiquity; second, the ideal of religious man, formed and handed down to us from Judaism through Christianity, and dominant in the civilization of authority that preceded the Enlightenment; third, the ideal of economic man...a transitional type, with the shortest life expectancy of all."[7] But as these earlier models have not occupied Rieff's attention to the same extent as "psychological man," he has left them as somewhat abstract constructs.

Like "psychological man," the religious, political and economic models pose all the difficulties associated with the use of ideal types, at once abstractions from multi-faceted reality and repositories of ideals, in historical analysis. Such vexations, however, should not be allowed to lead to a quick dismissal of models of human behaviour, for as Georges Duby has demonstrated, models of man—or, better, models of what should be the ideal behaviour of different groups of men—do emerge at different times and do play some role in influencing actual behaviour.[8] If Rieff's earlier models are to assume greater significance, their skeletal forms will have to be clothed in the kind of historical flesh provided by Duby. Only then will it be possible to situate properly "psychological man," whose physiognomy Rieff has portrayed in less than flattering detail, in relation to his predecessors. While at this point such an undertaking involves many more questions than firm answers, some suggestions can be made in regard to it.

Models of man have been constructed on the basis of the selection of a single dimension of experience as paramount in human affairs.[9] At least until the emergence of "psychological man," such models provided standards of conduct, legitimated demands for some degree of conformity with them, and presented both the solace associated with perceiving oneself as acting morally and the guilt connected with failing to do so. Serving as poles for intellectual discourse and emotional identification, these models seldom involved a complete repudiation of other facets of life. None of the models posited by Rieff, for instance, lacked a psychological dimension: not only did Aristotle accompany the *Politics* with *De Anima* and Locke buttress the *Two Treatises of Government* with the *Essay on Human Understanding*, but Augustine mused upon memory and Ricardo's *Principles of Political Economy and Taxation* found a complement in James Mill's *Analysis of the Human Mind*. But the other facets of life were ranked, explicitly or implicitly, in relation to the dimension deemed to be of fundamental importance. Differences in both the kind and degree of good and evil, happiness and unhappiness, could then be coupled with such rankings.

While different facets of experience have been ordered in different fashions within the different models, the subordinate elements within a single model have also been reordered on occasion. The latter process was facilitated to the extent that such models have not been rigid sociological constructs, but rather supple structures of beliefs and values which had to remain fluid in order to achieve and maintain hegemonic status within society. While such flexibility worked to ensure longevity by allowing for the incorporation of new kinds of experience, two checks have operated upon it. First, like extreme rigidity, excessive pliancy threatens hegemony: if the former opens a dangerously discernable gap between the ideal and the actual, the latter ends in the kind of incoherence which, at least before the emergence of the protean "psychological man," exercised scant ideological appeal. Second, not all facets of experience are available at any given time, a point well made years ago, in relation to a specific historical setting, by Lucien Febvre.[10]

Those engaged in the elaboration of models have also displayed a marked inclination to borrow features from other models to buttress the model of most concern to them. While "religious man's" perception of the deity as the supreme ruler provides an obvious example of this tendency, it has also operated in other areas, not least in connection with efforts to forge the model of "psychological man." This suggests that, while a dominant model usually constitutes the heart of intellectual discourse and the centre of emotional gravity, other models can and do coexist with it, especially within more pluralistic societies, either as legacies from the past, or challenges in the present, or prefigurations of the future. With the coexistence of several such models, it becomes possible to rally to any given one of them or to regard some or all of them with varying degrees of skepticism. Adopting Sir Isaiah Berlin's elegant shorthand, thinkers can be divided into "hedgehogs" and "foxes," with the former driven to "relate everything to a single vision, in terms of which they understand, think, and feel" and the latter inclined to "pursue many ends, often unrelated and contradictory."[11] While perhaps never banished from the scene, the "foxes" have been rarer creatures, until relatively recently, than the "hedgehogs" who rallied to a single over-arching concern, a single magnet for intellectual and emotional devotion, a single model of man which might be, at any given time, hegemonic.

Any appreciation of the historical roles played the different models of man must rest upon some comprehension of the structures and dynamics which have given rise to them. This entails, in turn, the need to arrive at an understanding of the social stratifications characteristic of particular societies. Such an effort is all the more important in that, while some models have been limited to providing an ideal of behaviour for a dominant elite, others have pointed in a more egalitarian direction. Particular models, moreover, can be interpreted in highly divergent fashions. While agreed upon what should be the central focus of concern, groups and individuals within an elite can still quarrel bitterly over the ramifications of that concern. And elements within the lower orders within a particular society can appropriate beliefs and values associated with an hegemonic model and put them to use in ways vastly different from those envisioned by their masters. Hence, even when agreement prevails in regard to what should be the focus of commitment, discourse in regard to it can degenerate into a bloody-minded business, a point underlain by a host of works like Luther's *Against the Murdering, Thieving Hordes of Peasants*.

Terms like "dominant elite," "lower orders" and "masters" beg many questions. But so too does the kind of class analysis which, especially when extended over centuries, would have, for example, "bourgeois ideologues" thinking, saying, and doing such and such. Efforts to escape that realm of caricature would have to take into consideration, along with others, questions which have to do with class identities and identifications, the particular mixture at any given time of coercion and conciliation in a ruling class' dealings with inferior classes, intra-class divisions at the higher and lower levels of society, the institutional settings in which the proponents of particular positions and interests find themselves, and the shifting balances between the ideological and the scientific contents of particular currents of thought. While such matters cannot be pursued here, it is still possible to uncover correlations—thought not one-to-one relationships—between particular models of man and the different phases in the development of capitalist society.[12]

Although the process could not have taken place without the impetus provided by the more powerful currents of socio-economic change, religion contributed mightily to the destruction of the hegemonic status of the religious model. If they challenged the Catholic variant of that model, none of the great reformers doubted the necessity of such a model, and each in his fashion endeavoured to supply it. Precisely because the great either/or, salvation or damnation, continued to exercise enormous influence over intellect and emotion, men proved all the more willing to kill each other over such matters as transubstantiation and consubstantiation. To recognize the intensity of religious convictions, however, is not to deny that, measured in sacred terms, the dirty secret of the Reformation was politics.

With the fracturing of the religious model, the terms of discourse eventually shifted. The religious, possessed of differing visions of sanctity and how to achieve it, either fell back upon political power to secure the imposition of their particular beliefs or discovered that the best they might achieve was toleration of their views by the secular authorities. The appeal of the religious model, of course, by no means was completely exhausted by these developments, and quite possibly Europe emerged as more Christian from the traumas of the Reformation and the travails of the Counter-Reformation. More Christian and less religious. But neither Calvinist economic ethics or even the new scientific spirit initially played the leading role in contributing to the growing secularization. The rise of "political man" to hegemonic status, in itself a reflection of the unfolding and collision of larger socio-economic forces, began the Weberian "disenchantment of the world."

The early steps toward the recreation of an hegemonic political model were taken in the northern Italy of the Renaissance. The relative weakness of feudalism and the vitality of urban life there, far more than the strength of capitalism at the time, favoured the drawing of parallels with, as well as lessons from, the classical world. That world had given rise to a model of "political man" which, however much misinterpreted by the Italian humanists, still provided them with critically important concepts and vocabulary, ideas and words like "citizen," "tyrant," and "commonwealth" which, if hardly unknown to the earlier Scholastics, had not played a crucial role in their religious discourse. Although hardly prototypical capitalist thinkers, the humanists made use of the classical political tradition when calling into question aspects of the religious model and, more important, when challenging a pivotal feudal model wholly overlooked by Rieff, the model of man-as-warrior.[13]

A balance has to be struck in assessing the contribution of the Renaissance to the emergence of "political man." Stronger in its mercantile and financial structures than in its productive structures, wealthy enough to attract the rapacity of northerners, divided into warring polities, with each of these divided into homicidal factions, the political frameworks of Renaissance Italy, provided a stimulus to political thinking, but at the same time proved incapable of generating an hegemonic model of "political man." Whatever the continuing creativity in other areas, the nascent political model suffered as the Medici smothered the institutions of the Florentine republic, as civic humanism gave way to neo-Platonism, as Machiavelli's *Discourses* came to have less relevance than Castiglione's *Book of the Courtier*. Moreover, the battles over the nature of religious man generated by the Reformation dwarfed, at least initially, the emergent "political man" of the Renaissance. But to leave the matter there would be to take an unduly narrow view of it, and J. G. A. Pocock quite rightly finds a "Machiavellian moment" beyond the spatial and temporal confines of Renaissance Italy.[14]

Unavoidably violating his richly detailed and subtle arguments, it can be suggested that the assumption of hegemonic status by "political man" constituted the essence of that "moment."

Events in seventeenth century England assured the hegemony of the political model. The revolutionary situation which developed there posed for some the question of control over the instruments of political power as, literally, a life-or death matter and, consequently, forced an eventual clarification of political relationships. If the theorists of monarchical sovereignty initially possessed theoretical advantages over ideologically confused parliamentarians, dissenting divines, and advocates of the common law, some more or less inchoate patterns can still be detected in the very confusions of the latter groups. Hobbes' mordant analysis of the "divers sorts" of "seducers" involved in the outbreak of the upheaval remains instructive: while he recognized both the continuing appeal of the religious model and its now fragmentary nature, he also noted the attraction exercised by two variant political models, one derived from the classical world and the other much more distinctly capitalist in features.[15] And once again religion worked to discredit the religious model: not only did antinomian frenzies leave a distaste for "enthusiasm" in their wake, but their paroxysms underlined the need to subordinate religion, through either the enforcement of outward conformity or the extension of toleration, to political considerations. Hobbes took the first path, Locke the second. Even Locke, however, invoked considerations of *raison d'état* when he excluded Catholics and atheists from his pleas for toleration.

Hobbes and Locke tried to provide an adequate model of "political man." Exposed to the social realities engendered during the phase of capitalist manufacture, both took a roundly comparable range of human striving into consideration and, transmuting them all too quickly into universal characteristics, both arrived at "the political theory of possessive individualism."[16] If upon close reading Locke's depiction of the state of nature was just as grim as that of Hobbes, it would be Locke's paradigm which would win assent. Hobbes' failure, however, still retains significance in that it casts light upon the particular social ramifications of the political model and, more generally, upon the workings of various models of man. Specifically, the ruthless egalitarianism central to Hobbes' *Leviathan* not only frightened both backers of the Stuarts and "commonwealth men," but could not be of much ideological use in situations where either an absolutist state served the interests of an aristocracy or a triumphant middle class had to defend itself against claims made from below.

Ideologically, Hobbes erred more fundamentally when, dispensing with the moral standards usually associated with models, he held up too reflective a mirror to the eternally calculating, endlessly striving, wholly insatiable social atoms engaged in the forging of the capitalist order. His stark image of man would continue to discomfort even those whose behaviour conformed most closely to it.[17] While less consistent than Hobbes, Locke provided a more appealing political model. Having recognized initial social equality only to negate it, he presented "political man" as a creature possessed of properties extending beyond his labour power; hence, possessed if rationality; and, consequently, possessed of the right to participate in the political forum in order to defend his properties and interests. His model lent itself to a dual usage in that it could be displayed to attack the existing order in societies where feudalism still lingered as a significant socio-political force, as in eighteenth century France, or to defend the *status quo* in societies, like that of eighteenth century England, where capitalism had become firmly established. In the French case, the contradictions within society worked to produce a "democratization" of the political model in the work of Jean-Jacques Rousseau. But if he admitted all males into the political forum, Rousseau, one of the supreme misogynists of the century, very consciously excluded women from it.[18]

If the continued decay of feudalism also stimulated economic speculation in the France of the Physiocrats, the workings of capitalism in England, buttressed by relatively liberal institutions legitimized by and legitimating the Lockean model, did more to encourage attempts at understanding the economic system. However in their efforts in that direction, Bernard Mandeville and others strayed too far towards the grim Hobbesian landscape and underlined, thereby, the extent to which, whatever the material and ideological comforts provided by the Lockean variant, the notion of the possessive social atom and that of the *res publica* had not been brought into complete congruence. The problem of the relations between self and society, one of capitalism's continuing ideological problems, had not been resolved.

With their awareness of that problem heightened by he first great impact of capitalism within their own society, the Scots theorists of the eighteenth century sought to resolve it by moving towards a more general comprehension of social dynamics and, indeed, towards a social model of man. Given the obstacles encountered on the social road, it is not wholly paradoxical that their most distinguished member should arrive at a wholly different model. Adam Smith, however, did not completely abandon the concerns of his fellows and, for a brief moment, brought together public and private interests in the course of showing how the rational pursuit of self-interest on the part of atomistic individuals contributed to the good of the whole; how the workings of the market at lamentable but necessary cost to some benefited society as a whole; and, less directly, how relations within the market reflected, in smaller but equally universal script, the relations among the atoms of great Newton's cosmos. "Economic man," the creature of the market, had emerged. Like political theory, economic thought now celebrated the calculating and calculable activities of the individual and lent itself to both justifications of an economic *status quo* and lent itself to attacks upon the domination of particular societies by pre-capitalist ruling classes. With their basically congruent models of man, political and economic Liberalism could be married in Political Economy.

As with many marriages, the harmonious facade disguised some fundamental tensions. As usual both partners brought problems of their own to a union, most certainly not made in heaven, which would only worsen in time. Most strikingly, the dimensions of the political arena and the economic marketplace failed to coincide. If the bourgeois, at once a political and economic creature, could move freely in both, those with only their labour power to sell in the market found themselves simultaneously excluded from its promise of wealth and from the right to participate in political life. Both models, moreover, lay open to appropriation, with revisions, by others in the service of ends scarcely intended by their authors. Reworking the classical image of "political man," Rousseau had already redefined citizenship in a manner which went not only beyond the musings of the ancients but also most of his contemporaries. The initial problems of the economic model, however, had more to do with the theoretical darkening of Smith's essentially optimistic presentation of the new construct. Already possessed of problematic aspects, the features of "economic man" turned harsher when elaborated upon by Thomas Malthus and David Ricardo. Moreover, an explosive device, the labour theory of value, had been built into the economic model from its beginning and lay open to appropriation by some of those appalled by the economic creature's features.

In order to neutralize threats generated internally and externally, viable models of man have to be flexible enough to subsume inconsistencies. But the French and Industrial Revolutions subjected the political and economic models to severe strains, at once weakening and buttressing them. Just as in England more than a century earlier, the outbreak of revolution in France posed the issue of possession of political power in life-and-death terms. But the more sweeping nature of the French upheaval radicalized further the terms of political discourse. Invoking the examples of classical heroes and republics, the proponents of the differing liberal and democratic images of "political man" clashed over the ideal dimensions of the forum. And despite the basic identity of interests revealed in the repudiation of the classical "agrarian law," Girondins and Jacobins collided violently over the issue of how, at least in times of crisis, "economic man" was to be treated. Was this model to be awarded an equal status with "political man," as the Girondins believed, or was it to be subordinated to political considerations, as the Jacobins urged?

The Industrial Revolution posed, in somewhat different terms, many of the same problems in Great Britain. Still, dwarfing in magnitude all economic changes other than those brought about when humans first settled down to agriculture millennia earlier and penetrating in a halting but sure manner to the deepest roots of society, the awesome nature of this upheaval still allowed for the kind of shielding of the political and economic models embodied in the Reform Bill of 1832 and the Poor Law of 1834. Such legislative enactments, however, no more ended the conflicts engendered by the Industrial Revolution than the bogus restorations sanctioned by the Congress of Vienna terminated the forces unleashed by the French Revolution. The nineteenth century, consequently, witnessed major efforts aimed at revitalizing older models or at creating new ones.

In the new circumstances forged by the Industrial and French Revolutions, the religious model could be put to a variety of uses. Hardly new in itself, the perception of religion as an instrument of social control reached a new level of clarity with Bonaparte and Andrew Ure.[19] The pallid secular religions spawned during the nineteenth century, those like Auguste Comte's Religion of Humanity, also aimed at providing a social cohesion which, in fact, involved social control. Yet the religious model could still function as Marx's "haven in a heartless world;" that is, it could provide some protection against the kinds of exploitation associated with other models. English workers who embraced Methodism, for instance, found within it not only some communal solace but also some shielding for personal identity against the claims made upon them by the economic model of man.

However, as E.P. Thompson has made abundantly clear, not only were the psychic costs of this kind of search for salvation likely to be high, but the emphasis upon "methodical discipline" worked to reinforce structures of exploitation which the economic model legitimated.[20] The religious model, in brief, now tended to function as a subordinate means of reinforcing the sway of other models. Hence, Kierkegaard's contempt for the conventional Christians of his day.[21] Yet changing conditions still allowed for some hopes in regard to a return of the religious model to a hegemonic status. If Pius IX's *Syllabus Errorum* (1894) had been heroic in its reactionary spurning of so many of the major tendencies of the nineteenth century, by its end Leo XIII could rest his supple efforts to revive the Catholic variant of the religious model upon a shrewd reading of the difficulties which had come by then to bevel the political and economic models.

Having become fused with revolutionary experience, the liberal versions of the latter models prospered or suffered in connection with differing appraisals of the French and Industrial Revolutions. If the revolutionary achievements seemed to some to consecrate the idea of progress in the political and economic realms, or for all spheres of life, others perceived their result to be a fragmented, conflict-ridden, squalidly disenchanted society, the very existence of which demanded a new vision of man. Drawing aid from a manipulative rationality, increasingly codified in a scientistic positivism, and from an irrationalism, shaped and sanctioned by a protean romanticism, much of the intellectual effort of the nineteenth century would be aimed at creating such a new model. But the results of this endeavour were either woefully incomplete or so complete as to be limited in their appeal and mutually exclusive. With multiple proffering of new models and new varieties of older models, confusion mounted and the number of Berlin's "foxes" increased.

As capitalism reaped its greatest successes, "economic man" did not prosper to a like degree. Finding scant comfort in the present, oscillating between mythic visions of past and future, suspicious of atomism and calculation, only momentarily satisfied with projections of heroic individuals and idealized communities, committed to diversity rather than universality, vaunting power and nursing impotence, the romantics united in heaping scorn upon the economic model. Largely oblivious to the links between capitalist economics and their own artistic creations, they posited such overlapping images of man as Prometheus, as criminal, as misunderstood genius, in opposition to "economic man" who often turned out to be, not only the exploiter in the economic realm, but also the Philistine in the expanding cultural marketplace. But the analogues of the romantic images who walked the streets of social reality—the bohemian, the dandy and the aesthete—proved susceptible to transformation into accepted stages of maturation or degeneration and, in any event, remained marginal to the larger business of capitalist life during the nineteenth century.[22]

No more capable of achieving a hegemonic status than the romantic images, the model of cultural man, the flower of *Bildung* cultivated by the German Idealists, embraced crippling contradictions of its own. In Central Europe the *Kulturträger* remained differntial in face of the sword-bearer who still tried to live up to the atavistic image of "man-as-warrior." There as elsewhere, moreover, cultivated scorn for the crassly economic required economic security. And even the most resolutely apolitical German burgher could not remained untouched by politics in a century which witnessed massive social change and the increasing appeal of nationalism. Still, the cultural model exercised an appeal which transcended Central Europe. It provided, for instance, the underlying motif of John Stuart Mill's *On Liberty*. Supremely a "fox," Mill managed to reduce many of the problems of "political man" to questions of mechanics in *Representative Government* and to soften the features of "economic man" to such an extent that the old model virtually disappeared from the successive editions of *Principles of Political Economy*.[23] Significantly, he proved unable to complete his *Logic* with a "Ethnology" or Sociology. But Mill could explain these and other problems as intrinsic to the "age of transition" which he inhabited.[24]

That kind of explanation emerged from the kind of historical consciousness so characteristic of the nineteenth century. With change accelerated by the French and Industrial Revolutions, with the sense of it sharpened by their ongoing effects, history entered upon a relatively brief reign as "queen of the sciences." While open to methods ranging from the romantic to the positivist, history's relation to the various models of man remained at best problematic. If Clio spread her treasures, with varying degrees of lavishness, in the service of multiple images of man, the differing gifts ended in raising questions about some of those images. The various strains of historicism, however defined, emphasized diversity rather than the elements of universality requisite to an adequate model of man. Significantly, by the end of the century, in very different fashions, Wilhelm Dilthey and Karl Lamprecht reached out to the developing new-comer, psychology, in efforts to shore up Clio's rapidly crumbling royal position. Still, with all allowance for history's shortcomings in buttressing models of man, much of the historical writings of the nineteenth century moved along political lines: didactic political history, which can be traced back to Thucydides, flourished as liberals and conservatives, as well as others, pondered and plundered the past in efforts to garb their own positions in Clio's prestige.

The political model had to be entirely rethought during the course of the nineteenth century. Despite intense resistance on the part of some, democracy and the nation now had to be taken into account. Exercising the genius of Tocqueville and scores of lesser figures, the problem of democracy would continue to haunt the ruling classes until the discovery that a broadening of the franchise would not necessarily lead from political democracy to social democracy and, indeed, might lead to a strengthening of their own positions. Although the democratic restructuring of the political model may have contributed in important respects to its ultimate weakening, the extent to which its reformulation took place within the context of the nation also served to strengthen it.[25]

If the nation served the needs of expanding capitalist productive forces, it also brought the benefits of a disguise for the market and the model of "economic man," a construct which had never roused mass ideological enthusiasm. With the internal market transformed into a nation, whether motherland or fatherland, emotion could be mobilized in support of disguised calculation. Moreover, whether trade followed the flag or the flag followed trade, some human sacrifices on the altar of the nation roused more sentiment than a bundle of merchandise on a distant dock.

Forged out of a variety of traditions more or less readily at hand and never solely a product of ideological conspiracy, the nation allowed for the survival of "political man" at best as citizen, at worst, especially between 1914 and 1918, as Frenchman, German, Englishman, and so forth. While the struggle begun in 1914 would make its own contribution to the lengthy process of disenchanting the political model, the intensity of the national allegiances revealed at all levels of society in that grim year testified to the role played by the nation in neutralizing those who had clung to older models, or more localized loyalties, or the horizontal thrust of class identity in face of vertically integrative claims. The nation, in brief, provided the ideological blanket, the sense of community, under which a variety of social divisions and conflicts could be, if not smothered, at least subsumed. But this socio-political construct could not resolve fully the greatest challenges posed in the nineteenth century.

The sociologist Simmel admitted rather grudgingly that, if the nineteenth century had any dominant concern, it lay with "society."[26] Given the century's welter of conflicting ideological currents, his hesitation is understandable, all the more so in that, despite enormous effort, to the very present capitalism has proven incapable of giving rise to a social model of man as generally persuasive as the political, economic, and psychological models. Still, the attempts to construct such a model not only defied the sway of the older political and economic models, but for a time offered a real, if ultimately abortive, challenge to "psychological man."

The opposition to *laissez-faire* capitalism, and the political and economic models intrinsic to it, came initially from conservatives and utopian socialists who stood at one in their searing critiques of the chaos spawned by it. Whatever the differences even within their own ranks, they shared a horror of the results of the French and Industrial Revolutions, a disgust with the liberal justifications of these results, a recognition of class struggle and a desperate desire to end it, a commitment to order, an interest in hierarchy, and a willingness to use religion, whether of the traditional sorts or more secular improvisations, as social cement. While they disagreed violently as to the nature of the ideal social organization, these theorists of class reconciliation agreed that society itself should take the place of the political forum and the economic marketplace as the focus of concern. The anarchists agreed with that focus, but went further in insisting that the small communities of society, knit together by federative threads, should also be the place of decision.

Others decided that, whatever the changes required, society had to be understood scientifically.[27] With extraordinary scientific advances taking place and the sciences being transformed into a reified Science, the prospect of a science of society could only dazzle. Seeking to meet the challenge, Comte embarked upon the construction of a "sociology"—his own neologism—which promised not only the fusion of "order and progress," but also the harmonization of the interests of bankers and workers. However, in the short run both the consistency and eccentricity of Comte's positivist vision precluded it from enjoying the kind of success in France which Spencer's version of sociology, with its fundamental congruence with the shibboleths of *lassez-faire* capitalism and opening to Social Darwinism, encountered in England. Yet, in Spencer's case, too much should not be made of success. Much had to change before the presumptuous new-comer, sociology, aspiring from birth to a long-lived reign as queen of the sciences, assumed academic recognition and realized its full intellectual and ideological potential.

The advent and consolidation of a much more organized and concentrated capitalism contributed, both positively and negatively, to the remarkable flowering of sociological thought in the *fin-de-siècle* when figures of the stature of Weber, Durkheim, and Pareto, as well as others, stepped forward to analyse, criticize, and justify the workings of increasingly complex societies. But despite all the genius expended in such endeavours, a hegemonic model of man, comparable in appeal to the earlier liberal political and economic models, did not emerge. The very complexity of the new kind of capitalist society either precluded an over-all simplification or, as with the later functionalists, ended in schema too general to serve as anything but crude justifications of the existing order.

Differences in what had become national traditions further complicated the matter: French positivism and German historicism could no more be easily reconciled than the republicanism of a Durkheim and the Hohenzollern loyalties of Weber. Existing socio-political structures, moreover, could thwart as well as stimulate: like Durkheim, Weber and Pareto were political creatures, but, unlike the Frenchman, supremely frustrated political creatures. None of the three, however, abandoned a concern with the doings of an "economic man" whose features had begun to change in light of new conditions: Durkheim investigated the division of labour; Pareto made his greatest contributions in economics rather than sociology; and at the end of his life Weber proudly identified himself as a political economist. Still, Weber's disenchanted judgment on his contemporaries, "specialists without spirit; sensualists without heart; this nullity," also marked the distance travelled away from the political and economic models of man.[28]

The classical image which had done so much to sustain the political model decayed as the nineteenth century waned. Terrified by the entrance into it of those whom Locke had so firmly barred from it, Nietzsche spurned the forum in favour of the psyche. As for the forum as marketplace, neither his Dioysius nor his Apollo were any more creatures of the *agora* than the archaic Furies who now began to haunt art and literature. Especially when faced with the challenge of a socialism which claimed to be scientific, others would follow Nietzsche in detecting the emergence of a "mass man" open to manipulation from below and, hence, in need of the firmest control from above. But the rejection of the political and economic models by self-proclaimed cultural elitists, a radicalization of earlier romantic tendencies, remained of less significance than the new efforts to counter the threat of socialism by integrating the working classes into national societies. As the nineteenth century ended, new ideologies aimed at class reconciliation proliferated: Social Darwinism (in its second, imperialist incarnation), Social Christianity, Socialism of the Chair, Social Imperialism, Social Liberalism, Fabian Socialism, and the like.

To the extent that such competing and overlapping ideological messages achieved legislative recognition, they contributed to the strengthening of the powers of the governmental bureaucracy at the expense of the very legislative power which sanctioned them and, hence, further sapped the political model of man. Under the pressure of social concerns, political debate gave ground to bureaucratic regulation, politics ceded territory to administrative control. Karl Mannheim put the matter succinctly in urging that "the reduction of the political element is essential for any form of planning."[29] Although still of inestimable value, the rights of citizenship proved more hollow than those who had fought for the democratization of the forum had believed. Indeed, whatever the resistance encountered, it might well be that the weakening of the forum contributed to a willingness to allow women into it. However that might be, the scene had been set for a more general acceptance of the forum as marketplace, the citizen as object, and politics as swindle. The apathy resulting from such perceptions would even be welcomed by some as a sign of the strength of democratic institutions.[30] In brief, if the institutionalization of the efforts to resolve "the social question" through the construction of the Social Welfare State eventually mitigated the sufferings of many, these endeavours neither rested upon nor brought about a hegemonic model of social man.

The National Socialist variant of Fascism actually went further towards the construction and, with the terms and media of discourse controlled tightly, the implementation of such a model. Fusing bits and pieces of debris derived from the streams of manipulative rationality and romantic vitalism which had opposed and interpenetrated each other since at least the nineteenth century, the Nazis' racist variant of the social model promised the integration of "mass man" into a hierarchically organized community from which the political and economic models would be banished finally and forever.[31] While it is misleadingly easy to interpret National Socialism in terms of psycho-pathology, it remains true that psychopaths still managed to gain and exercise enormous powers. More mundanely, in terms which Weber never foresaw, the specialists could make sure that the trains to the camps ran on time, the sensualists could become voluptuaries of violence, the nullities could strut as uniformed nihilists. Potent emotions could be harnessed to efficient techniques, and rationalized means could serve the most irrational of ends. And Martin Heidegger, hardly a Serenus Zeitblom, could meditate on Hölderlin none too far from Auschwitz. Along with much else, in a fashion which would have shocked John Locke, theorist of the *tabula rasa*, Fascism revealed the extraordinary plasticity of the human. Here it joined with, even while dividing itself from, the emergent "psychological man." In this instance, in a manner which Freud could not have wholly foreseen, the abnormal shed light upon that changing statistical average, the normal.

At least as much as history and sociology, psychology has lent itself to ideological use and abuse which Nietzsche hardly envisioned when he hailed it as the coming queen of the sciences.[32] But no more than other kinds of disciplined inquiry was it simply a ideological artifact deployed to answer the social needs of the moment. Long intertwined with philosophy as well as with the earlier models of man, psychology possessed an impressive pre-history. And with its autonomy finally achieved, it had to confront, just like any other discipline, problems intrinsic to its own development. Moreover, in order to establish their credentials as scientists, the new psychologists had to appropriate the great scientific advances of the nineteenth century, especially those brought about by Darwin and Helmholtz, and integrate them into their own work. But moving from the strictly scientific realm, they were also influenced by the century's dual legacy of manipulative rationality and romantic vitalism, and, indeed, continuing differences among psychological schools might still be defined in terms of the varying weights assumed by these currents within particular systems. Still, whatever the heritage from the past, the emergence of psychology as a distinct and increasingly important area of inquiry was but a part of a larger change within capitalist culture.

Towards the end of the nineteenth century, in Vienna and elsewhere, the *avant garde* of middle class intellectuals, in a rebellion which went far beyond that of the romantics, abandoned the convictions of their fathers and grandfathers that reality could be rationally understood and, once so understood, could be rationally manipulated in the service of either some human needs or the needs of some humans in areas like the political forum and the economic marketplace. In the course of so doing, they abandoned modernity in favour of modernism.[33] Often basing themselves upon a perception of life as flux, a view integral to the various forms of *Lebensphilosophie*, those caught up in the cultural shift moved in directions so multitudinous as to confirm a relativism more radical than that which had resided in historicism. While the new currents often ended in frank invocations of the irrational, they also stimulated major efforts at the rational understanding of the irrational. But whatever the perspective adopted, the result was a psychologizing of all realms of life and the emergence of "psychological man." While a crudely mechanical explanation of the cultural shift cannot do justice to its complexities, the change did not take place in a social vaccum and can be seen as a reaction, at once defensive and accommodating, to larger structural changes within capitalism.[34]

The structural transformation inevitably affected the fate of the already battered economic model which, while it would still be invoked, led an more precarious life in a marketplace increasingly dominated by corporate giants. The changes in the market, however, did allow for a softening of those features of "economic man" which had invoked so much dismay, contempt and hatred. Marginal utility thinking shifted the emphasis away from the labour theory of value, now dangerously appropriated by the Marxists, and at the same time, in face of the challenge posed by historical materialism, permitted the retention of the ahistorical perspective favoured by the classical economists in their depiction of "economic man." As the focus of concern moved from production to consumption, from objective calculation to subjective taste, the economic model tended to become more closely associated with the emergent psychological model. Although he depicted it as nothing more than a short-lived phase, even

Schumpeter acknowledged that "in the beginning, utility, both total and marginal, was considered a psychic reality, a feeling that was evident from introspection, independent of any external observation."[35] Whatever the balance to be struck in regard to that complicated matter, "economic man" survived better in another kind of relation to "psychological man."

No more than others could the new psychologists and psychiatrists escape the influence of their social settings: Jean-Martin Charcot's investigations of hysteria, for instance, had more than a little to do with railway accidents and litigation over accident claims and insurance payments. At a more subtle level, the psychologist/psychiatrists made use of analogies, metaphors and images derived from the surrounding society. In this respect, the idea of energy, of major scientific importance since Helmholtz, lent itself on occasion to uses which had much more to do with ideology than with the sciences. As early as 1869 the American neurologist George M. Beard brought together notions of energy, symbolized by the battery, with more distinctly economic analogies in attempting to explain the sources of his neologism, neurasthenia. T.J. Jackson Lears has noted the popularity of such imagery in the United States and related the message that "psychic wastrels could easily overdraw and bankrupt themselves" to a "scarcity therapy" which, with the changes in capitalism, began to give way around the turn of the century to "a new faith in psychic abundance."[36]

William James propounded that message of abundance. Convinced of the existence of an "energy budget," he also detected a relationship between energy and "a very practical problem of national economy, as well as of individual ethics…In rough terms, we may say that a man who energizes below his normal maximum fails by just so much to profit from his chance of life; and that a nation filled with such men is inferior to a nation run at higher pressure."[37] But his commitment to psychic abundance impelled the fox-like James to steer away from the economics of energy with its implications of possible scarcity. Viewed in light of its relation to capitalism, his real achievement was to present the old "possessive individualism" in new psychological guise: *In its widest possible sense…a man's Self is the sum total that he* CAN *call his*, not only his body and psychic powers, but his clothes and house, his wife and children, his ancestors and friends, his reputation and works, his lands and horses, his yacht and bank-account."[38]

Although Pierre Janet acknowledged his debt to James' essay on energy, the French psychiatrist remained faithful to the older concern with scarcity. Having begun his eminent career with the brief *Fondement du droit de propriété* (1883), which had nothing and perhaps everything to do with his later psychology, Janet went on to develop in obsessive detail permutations of the equation of psychic energy with psychic capital. Indeed, in his massive compendium on "psychological healing," he devoted more than three hundred pages to "Psychological Economics" and close to five hundred pages to "Psychological Acquisitions."[39] Arguing that "most neuropaths…are on the verge of bankruptcy," Janet concluded that psychotherapists had "to take up the problem of the economic administration of the mind's forces.[40] Holding out the prospect that it would eventually become possible to "know how to establish the balance and budget of a mind as we establish that of a business firm," he thought that the psychiatrist would then not only "be able to make good use of slender resources by avoiding useless expenditure," but, even better, would be able "to teach his patients to increase their resources and enrich their minds."[41] Janet posited, in brief, the psychotherapist as at once receiver in bankruptcy and portfolio manager.

If his imagery tended more towards the martial, economic comparisons did not frighten Freud. In *The Interpretation of Dreams*, he proclaimed confidently that "daytime thought may very well play the part of *entrepreneur* for a dream; but the *entrepreneur*, who...has the idea and the initiative to carry it out, can do nothing without capital; he needs a *capitalist* who can afford the outlay and the capitalist who provides the psychic outlay for the dream is invariably and indisputably...*a wish from the unconscious*."[42] Pursuing the parallel, he allowed that "sometimes the capitalist is himself the *entrepreneur*," before going on to consider the instances in which "the *entrepreneur* may himself make a small contribution to the capital; several *entrepreneurs* may apply to the same capitalist; several capitalists may combine to put up what is necessary for the *entrepreneur*."[43] A few years later Freud developed an equally detailed "comparison between psychical economy and a business enterprise."[44] Although the source of the story cannot be considered unbiased, this kind of thinking might have led him to remark to Emma Jung that his marriage "had long ago been 'amortized.' "[45]

Fundamental suppositions, acknowledged and unacknowledged, lay behind such language. Suspicions of the American promise of abundance, psychic and otherwise, and acutely aware of the conflicts engendered by conditions of scarcity, this "biologist of the mind" echoed Malthus: "The motive of human society is in the last resort an economic one: it does not possess enough provisions to keep its members alive unless they work, it must restrict the number of its members and divert their energies from sexual activity to work."[46] If Janet moved swiftly to the equation of psychic energy with capital, Freud proved more faithful to the etymology of "energy" and concentrated quite as much upon labour as conflict in the construction of his system.[47] It might even be argued that Freud's version of "psychological man" rested upon a genuine, though trans-valued and unrecognized, labour theory of value.[48] Be that as it might, more than Janes or Janet, Freud came to the rescue of "economic man," increasingly banished as an individual from the marketplace, and, absorbing the construct into his system, set the creature free to stalk the convoluted corridors of the psyche.

Motivated by the larger suppositions inherited from the Enlightenment, as well as by their more specific positivist re-workings, Freud remained faithful to the economic model in his firm rejection of "religious man." Although scarcely as virulent, his treatment of "political man" was, in its essentials, equally harsh. Despite the incorporation into his system of elements like censorship, clearly derived from his Viennese background, he turned his back upon the struggles of that hapless creature. Influenced in part by what he saw as the implications of the Darwinian revolution, in part by the changing political situation in Vienna, and perhaps in part by the more general decline of the political model, this apolitical Liberal dealt a blow to "political man" which still reverberates. The reverse of that achievement lay in Freud's extension, to at least some wealthy enough to afford it, of some degree of protection against the claims asserted by the larger community. Ironically, there are those like Rieff who, while profoundly influenced by Freud, have lamented the loss of the sense of community which accompanied the rise of "psychological man."

When that construct achieved hegemonic status within society deserves further investigation.[49] But it appears that "psychological man" stands at the end of a long process of development which began when the workings of capitalism undermined a religious model rooted in non-capitalist conditions. "Political man," a model rooted in the classical world but one which underwent profound revisions in the seventeenth century. constituted the first viable alternative to "religious man." More than a century later "political man" found a worthy, though perhaps less attractive, complement in "economic man." These two models, however, encountered challenges from a variety of directions in the nineteenth century. Shaken by change on a hitherto unknown scale, that period witnessed the rise of competing efforts either to rework the religious, political and economic models or to provide hegemonic alternatives to them. If the most significant of the latter endeavours had to do with the search for a generally acceptable social model of man, even the more highly concentrated and socialized capitalist conditions which had begun to take shape by the end of that century worked to preclude the emergence of such a model. While the increased wealth of some societies then began to allow for the incorporation of a social dimension into the political model, that very process further weakened the political model's once eminent position. The model of "economic man," the starkness of which had done much to stimulate the quest for "social man," also managed to survive, but at the price of also losing its former eminence and of having some of its most distinctive features incorporated into the emergent psychological model.

Given the consecration of a transfigured individualism intrinsic to it, the advent of that construct might be taken as the final triumph of Berlin's "foxes." This protean creature, "psychological man," seems to have escaped, not only the kind of constraints central to the earlier models, but constraints of all sorts and, hence, might be taken as the supreme figure of "post-modernism," itself ultimately an expression of capitalist dynamics. But like the social atoms of the political and economic models, the newer atoms also undergo a process of socialization sanctioned by a model which, providing a focus for intellectual discourse and a magnet for emotional identification, awards a privilege status to one dimension of experience at the expense of others and, thereby, eases some tensions while exacerbating others. Whether one reviles "psychological man" or empathizes with his real and illusionary agonies, or delights in his multi-faceted and constantly changing character, or simply accepts him as the dominant figure of the cultural landscape of the late twentieth century, the full measure of Schorske's "dangerous and mercurial creature" has no more been taken adequately than have the intricate ties which bind this model of man, like the earlier ones, to a particular socio-economic setting.

Notes

1. Carl E. Schorscke, *Fin-de-siècle Vienna: Politics and Culture* (New York: Alfred A. Knopf, 1980), p. 4.

2. *Ibid.*, p. 5.

3. *Ibid.*, p. 8. Christopher Lasch, *The Culture of Narcissism: American Life in an Age of Diminishing Expectations* (New York: Warner Books, 1979), pp. 38, 4. For a brief review of discussions of "psychological man," see Peter Homans, *Jung in Context: Modernity and the Making of Psychology* (Chicago: University of Chicago Press, 1979), pp. 1-5.

4. Rieff, *Triumph*, pp. 241-42.

5. Rieff, *Triumph*, p. 5.

6. An extensive bibliography would be out of place here, for outstanding, though very different, efforts of this sort, see Robert N. Young, *Mind, Brain and Adaptation in the Nineteenth Century. Cerebral Localization and its biological context from Gall to Ferrier* (Oxford: Clarendon Press, 1970); Dorothy Ross, *Stanley Hall: The Psychologist as Prophet* (Chicago: University of Chicago Press, 1972); and Frank J. Sulloway, *Freud, Biologist of the Mind: Beyond the Psychoanalytic Legend* (New York: Basic Books, 1979).

7. Philip Rieff, *Fellow Teachers* (New York: Dell Publishing, 1975), p. 391. See also the "Epilogue" to the third edition (1979) of Philip Rieff, *Freud: The Mind of the Moralist* (Chicago: University of Chicago Press, 1959).

8. Georges Duby, *Les trois ordres ou l'imaginaire du féodalisme* (Paris: Editions Gallimard, 1978). The very mention of feudalism brings to mind a remarkably long-lived model curiously neglected by Rieff, "man as warrior".

9. While the matter is of great importance, no effort will be made here to explore the relations of images of woman to the models of man. But it might be suggested that women came to play a greater role in relation to male models only when those models had begun to lose hegemonic status: women, for instance, gained the vote at the time when electoral politics were coming to be overshadowed by the growth of administrative machinery. Moreover, it might be suggested that, given its protean character and relatively recent assumption of primacy, the role assigned to women within the psychological model poses exceptionally complex problems. Those problems are all the more difficult in that the model of "psychological man" was initially constructed on the basis of psychologists" and psychiatrists' experiences with and experiments upon women.

10. Lucien Febvre, *Le problème de l'Incroyance au XVIe siècle. La religion de Rabelais* (Paris: Editions Albin Michel, 1942).

11. "The Hedgehog and the Fox," Isaiah Berlin, *Russian Thinkers* (Harmondsworth: Penguin Books, 1979), pp. 22-81, p. 22.

12. The various Marxist weighting of the elements central to the capitalist models of man deserve separate attention. Social Democrats tended to profile their own model of "economic man"; Leninists, their version of political man. Although his emphasis on different models could and did shift, Marx remained enough of a Hegelian to be primarily concerned with the *totality*.

13. Machiavelli and others, of course, tried to rework the warrior model, by relating it to classical notions of citizenship. But the cult of the sword and the horse, of the officer and the gentleman, though persisting long after the Renaissance, never quite lost its feudal character. Rieff's failure to do anything with this long-lived model is all the more striking in that, like other commentators, he is fully aware of Freud's penchant for martial imagery. Whatever one might think of his interpretation of imperialism, another Viennese was fully aware of the atavistic attitudes and behavior which characteristic of "man-as warrior." See Joseph Schumpeter, *Imperialism and Social Classes: Two Essays* (New York: Meridian Books, 1955).

14. J.G.A. Pocock, *The Machiavellian Moment: Florentine Political Thought and the Atlantic Republican Tradition* (Princeton: Princeton University Press, 1975).

15. Thomas Hobbes, *Behemoth* (New York: Barnes and Noble, 1969), p. 2.

16. B. McPherson, *The Political Theory of Oossessive Individualism: Hobbes to Locke* (Oxford: Clarendon Press, 1962).

17. Even in the nineteenth century, when capitalist behaviour most closely approximated it, the utilitarian message, whether in Bentham's raw formulation or John Stuart Mill's sterilized version, never commanded wholehearted assent within the ranks of the bourgeoisie. Not until the twentieth century, and then largely shorn of its explicitly political focus, would the Hobbesian pleasure-pain caculus, transformed into the stimulus-response of behaviourist psychologists find its realization in B. F. Skinner's *Beyond Freedom and Dignity* (1971) and the degree of repression central to *Leviathan* find another kind of vindication in *Civilization and Its Discontent* (1930). Even now, however, the reworked Hobbesian image of man seems to require the cushioning provided by "the triumph of the therapeutic."

18. For Rousseau's pronounced misogyny, see the forthcoming work of Louise Gavard.

19. "Society is impossible without inequality, inequality intolerable without a code of morality, and a code of morality unacceptable without religion." Napoleon Bonaparte, quoted in George Rudé, *Revolutionary Europe, 1783-1815* (London: Collins, 1964), p. 237. "It is in the interest of every mill-owner to organize his moral machinery on equally sound principles with his mechanical, for otherwise he will never command the steady hands, watchful eyes, and prompt co-operation, essential to the excellence of product. There is, in fact, no case in which the Gospel truth, 'Godliness is great gain,' is more applicable than to the administration of a great factory." Andrew Ure, quoted in E.P. Thompson, *The Making of the English Working Class* (London: Victor Gollanz, 1963), pp. 361-62.

20. *Ibid.*, pp. 350-400.

21. If religious accommodations with the political and economic models proved to be very much the order of the day in the nineteenth century, another kind of shift in the religious perspective appears to be more significant in light of twentieth century developments. In psychologizing religion, Kiekegaard carried further a process already begun by Friedrich Schliermacher for whom, incidently, Hegel had infinite contempt. By 1857 an Anglican clergyman, destined to become Archbishop of Canterbury, could argue that "theology has been cast in a scholastic mode, *i.e.* all based on logic. We are in need of, and are being gradually forced into, a theology based upon psychology." Frederick Temple, quoted in L.S. Hearnshaw, *A Short History of British Psychology, 1840-1940* (London: Methuen and Co., 1964), p. 292.

22. Such transformations at best papered over tendencies whose full results would only be reaped in the twentieth century. George Steiner has found "the most haunting, prophetic outcry of the nineteenth century" in Theophile Gautier's *"plus la barbarie que l'ennui."* George Steiner, *In Bluebeard's Castle: Some Notes Toward the Redefinition of Culture* (New Haven: Yale University Press, 1971).

Boredom's relation to the models of man, the confusion, provoked by the lack of such models, and the eventual emergence of "psychological man" calls for further study. For suggestive analyses, moving from the specific to the more general, see Walter Benjamin, *Charles Baudelaire: A Lyric Poet in the Era of High Capitalism* (London: New Left Books, 1974); Mario Praz, *The Romantic Imagination* (London: Oxford University Press, 1970); and Reinhard Kuhn, *The Demon at Noontime: Ennui in Western Literature* (Princeton: Princeton University Press, 1976).

23. As early as 1836 Mill reduced "economic man" to simply an analytical device. "On the Definition of Political Economy; and on the Method of Investigation Proper to It," John Staurt Mill, *Essays on Economics and Society, 1824-1845, Collected Works*, IV (Toronto: University of Toronto Press, 1967), pp. 309-39, p. 322.

24. John Stuart Mill, *Autobiography* (Indianapolis: Bobbs-Merill Co., 1957), p. 3. See also "The Spirit of the Age," John Stuart Mill, *Essays on Politics and Culture*, edited with an Introduction by Gertrude Himmelfarb (Garden City: Doubleday and Co., 1962), pp. 3-50.

25. For a searching investigation of one instance of this kind of process, see Sanford Elwitt, *The Making of the Third Republic: Class and Politics in France, 1868-1884* (Baton Rouge: Louisiana State University Press, 1975).

26. "The Conflict in Modern Culture," Georg Simmel, *The Conflict in Modern Culture and Other Essays* (New York: Teachers College Press, 1968), pp. 11-26, p. 14.

27. Marx might be placed within this current, but for his insistence on the totality of analysis, inherited from Hegel, and radical transformation, definitely not inherited from Hegel. That did not prevent subsequent Marxists have placing undue emphasis on different dimensions of human experience.

28. Max Weber, *The Protestant Ethic and the Spirit of Capitalism* (New York: Charles Scribner's Sons, 1956), p. 182.

29. Karl Mannheim, *Man and Society in an Age of Reconstruction: Essays in Modern Social Structure* (London: Routledge and Kegan Paul, 1940), p. 360.

30. Herbert Tingsten, *Political Behaviour: Studies in Election Statistics* (London: P.S. King and Son, 1937), pp. 225-26; W.H. Morris Jones, "In Defence of Political Apathy," *Political Studies*, 2 (1954), pp. 25-37.

31. Political and economic life, of course, continued, but in theoretical subordination to the dominant racist social model which, in fact, allowed both elements to become far bloodier. For very different interpretations of the subordination of the political and economic models, see Franz Neumann, *Behemoth: The Structure and Practice of National Socialism, 1933-1944* (New York: Oxford University Press, 1944), pp. 459-70 and Peter F. Drucker, *The End of Economic Man: A Study of the New Totalitarianism* (New York: John Day, 1939).

32. For studies of the ideological use and abuse of psychology, see Stephen Jay Gould, *The Mismeasure of Man* (New York: W.W. Norton, 1981).

33. Irving Howe has noted that *"modernism despairs of human history...yet within its own realm is committed to ceaseless change, turmoil and recreation.* Emphasis in the original. "Introduction. The Idea of the Modern." Irving Howe (ed.), *The Idea of the Modern in Literature and the Arts* (New York: Horizon Press, 1967), pp. 11-40, p. 17. In Philip Rieff's formulation, "to be radically contemporaneous...is to achieve a conclusive, unanswerable failure of historical memory. This is the uniquely modern (sic) achievement." Rieff, *Fellow Teachers*, p. 391. Rieff, in fact, means modernist and, perhaps in an extension, its popularization in post-modernism.

34. For a stimulating but excessively mechanical analysis of the cultural change, see George Lukács, *Die Zerstörung der Vernunft* (Berlin: Aufbau, 1933).

35. Joseph A. Schumpeter, *History of Economic Analysis* (New York: Oxford University Press, 1954), p. 1060.

36. T.J. Jackson Lears, *No Place of Grace: Antimodernism and the Transformation of American Culture, 1880-1920* (New York: Pantheon Books, 1981), pp. 52-53.

37. "The Energies of Men," William James, *Memories and Studies* (London: Longmans, Green, and Co., 1912), pp. 227-64, 231, 233-34.

38. Emphasis in original. William James, *The Principles of Psychology*, I (New York: Dover Publications, 1950), p. 291.

39. Pierre Janet, *Psychological Healing: An Historical and CLinical Study*, I and II (New York: The Macmillan Co., 1925), pp. 371-1205.

40. *Ibid.*, p. 456; Pierre Janet, *Principles of Psychotherapy* (London: George Allen and Unwin Ltd., 1926), p. 313.

41. *Ibid.*, pp. 313-14.

42. Sigmund Freud, *The Interpretation of Dreams* (Harmondsworth: Penguin Books, 1976), p. 714. Emphasis in original.

43. *Ibid.*

44. Sigmund Freud, *Jokes and Their Relation to the Unconscious* (Harmondsworth: Penguin Books, 1976), pp. 210-11.

45. Emma Jung to Sigmund Freud, Nov. 6 (1911), *The Freud/Jung Letters. The Correspondence between Sigmund Freud and C.G. Jung*, edited by William McGuire (Princeton: Princeton University Press, 1974), pp. 455-57, p. 456.

46. Sigmund Freud, *Introductory Lectures on Psychoanalsis* (Harmondsworth: Penguin Books, 1973), pp. 353-54.

47. David Riesman remarked drily that "just as Freud 'allowed himself' his book-collecting and other hobbies for their re-creative functions, so he 'allowed' mankind the apparent frivolity of foreplay for its procreative functions." "The Themes of Work and Play in the Structure of Freud's Thought," David Riesman, *Selected Essays from Individualism Reconsidered* (Garden City: Doubleday Anchor Books, 1955), pp. 175-205, p. 197.

48. In other words, Freud might be seen as a late Ricardian who, at the time of the waning of the domestic *laissez-faire* market, internalized its dynamics within the individual while others, who shared his penchant for martial imagery, externalized them further through imperialist expansion. The isolation of a Ricardian element in Freud's thought might also help unravel a more minor problem. H. Stuart Hughes has noted that Herbert Marcuse in dealing with "surplus repression" in *Eros and Civilization* (1955) "put on a spectacular performance...more particularly since Marx's name never appeared in his pages." Neither did Ricardo's name. But if there is a Ricardian strain buried in Freud's system, then Marcuse's *tour de force* becomes more readily understandable. H. Stuart Hughes, *The Sea Change: The Migration of Social Thought, 1930-1965* (New York: Harper and Row, 1975), p. 177.

49. Cases of "shell-shock" in World War I accelerated the acceptance of the psychological model. Its possible demise is equally debatable. Whereas one commentator has already relegated "psychological man" to the past, another has contended that "the creature is only half-way out of the shell." The latter argument rests upon the view that "the world ideological situation...is still dominated by 'economic man'—especially by Marx's version, the most powerful non-psychological and in effect anti-psychological ideology of the day." John Caroll, *Puritan, Paranoid, Remissive: A Sociology of Modern Culture* (London: Routledge and Kegan Paul, 1977); Jack Jones, "Five Versions of Psychological Man," Robert Boyers (ed.), *Psychological Man* (New York: Harper and Row, 1975), pp. 57-64, p. 57.

8

THE PROBLEMATIC BOURGEOISIE [1]

A review of Peter Gay, *The Bourgeois Experience: Victoria to Freud*, Vol. I, *Education of the Senses* (New York: Oxford University Press, 1984). Page references to this work will appear in the text. All emphases appear in the original.

Peter Gay has begun a "symphonic treatment" of "the bourgeois experience from Victoria to Freud" (p. 1). This multi-volume endeavor is to be "constructed…on the fundamental building blocks of the human experience—love, aggression, and conflict" (p. 6). While the first volume is devoted to "the bourgeois sensual life," the second will be concerned with expressions of love and desire "in the so-called higher reals of culture" (p. 6). Gay notes, however, that "in both volumes, love and sex are interwoven" and that, solely because of the richness of the material, he made a "tactical" decision to divide it (p. 6). Subsequent volumes will treat of aggression, conflict, and, initially, "the travail of liberal culture" (p.7). Requiring erudition, sensitivity and courage, qualities which Gay has amply displayed in other works, the projected undertaking is awe-inspiring. And anything approaching a final judgment in regard to it must await the last note of the symphony. But the recently published first volume prompts, along with appreciation of the wealth of detail, a good measure of doubt. The book is learned, provocative, and, in a fashion, daring. It is also flawed. A work of such scope, of course, will always lead to quarrels over details which, however stimulating, are not in the end that important. Unfortunately, the fundamental faults of *Education of the Senses* have to do with more important matters of method.

Gay seeks to combine two of the now fashionable currents of historical analysis: historical cultural anthropology and psycho-history. He informs his readers: "The word 'culture,' which I use in the comprehensive way of anthropologists, requires some words of caution. Every human artifact that contributes to the making of experience belongs under this capacious rubric: social institutions, economic developments, family life, moral and religious doctrines, the anxieties of physicians, the tides of taste, the structure of the emotions, even politics" (p.4). But Gay does not reveal how the historian is to establish rankings of importance among the variegated facets of human experience. And the coy "even politics" cannot disguise an equally basic problem:

as Ranke, Marx, and other now less fashionable historians would have agreed, there are distinct limits to what can be achieved through the kind of analysis which slights the workings of political power within society. The exercise of power, moreover, is hardly confined to the political process.

Consequently, one is not altogether reassured when Gay proclaims: "My leading men and women are physicians, merchants, teachers, housewives, novelists, painters, politicians, the occasional prosperous artisan who has secured a measure of economic independence and social responsibility, and the rare aristocrat whose credentials are dubious and whose very posture is supremely bourgeois" (p. 4). These are all, to be sure, worthy bourgeois types. There were also others. The painter Thomas Uwins, whom Gay quotes, remarked: "The old nobility and landed proprietors have gone out. Their place is supplied by railroad speculators, iron mine men, and grinders from Sheffield, etc., Liverpool and Manchester merchants and traders" (p. 388).

While he must devote some attention to the railway, Gay ignores the industrialists in his analysis of the century, which was, after all, the century of the Industrial Revolution. However busy the captains of industry, some of them also left the sort of intimate sources especially favored by Gay, diaries and family letters. And they do appear in other works: for instance, in Bonnie G. Smith's *Ladies of the Leisure Class*, which makes the kind of point too often slighted by Gay: we must "remember what nineteenth-century men never failed to recognize: the culture of the home often stood in opposition to the imperative of industrial progress."[2] But perhaps Gay's resolution of such problems will only become apparent when he has completed the massive work which will not be psycho-history but rather "history informed by psychoanalyzed" (p. 8).

Whatever the worth of that distinction, Freudianism provides the theoretical spine of *Education of the Senses*. Gay takes it as a given that "having traversed the Oedipus complex, the child comes to repress much of what he has learned. There are good reasons for these intense acts of forgetting: the little boy would just as soon not be reminded of open or fancied threats to his cherished penis, the little girl as soon deny her dismay at discovering that she has no penis to lose" (p. 278). According to Gay, many bourgeois resolved their Oedipal struggles successfully, the result being "happy sensual marriages among the middle class in the nineteenth century" (p. 331). Happy sensual marriages there were: the Kingsleys stand in pleasant contrast to the Ruskins. But whether such marriages can be explained primarily in terms of the surmounting of the fear of castration and the overcoming of the resentment engendered by the lack of a male organ remains open to question.

Gay dutifully supplies two examples of penis envy. Having discovered as a child the genital difference between the sexes, Sigrid Undset later recalled that she "paid tribute to the superior equipment of boys, meekly and without envy" (p. 331). One does not have to be a Freudian to realize that denials can be revealing, but Gay is too ready to conclude that "she must have envied boys more than she later remembered" (p. 331). The case of Victoria Benedictesson is much more complex, but Gay is equally ready to decide that "her frigidity was entangled in fundamental sexual confusion and in her ultimate grievance: she felt herself to be a castrated man, furious and, even more, depressed at being enslaved in a woman's body" (p. 116). Quoting a diary entry, Gay argues that she "dreaded only one thing: 'to be deprived of' " (p. 116). He then asserts that "we are entitled…to complete that sentence: it was dreadful to be deprived of a penis, source and symbol of power" (p. 116). Such entitlements proliferate throughout the book and contribute to shaping it in two somewhat contradictory fashions: they allow Gray to extrapolate beyond what his sources reveal, but they also dictate a choice of sources which lend themselves to this kind of interpretation. Freudianism underlies both tendencies. In this particular instance, Gay not only accepts penis-envy but also asserts that "most girls learn to reconcile themselves to their biological destiny, resigning themselves to or even revealing in their femininity" (p. 117). He has returned, in brief, to that world in which "Anatomy is Destiny."[3]

Too sophisticated to ignore Freud's misogyny, Gay quotes from the notorious letter to Freud's fiancé of November 15, 1883 in which he proclaimed that, for all his merits, John Stuart Mill "lacked the sense of the absurd on several points, for instance in the emancipation of women and the question of women altogether."[4] But one as concerned as Gay with "sweet bourgeois communions" might have included Freud's conclusion that "the position of woman cannot be other than it is: to be an adored sweetheart in youth, and a beloved wife in maturity."[5] Still, whatever the implications of such bourgeois commonplaces for the later development of psychoanalysis, an impressionistic survey of the psychological literature of the turn-of-the-century suggests that Freud was no more misogynist than most of his colleagues and quite possibly less so than many of them.

The recent "trouble in the archives," however, indicates that the issue is more complex.[6] While this tale of credulity, opportunism, and obsession is hardly edifying, it once again raises questions about the scientific validity of Freud's work and the consequences of that work for women. Reducing the matter to its essentials, Jeffrey Masson, who served briefly as projects director of the Sigmund Freud Archives, has argued that, driven by a variety of pressures which had nothing to do with science, Freud abandoned his acceptance of actual sexual violations of children in favor of the universal fantasies which constitute the Oedipal complex, the keystone of the psychoanalytical system. Masson also asserts that Freud continued to recognize instances of "seduction" and remained ambivalent about these threats to his larger theoretical structure. Some of Freud's disciples, according to Masson, later embarked upon the censoring of his letters to Wilhelm Fliess which resulted in the further damage of already severely traumatized patients, the majority of them women. More generally, but hardly originally, Masson charges: "By shifting the emphasis from an actual world of sadness, misery and cruelty to an internal stage on which actors performed invented dramas for an invisible audience of their own creation, Freud began a trend away from the real world which…is at the root of the present-day sterility of psychoanalysis and psychiatry throughout the world."[7]

Peter Gay, the historian who spent seven years as a "Research Candidate" at the Western New England Institute for Psychoanalysis, may have known of the burden of Masson's case before it became public knowledge.[8] In any event, while the Oedipus complex remains the pivot of his arguments, Gay makes some concessions in regard to the molestation of children:

The case books of late-nineteenth-century psycho-pathologists record harrowing accounts of early seductions, by no means all of them imaginary. Even after Sigmund Freud abandoned his sweeping theory that all neuroses are caused by the seduction of young girls by their fathers, he continued to recognize that reports of such seductions were often enough true. Certainly the incidents that left their traces in the medical records represent only a modest fraction of precocious initiations into sexual activity, for most of these never came to the attention of a priest or psychiatrist (p. 333).

In other words, sexual violations of children took place and possibly on a scale which Freud refused to recognize after his abandonment of the "seduction" theory. But having accepted the Oedipus complex, Gay cannot easily discriminate between the real and the imaginary.

The issue is significant enough for Gay to return to it: "As is only too well known, Sigmund Freud developed his theory about the centrality of fantasies in mental life by by learning to discount the reports of his female hysterical patients that they had been seduced by their fathers" (p. 494). The phrase, "as is only too well know," might be pondered, but without faltering, Gay goes on to maintain that "nothing...that Freud wrote in 1897, when he made his discovery that these confessions were indeed fantasies, or anything he said later, led him to complete skepticism about such reports" (p. 494). Gay admits that "Freud's record on the issue is complicated by his denying twice—in two early case histories of hysteria—that it had been the patient's father who had assaulted or mistreated her. He made amends with some severe self-criticisms, in the second edition of 1924" (p. 494). Some severity is to be found there:

I venture after the lapse of so many years to lift the veil of discretion and reveal the fact that Katerina was not the niece but the daughter of the landlady. The girl fell ill, therefore, from several attempts on the part of her own father. Distortions like the one I introduced in the present instance should be altogether avoided in reporting a case history.[9]

That seems categorical enough, but one is still left wondering why Freud should have drawn "the veil of discretion" in the case of a serving girl encountered briefly at a mountain inn. The second correction of 1924 simply reads: "In this instance, too, it was in fact the girl's father, not her uncle."[10] There have been harsher self-criticisms in the twentieth century. Some were a good deal less well justified.

The fundamental problem has to do with the relations between the internal and the external, psyche and society. At the most basic level, in Gay's unimpeachable formulation, "experiences...testify to the uninterrupted traffic between what the world imposes and the mind demands, receives and reshapes" (p. 12). But once that has been said, matters become considerably more complicated. While Gay dismisses the views of those like Harry Stack Sullivan and Erich Fromm who have stressed the role of social forces in the shaping of the psyche, he also insists, quite properly, that Freud never abandoned a concern with the influence of society upon the individual. Contrary to Masson and others who point to Freud's retreat from reality into fantasy, that could never be wholly the case with one who stoutly maintained: "The motive of human society is in the last resort an economic one: since it does not possess enough provisions to keep its members alive unless they work, it must restrict the number of its members and divert their energies from sexual activity to work."[11] There spoke the nineteenth century or at least one of the most influential—and distinctly bourgeois—currents within it. But Gay does not cite that that quotation, for, if nothing else, it poses questions his strenuous contention that the bourgeois sexual experience of that century was considerably richer and happier, less convoluted and hypocritical, than that suggested by his arch-villain, Steven Marcus, in *The Other Victorians: A Study of Sexuality and Pornography in mid-Nineteenth Century England* (1966).[12]

Turning towards external reality, Gay contends, in orthodox Freudian terms, that "the psychoanalyst's individual is a social individual" (p. 16). Having placed his emphasis upon the individual, he acknowledges special theoretical debts to the Freudian ego psychologists, Heinz Hartmann, Ernst Kris and Hans W. Lowald. He draws upon their positions in making "strong claims for the authority of external reality and for the competence of mind" (p. 12). Those claims are laudable. They echo Gay's beloved Enlightenment. They are also the result of Freud's ideal, "Where id was, there shall ego be."[13] But an irony resides here. Gay has set out to overturn "the popular perception of comfortable bourgeois...as cold machines for profit making," but he intends to do so with the aid of those theories which emphasize "man's ego, endowed with capacities for thinking, calculating, and anticipating" (p. 440). Put more bluntly, the psychoanalytic ego is very much like a good nineteenth-bourgeois: "the great negotiator and compromiser which induces the individual to give up lesser and richer pleasures now for greater and safer pleasures later. The ego's ultimate task is to reach accommodation with the world and, at best, to manipulate it and to master it" (p. 227). But Gay carries the individualist thrust much further: "Only the individual loves and hates, develops tastes in painting and furniture, feels content in moments of consummation, anxious in times of peril, and furious at agents of deprivation; only the individual glories in mastery or revenges himself upon the world. The rest is metaphor" (p. 15).

The chilling last sentence poses three kinds of problems: those which spring from the role of metaphor and the like in thought and expression; those rooted in the part played by language and symbolism within the Freudian system; and those which have to do with the Freudian view of human relations.

This is not the place to discuss the question of the role of metaphors and similar constructs in thought, including scientific thought, at any length.[14] It might be well to note, however, some of the positions which have been taken in regard to it. According to Terence Hawks, "there is...no way in which language can be 'cleaned' of metaphor."[15] But viewing them as obstacles to scientific thinking, Gaston Bachelard has warned strongly against them: *"Qu'on le veuille ou non, les métaphors seduisent le raison."*[16] Max Black's position is more balanced: "No doubt metaphors are dangerous—and perhaps especially so in philosophy. But a prohibition against their use would be a wilful and harmful restriction upon our powers of inquiry."[17] Extending his discussion to models and archetypes, he maintained that "all intellectual pursuits, however different their aims and methods, rely firmly on such exercises of the imagination."[18] But Black also cautioned that, "the more persuasive the archetype, the greater the danger of its becoming a self-certifying myth."[19] In brief, while the results of metaphorical and analogical transferences can be enlightening, they can also be intellectually and socially dangerous dangerous.[20] Much the same, of course, could be said about language itself.

Freud understood very well that "even in its caprices the usage of language remains true to some kind of reality."[21] That proposition cuts in two directions. It involves the untangling of the linguistic and symbolic associations displayed in *The Psychopathology of Everyday Life* (1901) and *Jokes and Their Relation to the Unconscious* (1904) and, through the use of free association and dream interpretation, therapeutic technique. It also points toward the difficulties involved in explicating what Freud believed to be psychic realities in terms of images derived from external reality. That exercise requires the use of metaphors, similes, and analogies. Freud, a master of language, does not shrink from them. And as Gay argued elsewhere. "at least some of the metaphors, comparisons, and analogies that Freud so vigorously employed were, in this mind, almost literally descriptive: to assimilate mental life to warfare, like assimilating psychoanalysis to archeology, said something that was true rather than just picturesque...Analogies disclosed substantial relationships."[22]

Gay shows no interest in Freud's economic analogies.[23] He scorns those who "have made much of the English colloquialism for having an orgasm—'to spend'—and argued that a high-capitalist culture must naturally regard seminal emissions as a loss and must naturally speak as though it were a financial transaction" (p. 317). Certainly the comparison occurred in some pre-capitalist societies possessed of currencies, much as the sexually intended "ploughing" continues to appear in industrial societies, which still carry a linguistic burden derived from an agricultural past. One takes one's comparisons from tradition and surrounding circumstances, and blending Freud's military and economic imagery, Gay himself lauds those who "found targets worthy of whole-hearted investment" (p. 280). Seen in strict terms, such "investment" has to do with the deployment of libido, but such words carry larger cultural resonances which echo, even in their "caprices," larger social realities.

The fundamental problem in this area, however, lies at a deeper level and has to do with the extent to which social relations are perceived, consciously or unconsciously, as object relations. According to Charles Rycroft, *A Critical Dictionary of Psychoanalysis*, an "object" is:

> That towards which action or desire is directed, that which the SUBJECT requires in order to achieve instinctual SATISFACTION, that to which the subject relates himself. In psychoanalytical writings, objects are nearly always persons, parts of persons, or SYMBOLS of one or the other. The terminology confuses readers who are more familiar with "objects" in the sense of a "Thing," i.e. that which is not a person.[24]

While the concept of "reification" has been much abused in recent decades, the uses to which Hegel and Marx put it still demand attention and respect. More to the point here, never before the nineteenth century had so many been perceived as things, as "hands," and, in the case of the younger Freud, as symbolic of what would become the "id."[25] This does not imply that those exposed to the full horrors of the Industrial Revolution were ever fully reduced to the status of passive objects, much as that might have been hoped for by some members of the bourgeoisie. It but calls for a recognition that specific kinds of perceptions arose out of particular kinds of class relations.

Favoring the English usage "middle classes," Gay is not prepared to explore the social relations of production in forging primary class identities, let alone to move on to the difficult questions which have to do with how other kinds of social relations reinforce or distort these primary identities. Although well aware that "bourgeois populations...swam in a sea of poverty," he only promises to provide, in the second volume, an account of the "invidious comparisons" through which "the nineteenth-century bourgeoisie defined itself erotically at least in part by observing the aristocracy, the working class, and the peasants of its time" (p. 24, n. 62, p. 442). So far he has confined himself, aside from the occasional servant, to a group which, shorn of the larger social relations vital to its existence, is hardly revealed in its full class character. Ironically, despite all his sympathy for the bourgeoisie, Gay has inflicted a major historical injustice upon it.

Even if one accepts Gay's narrow focus, the problem of object relations as social relations re-emerges. Rycroft defines:

Object, need-satisfying" as "an object whom the subject 'loves' solely on account of its capacity to satisfy needs and whom the subject fails to recognize as a person. The terms is only used when discussing the nature of an infant's attachment to its *mother*.[26]

Surely that usage is too restrictive, for throughout the nineteenth century one often enough finds wives—and mistresses and prostitutes—perceived in precisely that fashion. But one must wait for the second volume, *The Tender Passion*. for Gay to arrive at matters such as prostitution. In the meantime, the puzzling results of his "tactical" decision to divide his material have already begun to become apparent. If prostitutes are missing from *Education of the Senses*, Gay does include those "offensive women" who range from feminists to the "demonic and destructive" creatures who made their appearance in art and literature (p. 201). Largely following int the wake of Mario Praz, *The Romantic Agony* (1930), he lends to the discussion of the latter group a special concern with the *vagina dentata*. More generally, Gay is especially alert to the reactions of males threatened, in one fashion or another, with castration.

The division of material may also explain the curious treatment of Gladstone. The great statesman is presented massaging his wife's breasts after childbirth and grieving over ill and dying children. But Gay passes over in silence whatever may have been involved in Gladstone's personal efforts to reform and/or redeem prostitutes. He also eschews the obvious temptation of a Freudian reading of Gladstone's diaries. Gay settles instead for a celebration of a marriage in which "William Ewart and Catherine Gladstone, that ideal bourgeois couple, sang of an evening, took long walks, played chess, talked over everything including politics, catechized their children in religion and Latin, and loved one another" (p. 442).

The Gladstone marriage stands in marked contrast to that of the Todds which so fascinates Gay. Certainly Mabel and David Todd seemed to have derived great sexual satisfaction from each other during the early years of their marriage; and Gay makes use of that in order to deny "the received wisdom...that the nineteenth-century middle class male split his love life into two, that some of his women were angels, others were whores" (p. 89). But when the Todds settled in Amherst, Massachusetts, Mabel acquired a lover. While the situation created problems within the marriage, Gay knows that David Todd "on the most obscure, the most tenaciously defended levels of his unconscious...must have taken considerable erotic pleasure in the emotional intimacy that Austin Dickinson's affair with his wife permitted him with her lover" (p. 95). Moreover, believing that "highly scandalous exceptions apart, girls must lose the initial Oedipal combat and yield the father to the mother" and aware that Dickinson was almost the age of Mabel's beloved father, Gay can conclude that "for a young woman to carry off in triumph an older man, and a married man at that, was to win that combat doubly, if vicariously" (p. 101). But there was, according to Gay, very little scandal in regard to the affair itself: "far more important than the town's complaisance about the man was its toleration of the woman" (p. 106). Hence, he can use the case to argue that the "boundaries around the passions" constructed by the bourgeisie of the nineteenth century were more flexible than is sometimes perceived from the perspective of the twentieth century (p. 107).

Mabel Todd is, in effect, the heroine of *Education of the Senses*. And Gay's problems with the selection and interpretation of sources appear most clearly in connection with her case. Her diary entries reveal a remarkable woman and lend themselves readily enough to Freudian interpretation.[27] They allow Gay to present her in terms of the realization of purportedly generalized fantasies, but they provide no grounds for judging just how typical or atypical her experiences may have been. Other diaries provide quite different stories. In repard to such problems, historical cultural anthropology does have contributions to make, but much more digging will have to be done in a much wider range of sources before it can do so. In any event, to his credit, Gay does not forget the long-lasting suffering visited about Mabel's daughter by the affair.

In Gay's view, whatever the particular experiences encountered, the nineteenth-century bourgeois family was inevitably problematic:

> ...the modern middle-class family was a breeding ground for sexual rivalries. Intimate love, intimate hatred, are timeless. Freud did not name the Oedipus complex after an ancient mythical hero for nothing. But the nineteenth-century middle-class family, more intimate, more informal, more *concentrated* than ever, gave these universal human entanglements exceptional scope and complex configurations (p. 444).

But he also insists that "the bourgeois experience was far richer than its expression, rich as that was; and it included a substantial measure of sensuality for both sexes, and of candour—in sheltered surroundings. It would be a gross misreading of this experience to think that the nineteenth-century bourgeois did not know, or did not practice, or did not enjoy what he did not discuss" (p. 458). Hence, Gay excoriates Stendhal, Heine, Flaubert, Ibsen, Marx, Engels, and Steven Marcus who accused the bourgeois of hypocrisy.[28] Even Freud is taken to task in this regard. The basic mistake, according to Gay, is to confuse the bourgeois concerns with propriety and privacy with hypocrisy.

Gay acknowledges that "the conflicts generated by middle-class definitions of propriety were exacerbated by banal but often ferocious boundary disputes about the standards appropriate to men and women" (p. 453). He is also well aware that, when it came to marriage, "love and profit went hand in hand" (p. 443). But while making use of a method which claims special sensitivity to the nuances of language, he does nothing with the linguistic association between "property" and "propriety."[29] He is more interested, in any event, in privacy. In his view, "the nineteenth-century middle-class family was the supreme haven of privacy" (p. 445). But Gay remains insensitive to a point made by Christopher Lasch: "The concept of the family as a haven in a heartless world took for granted a radical separation between work and leisure and between public life and private life."[30]

Focusing on the latter factor, the Genoveses have extended that argument to the realm of historiography in a manner which might well relate to Gay's ambitious undertaking: "The burgeoning interest in the history of marriage and the family owes much to the preference for private over public purpose; to the perception of a corrupt and bureaucratic state upon which political processes, and even socialist revolutions, seem to make little impact; and to the cries of anguish from within the Western family itself."[31]

Nobody, of course, denies the importance of the family. And despite his troubles with balancing tensions intrinsic to it against idyllic achievements, Gay has rendered a real service in furnishing a wealth of detail in regard to the bourgeois family of the nineteenth century. Some of that detail is harrowing. The clitoridectomy performed in Cleveland, Ohio in 1894 may have been exceptional, but there were much more common costs and risks associated with sexual pleasure: "Through the nineteenth century...the processes of pregnancy and giving birth were attended by pain and often by excruciating sufferings, and the ever present threat of death to child and mother alike" (p. 231). In that respect nineteenth-century graveyards remain instructive. Gay also notes that when the use of chloroform became feasible, there were those who opposed it on the basis of the Biblical condemnation of women "to bring forth in sorrow" (p. 231). He fails to remark, however, that the Royal Medical and Chirurgical Society had decided earlier that pain was a necessary and beneficial accompaniment of any operation. It would be interesting to learn whether, despite the example set for women by Queen Victoria, males benefitted more quickly from the lifting of the ban on pain-killers. In any event, one can understand the gratitude, at once physical and economic, with which the condom was greeted by loving bourgeois couples.

Yet liberation from some fears could spawn other problems. Gay has "reservations" in regard to birth control: "It compromised the spontaneous gratification of desire by bringing calculation to bear on the passions; it imported ego into the domain where the id had once reigned more or less supreme, and invited the reality principle to intervene in the working of the pleasure principle" (p. 274). But while he cites Freud's remarks on birth control in "Draft B, The Aetiology of the Neuroses," he does not fully cite the following:

> The first part of this task, the prevention of sexual noxia of the first period, coincides with prophylaxis against syphilis and gonorrhea, for these are the noxia which threaten anybody who gives up masturbation. The only alternative would be free sexual intercourse between young

males and respectable girls; but this could only be resorted to if there were innocuous preventive methods. The alternatives are: masturbation, with neurasthenia in males and hystero-neurasthenia in females, or syphilis in the next generation, or gonorrhea in males, with gonorrhea and sterility in females.

The same problem—how to find an innocuous method of preventing conception—is set by the sexual noxa of the second period, for the condum provides neither a safe solution nor one which is tolerable to anyone who is already neurasthenic. In the absence of such a solution society seems doomed to fall victim to incurable neuroses which reduce the enjoyment of life to a minimum, destroy the marriage relation and bring hereditary ruin of the whole coming generation.[32]

Whatever this sweeping diagnosis reveals about Freud, it would be better to take it, with all its revealing obscurity, as an enlightened physician's expression of the sexual fears which haunted the bourgeoisie.

The dialectic between liberation and control, in the sexual and social realms, was even more complex than Gay's reservations and Freud's formulations allow. Gay at least does pay attention to one group who brought together sexual and social concerns, the eugenicists, and he is quite right in arguing "they were rarely quite certain whether it was more urgent to encourage the intelligent and the prosperous to reproduce their number or to prevent the idiotic and the indigent, who were breeding like rabbits, from swamping and conquering the world with their inferior blood" (p. 271). But again the failure to explore class relations damages his argument, for he cannot fully convey the contradictions embodied in a situation where members of the bourgeoisie urged birth control upon the restless masses below them, but practiced it themselves to an extent which threatened to reduce their own numbers. The views of the Webbs in this regard—one hesitates to say "practice"—are not without significance.

Still, Gay has accomplished a *tour de force*: he reached the eugenicists without mentioning Darwin whose name only appears once, and then in passing, in this stout volume. That oversight has nothing to do with the exclusion of theorists from *Education of the Senses*, for he devotes considerable attention to those conservative defenders of the traditional family, Fréderic Le Play and Wilhelm Heinrich Riehl. Whatever its cause, this omission damages Gay's book. Although far more humane and cautious than the eugenicists, Darwin shared their fears:

A most important obstacle in civilised countries to an increase in the number of a superior class has been strongly insisted upon by Mr. Greg and Mr. Galton, namely, the fact that the very poor and reckless, who often degraded by vice, almost invariably marry early, whilst the careful and frugal, who are generally otherwise virtuous, marry late in life, so that they may be able to support themselves and their children in comfort.[33]

To put a point on the matter, Darwin went to quote W.R. Greg:

The careless, squalid, un-aspiring Irishman multiplies like rabbits, and the frugal, foreseeing, self-respecting, ambitious Scot, stern in his morality, spiritual in his faith, sagacious and disciplined in his intelligence, passes his best years in struggle and celibacy, marries late, and leaves few behind him.[34]

The Scots, it seemed, possessed all of the great bourgeois virtues, but those very virtues worked biologically against them. The bourgeois world was even more complex than Gay, no stranger to complexity, recognizes.

The omission of Darwin hurts the book in yet another fashion. Gay devotes some fine pages to the obstacles encountered by women in search of higher education, but he fails to perceive how the most advanced scientific ideas of the age could be joined with masculine prejudice in the justification of those barriers. Darwin proclaimed that "the chief distinction in the intellectual powers of the two sexes is shown by man's attaining to a higher eminence, in whatever he takes up, than can woman."[35] The great naturalist also asserted that "with woman the powers of intuition, of rapid perception, and perhaps of imitation, are more strongly marked than in man; but some, at least, of these faculties are characteristic of the lower races."[36] Darwin moved, in other words, toward an equation of the female with the primitive.

Relying partially on the authority of the reactionary Gustave Le Bon, Freud equated, in *Group Psychology and the Analysis the Ego* (1911), children, savages and neurotics. He had already asserted elsewhere the "greater proneness of women to neurosis and especially to hysteria."[37] But the implied comparison of neurotic women with savages does not constitute the core of the problem. Freud argued that savages, like children, displayed "the weakness of intellectual ability, the lack of emotional restraint, the incapacity for moderation and delay, the inclination to exceed every limit in the expression of emotion."[38] Turning to women in general, he did not hesitate to recast traditional male perspectives in light of his own theories: "Character-traits which critics of every epoch have brought up against women—that they show less sense of justice than men, that they are less ready to submit to the great exigencies of life, that they are more often influenced in their judgments by feelings of affection or hostility—all these would be amply accounted for by the modification in the formation of their super-ego."[39] Although Freud came to admit that "psychology...is unable to solve the riddle of femininity," he still maintained that "women must be regarded as having little sense of justice...as weaker in their social interests and having less capacity for sublimating their instincts than men."[40] In brief, Freud elaborated upon the equation of females and primitives, and at least in this respect Ernest Jones was quite right in calling him "the Darwin of the Mind."[41]

Those characterized as primitives or savages seldom appear in *Education of the Senses*. But more the ever before Europeans and North Americans were meeting these and other non-Western peoples during the course of the nineteenth century. The encounters had cultural and sexual consequences. Gay does very little with this dimension of the bourgeois experience and even then tends to misread or ignore evidence. One needs, along with the discussion of the appeal of Canova's statues, an appreciation of the appeal of Fitzgerald's translation of the *Rubáyát*. Concerned with distancing in time and space as a means of imparting carnal knowledge, Gay conflates the classical and the exotic:

A provocative, barely clothed girl lounging in an Algerian doorway was exotic; the same girl in the same attitude in a Parisian doorway would have been obscene. A suggestive nude displaying her flawless body and called "Venus" was a work of art; the same nude in the same posture but obviously of domestic provenance would have outraged many museum-goers (p. 392).

The matter is more complex. On the one hand, it was all too easy for the bourgeoisie to make the transition from the exotic to the familiar. Paris abounded in the late nineteenth century with "street arabs" and "apaches," and Le Bon, colonial theorist and social psychologist, did little more than codify a common bourgeois perception when he proclaimed: "*La foule n'est pas seulement impulsive et mobile. Comme le sauvage, elle n'admet pas d'obstacle entre son désir et la la réalisation de ce d'esir.*"[42] On the other hand, there were significant disjuncture between the classic and the exotic. Whatever titillation the classics may have provided int the schools, one encounters few pieces of pornography with classical settings. But the exotic settings, with all their potentialities for the fantasies of control intrinsic to sadism, appear again and again.

The nineteenth-century bourgeoisie engaged itself, directly or indirectly, in a variety of forms of imperialist rape. The very language of imperialism, with its piercing, penetrations, carvings and so forth, carried distinctly sexual connotations. Imperialist activity, moreover, probably reinforced those images of scientific conquests and of scientists as explorers, adventurers, and conquerors which came so readily to Freud and others. In more concrete terms, Dr. Iwan Bloch's *Anthropological Studies in the Strange Sexual Practices of All Ages, Ancient and Modern, Oriental and Occidental, Primitive and Civilized* (1902-1903) was just as much a manifestation of the age of the imperialism as the plantations which provided the raw material for condoms. At a more important level, sexual relations within the colonies and semi-colonies, hitherto largely the preserve of novelists, still await generalized treatment. Whoever takes up that task will find it no more easy to untangle the convoluted inter-weaving of sexual desire and racial antipathy than to judge the extent to which political control allowed fantasy to escape other forms of control and to realize itself in life. The imperialist world was in the sexual realm, as in so many other areas, very much a world of masters and victims.

Gay has written elsewhere of "masters and victims in modernist culture."[43] Modernism claims to both express and to master ambiguities. But ambiguity itself continues. It is central to Gay's undertaking. His credentials as a master of the historical craft have not hitherto been in doubt. But this elegant historian of and spokesman for the Enlightenment has been at least partially victimized by post- and anti-Enlightenment currents of modernism. Growing in strength since the beginning of this century, such modernism spurned the past and, by extension, any effort to arrive at an understanding of it. Hence, modernism poses major problems for the historian. One response, in a now largely historically lobotomized society, is to compromise with the various currents intrinsic to modernism. Consequently, much of the newer historical cultural anthropology, like modernism itself, supplies much superficial movement and riveting detail, but usually spurns the issue of the exercise of power, provides little sense of the direction of change, and renders the discrimination of the differing degrees of importance attached to the various facets of life unnecessarily difficult. Another modernist current, however, insists upon the primacy of the internal workings of the psyche. Sigmund Freud lent a powerful impetus to that modernist thrust. But despite its claims to a scientific status, Freud's method cannot resolve adequately the problems posed by a bourgeois experience which was more heroic and tragic, more prosaic and squalid, more complex and simple than Gay allows. Metaphors, even that of the symphony, are of even less use in this domain than historical cultural anthropology. Gay proffers, along with speculation turned into fact, illuminating detail and restless movement. But the ambiguity remains. More than anything else, *Education of the Senses* expresses, in unintended fashions, the now long-lasting crisis of liberal culture.

Notes

1. *Historical Reflectiona / Réflexions historiques*,11, (Summer, 1984). pp. 154-72.

2. Bonnie G.Smith, *Ladies of the Leisure Class: The Bourgeoises of Northern France in the Nineteenth Century* (Princeton: Princeton University Press, 1981), p. 7.

3. Sigmund Freud, "The Dissolution of the Oedipus Complex," in *On Sexuality* (1924; reprint ed., Harmondsworth: Penguin Books, 1979), pp. 313-22.

4. Sigmund Freud to Martha Bernays, 15 November 1883, *The Letters of Sigmund Freud*, Ernst Freud, ed. (New York: Basic Books, 1975), p. 75.

5. *Ibid.*, p. 76.

6. Janet Malcolm, "Annals of Scholarship: Trouble in the Archives," *The New Yorker*, 5 December 1983, pp. 59-152; 12 December 1983, pp. 60-119.

7. Jeffrey M. Masson, "Freud and the Seduction Theory," *The Atlantic Monthly*, February 1984, pp. 30-60. Gay would probably classify this reviewer in light of "the sheer defensiveness that angry historians have displayed in attempting to stifle psycho-history" (p. 464). But however much one might like to see Freudian assumptions undermined, one must acknowledge that neither Masson's article nor his more recent *The Assault on Truth. Freud's Suppression of the Seduction Theory* (New York: Farrar, Straus and Giroux, 1984), has accomplished that feat. The controversy provoked by Masson, however, throws light upon "the use and abuse of history" in contemporary society. Involving the hustling Sanskritist Masson, the over-trustful analyst Kurt Eissler, the very quick and now dead Anna Freud, and the self-proclaimed "punk-historian" Peter Swales. the affair partakes more of psycho-drama than of serious historical investigation, for although the matters in dispute are primarily historical in nature, none of the major participants in the dispute appears to have received any historical training. The judgment delivered by the *New York Times* in regard to the controversy also gives pause: "As for Freud himself, as historians of science are well aware, those who introduce a major new theory in an atmosphere of opposition often overstate their case. In the process they bury their doubts and gloss over some bits of evidence to the contrary, all in the service of making their point. Galileo, Newton and Mendel are now known to have done so; to that list, it appears, we can now add Freud. To be so included does not negate his very real contributions, but shows that he too has followed a pattern that seems inherent in the social forces that shape the sciences." Daniel Goleman, "Psycho-analysis appears stung but little harmed," *New York Times*, 24 January 1984, pp. C1, C4, Although too much should not be expected from scientific journalism, that passage poses several problems. As Frank J. Sulloway demonstrated in *Freud: Biologist of the Mind: Beyond the Psychoanalytic Legend* (New York: Basic Books, 1979)m Freud considerably exaggerated the opposition which he encountered. Moreover, whereas the achievements of Galileo, Newton and Mendel are not in dispute, those of Freud remain very much so. Finally, whatever the failings of the former three, their shortcomings did not entail immediate human consequences.

The "orthodox" version of the Freud-Fliess relationship can be found in Ernest Jones' *The Life and Work of Sigmund Freud* (1953, 1955, 1957), described by Gay as "partisan, unstylish, but beautifully informed" (p. 464). Gay characterizes Sulloway's book as "over-argued, irritatingly self-indulgent," but he admits that it does "suggest some revisions of the Freud-Fleiss relationship" (p. 464). In general, when compared to the magisterial surveys of the relevant literature incorporated into Gay's volumes on the Enlightenment, the bibliographical essay in *Education of the Senses* is distinctly more partisan and, on occasion, ill-tempered and mean-spirited. It may be that psycho-historians are at least as defensive as their historical critics.

8. The Yale Professor might have attended in the early summer of 1981 Masson's lecture to a meeting of the Western New England Psychoanalytical Society, held in New Haven, in which he used precisely the same formulation in regard to the shift from the external world of misery to the internal world of fantasy. Gay certainly frequents the circles in which Mason's views have made such a stir.

9. Joseph Breuer and Sigmund Freud, *Studies on Hysteria* (1924; reprint ed., Harmondsworth: Penguin Books, 1974), n. 2, p. 201.

10. *Ibid.*, n. 1, p. 242.

11. Sigmund Freud, *Introductory Lectures On Psychoanalysis* (1916-1917; reprint ed., Harmondsworth: Penguin Books, 1973), pp. 353-45.

12. Again irony intrudes: along with Lionel Trilling, Marcus edited the abridged edition of Jones' biography of Freud. A detailed comparison of the views of Marcus and Gay would be useful, but cannot be undertaken here.

13. Sigmund Freud, *New Introductory Lectures on Psychoanalysis* (1933, reprint ed., New York: W.W. Norton, 1963), p. 71.

14. This problem has recently been raised again in a delightfully unexpected context. See Donald n. McCloskey, "The Rhetoric of Economics," *Journal of Economic Literature*, 21 (1983), pp. 481-517.

15. Terence Hawks, *Metaphor* (London: Methuen, 1972), p. 55.

16. Gaston Bachelard, *La formation de l'esprit scientifique: Contribution à une psychoanalyse de la la connaissance objective* (Paris: Librairie Philosophique J. Vrin, 1969), p. 78.

17. Max Black, *Models and Metaphors: Studies in Language and Philosophy* (Ithaca: Cornell University Press, 1962), p. 47.

18. *Ibid.*, p. 242.

19. *Ibid.*

20. To take an example from Gay's chosen century, the adventures of the idea of the division of labour are instructive, Although resonant with ideological connotations from the first, its elaboration by the Classical Economists constituted a genuine analytical breakthrough. That advance, in turn, provided stimulus during the first half of the nineteenth century to the more strictly scientific work of Milne-Edwards and others on the physiological division of labour among the bodily organs. Seizing upon the economic and biological analyses and extending them analogically and metaphorically, Herbert Spencer and Emile Durkheim transformed the division of labour into a principle informing the entire development of society. As a result of that exercise, they both succeeded in providing justifications for existing society. In other words, through the use of analogy, they transformed scientific advance into ideological mystification. But despite their common specific starting point and their more general shared ending, their visions of capitalist society, as well as their prescriptions for it, differed substantially. Seen in the most general terms, such differences lay rooted in the differing structures of nineteenth century England and Third Republic France nd the consequent differing ideological weights assigned to factors like *laissez-faire* and *solidarité*. These variations, in turn, shaped the uses made of the metaphors and analogies. See Herbert Spencer, *The Study of Society* (1873; reprint ed., Ann Arbor: University of Michigan Press, 1961), pp. 301-306; and Emile Durkheim, *The Division of Labor in Society* (1893; reprint ed., New York: The Free Press, 1964), pp. 40-41.

21. Sigmund Freud, *Group Psychology and the Analysis of the Ego* (1921; reprint ed., New York: W.W. Norton, 1959), p. 43.

22. Peter Gay, *Freud, Jews and Other Germans: Masters and Victims in Modernist Culture* (Oxford: Oxford University Press, 1978), p. 54.

23. To be fair to Freud, he made much less use of economic analogies than his French contemporary, Pierre Janet. See Jonh F. Laffey, "Society, Economy, and Psyche: The Case of Pierre Janet," *Historical Relections / Réflexions historiques*,1l0(1983), pp. 269-294.

24. Charles Rycroft, *A Critical Dictionary of Psychoanalysis* (Harmondsworth: Penguin Books, 1972), p. 100.

25. "...the mob gives vent to its pleasures and we deprive ourselves." Freud to Martha Bernays, 29 August 1883, Freud, ed., *Letters*, pp. 50-52.

26. Fycroft, *Critical Dictionary*, p. 101.

27. In dealing with Mabel Loomis Todd, Gay reveals his own limits in the Freudian reading of symbols. Describing the first months of the marriage, he notes: "There were those figs in the and grapes in the morning, and, at times, even more suggestive foods. 'Ice cream on the way home --.'" Gay cited earlier Freud's remark that "love...makes things wet," but to indulge for once in the language of psychoanalytic history, Freud would have been as interested in the grapes and undoubtedly even more so in the figs (p. 76). More seriously, in a volume devoted to sensual experience, next to nothing is done with food and drink. The great chef Auguste Escoffier is quoted in regard to the passion for novelty, but nothing is said about the repasts which fuelled the bourgeoisie in a century profoundly concerned with the forms of energy.

28. Stendhal is also singled out for having begun the practice of attaching "ingenious, picturesque, and, strictly speaking, illogical labels to important elements in the middle class" (p. 29). He purportedly erred in asserting: "The banks are masters of the state. The bourgeois has replaced the Faubourg Saint-Germain, and the bank is the aristocracy of the bourgeois class" (p. 29). But the novelist simply repeated what the masters of the July Monarchy, lacking hypocrisy or perhaps propriety, openly proclaimed.

29. In light of the fusion of love and profit, some attention might also be paid to the various uses, in French and English, of "commerce." See Albert o. Hirshman, *The Passions and the Interests: Political Arguments for Capitalism before its Triumph* (Princeton: Princeton University Press, 1977), pp. 61-62.

30. Christopher Lasch, *Haven in a Heartless World: The Family Beseiged* (New York: Basic Books, 1977), pp. 7-8.

31. "The Political Crisis of Social History: Class Struggle as Subject and Object," Elizabeth Fox-Genovese and Eugene D. Genovese, *Fruits of Merchant Capital: Slavery and Bourgeois Property in the Rise and Expansion of Capitalism* (Oxford: Oxford University Press, 1983), p. 200. This author is bemused and amused by his old comrades flirting nervously with the notion of "bureaucratic collectivism."

32. "Draft B, The Aetiology of the Neuroses," 8 February 1893, Sigmund Freud, *The Origins of Psycho-Analysis: Letters to Wilhelm Fliess, Drafts and Notes*, (New York" Basic Books, 1954), pp. 71-72.

33. Charles Darwin, *The Descent of Man and Selection in Relation to Sex*, in *The Origin of Species by Means of Natira; Selection or the Preservation of Favored Races in the Struggle for Life and the Descent of Man and Selection in Relation to Sex* (New York: The Modern Library, n.d.), p. 505.

34. *Ibid.*

35. *Ibid.*, p. 873.

36. *Ibid.*

37. "The Transformations of Puberty" (1905), Freud, *On Sexuality*, p. 144.

38. Freud, *Group Psychology*, p. 49.

39. "Some Psychical Consequences of the Anatomical Distinction Between the Sexes" (1925), Freud, *On Sexuality*, p. 342.

40. Freud, *New Introductory Lectures*, p. 102, 119.

41. Ernest Jones, *The Life and Work Sigmund Freud*, vol. 3, *The Last Phase, 1919-1939* (New York: Basic Books, 1957), p. 304.

42. Gustave Le Bon, *Psychologie des foules* (1895; reprint ed., Paris: Presses universitaires de France, 1963), p. 18.

43. See n. 22.

9

ECONOMY, SOCIETY, AND PSYCHE:
THE CASE OF PIERRE JANET[1]

Sigmund Freud, in the most ideologically explicit of his efforts, still had the good sense to observe that "even in its caprices the usage of language remains true to some kind of reality."[2] But "kind of reality" begs a multitude of questions, for language can be used to clarify or to mystify. Special problems are posed by analogies, metaphors, similes, images and models, all of which readily lend themselves to both usages. Playing major roles in the production and appropriation of the sciences and ideologies, these devices cause the most trouble when they appear in the borderlands between the two domains. But whether their usage be strictly scientific, or distinctly ideological, or some combination of the two, their employment implies the existence of an audience which understands the terms of discourse. Sharing a common cultural heritage, that public may also possess a more restricted class or professional character. Difficulties multiply when one endeavours to introduce new ideas to such a group, and then it often becomes imperative to fall back upon references familiar to it. Such problems appear to be simplified when, in the very course of formulating these ideas, one has drawn upon the stock of the commonplace. But such common sense, as Antonio Gramsci recognized, is likely to be "ambiguous, contradictory and multiform," precisely the qualities which appear in the sloppier analogies, metaphors and the like. Primarily concerned with the distorting impact of common sense at the popular level, Gramsci did not pursue in any detail the ways in which its "crudely neophobe and conservative tendencies" could be made use of in the forging of new ideas or systems, in making these acceptable to members of a ruling class, and, hence, in the buttressing of that class' ideological hegemony.[3]

As psychology came to occupy a more aggressively independent position in the borderlands of the scientific and ideological endeavours of the late nineteenth century, its practitioners framed various and sometimes vital parts of their messages in images appropriated from life within capitalist society. Often ideologically precocious in such undertakings, the Americans appear to have been the first to move in this direction. Developing ideas initially laid down in 1869, the neurologist George M. Beard found the sources of his neologism, "neurasthenia," in the stresses and strains imposed by an increasingly mechanized life and predicted that this peculiarly American disease would spread elsewhere as the tempo of economic life accelerated. Bringing together notions of energy, symbolized by the battery, with more distinctly economic images, he insisted that "the man with a small income is really rich as long as there is no overdraft on the account" and that "a millionaire may draw very heavily on his account and yet keep a large surplus." Viewed in such terms, neurasthenia was but "nervous bankruptcy."[4] T.J. Jackson Lears has recently pointed to the popularity of such imagery in the United States and related the message that "psychic wastrels could easily overdraw and bankrupt themselves" to a "scarcity therapy" which, with changes in the nature of capitalism, began to give way around the turn-of-the-century to "a new faith in psychic abundance."[5] Lacking the vistas opened by the tremendous expansion of American capitalism, those inclined to deal in such comparisons in Austria-Hungary and France tended to cling to the older model of scarcity.

Peter Gay has remarked that "at least some of the metaphors, comparisons, and analogies that Freud so vigorously employed were, in his mind, almost literally descriptive: to assimilate mental life to warfare, like assimilating psychoanalysis to archeology, said something that was true rather than just picturesque....Analogies disclosed substantial relationships."[6]

But one can all too easily pick and choose among the images one finds in Freud's complex and changing thought, and for his illustrations Gay for two of the most common, though not necessarily the most significant. To be at all fair to a theorist with a decided flair for symbolism, one would have to weigh the balance between his martial and economic comparisons, discriminate between notions of economy derived from physics and those extracted from the marketplace, explore his own discussions of analogy, metaphor and "scientific myth," and address a host of questions having to do with his social position and social attitudes. But for our purposes here, only two points need be made. First, Freud's social views rested upon a basis of scarcity: "The motive of human society is in the last resort an economic one: since it does not possess enough provisions to keep its members alive unless they work, it must restrict the number of its members and divert their energies from sexual activity to work."[7] Second, economic analogies and similes did not frighten Freud.

In *The Interpretation of Dreams*, Freud confidently proclaimed that "daytime thought may very well play the part of *entrepreneur* for a dream, but the *entrepreneur*, who...has the idea and the initiative to carry it out, can do nothing without capital; he needs a *capitalist* who can afford the outlay, and the capitalist who provides the psychical outlay for the dream is invariably and indisputably...*a wish from the unconscious*." Pursuing the parallel, he allowed that "sometimes the capitalist is himself the *entrepreneur*, and indeed in the case of dreams this is the commoner event" before going on to consider the instances in which "the *entrepreneur* may himself make a small contribution to the capital; several *entrepreneurs* may apply to the same capitalist; several capitalists may combine to put up what is necessary for the *entrepreneur*."[8] A few years later he developed an equally detailed "comparison between psychical economy and a business enterprise."[9] Although the source of the story cannot be considered unbiased, this manner of thinking could have led him to have remarked to Emma Jung that his marriage "had long ago been 'amortized.' "[10] Yet, in all fairness to Freud, he made much less use of such language than did his French contemporary, Pierre Janet (1859-1947).

Despite the fascination with hysteria which they initially shared, Freud and Janet developed over time a marked distaste for each other's ideas.[11] While their disagreements involved matters of genuine intellectual substance, differences in the social and professional experiences of the of these two eminently bourgeois gentlemen undoubtedly exacerbated their mutual dislike. If Freud exaggerated the professional resistance to his work, his early struggle for comfort was real enough, and in the dual monarchy and the succeeding rump state the ease of a Jewish professional man always remained precarious. Janet, on the contrary, was born into the Parisian upper bourgeoisie and, after the usual time spent teaching in provincial *lycées*, joined the ranks of an academic mandarinate where an uncle had already distinguished himself with a series of works reinforcing, with flexibility and a consequent vagueness, the hegemony of that bourgeoisie.[12] Yet Janet acquired far more clinical experience than Freud and, hence, encountered a far greater social range of patients.[13]

Both physicians, of course, met many of the same bourgeois types among their patients, male and female. But differences in theoretical orientations entered into their perceptions and treatments of even these patients. Where Janet saw a patient whose problems, partially manifested in the feeling that "the least of my employees is more capable than I am," sprang from having to take over the management of a family business, Freud undoubtedly would have been more interested in the troubles appearing after the death of the patient's father.[14] One wonders too what Freud would have made of the former chief bank clerk who, unable to handle the increased responsibilities of a new managerial position, slid into the "severe melancholic depression" from which Janet rescued him by simply arranging "for him to take up his earlier post once more."[15] Certainly in Janet's intellectual world psychic crises were more likely than in Freud's to be triggered by "losses of money in business" or "a factory...in financial difficulties."[16]

Although he refused to "dwell on the obsessions and phobias to which lawyers, doctors, dressmakers, or barbers, are liable to succumb," Janet also displayed far more interest than Freud in occupational psychoses. [17] The range of occupations so briefly noted is significant. Janet not only had patients exhausted by study and violin practice, but also those prostrated by more immediately brutal forms of overwork.[18] There was nothing in Freud's experience to match Janet's professional acquaintance with servant girls from the country disoriented by city life, cashiers and concierges, shop assistants and shopkeepers, travelling salesmen and merchant seamen, locomotive engineers and firemen, bookkeepers and commercial clerks, the maker of doll's eyes and the victim of "an occupational chorea" who "persistently made ironing motions."[19] Given the sympathetic tone of Janet's comments on overwork, it is unlikely that this grander bourgeois would have penned Freud's version of the servant problem: "Our servants are dominated by a mute hostility towards the manifestations of art, especially when the objects (whose value they do not understand) become a source of work for them."[20]

Be that as it may, Freud could contrast fictionally a caretaker's daughter with the landlord's daughter and blithely conclude that the former "will go through her life undamaged by the early exercise of her sexuality and free from neurosis."[21]

But Janet had to treat Irène. True, in good Freudian terms, she had been raised in an "easy-going proletarian environment" and had come to enjoy a normal sex life. But the matter was not quite so simple. As a result of the alcoholism of her father, her mother's death from pulmonary tuberculosis, and exhaustion by "poverty, overwork, and sleepless nights," she had developed "a succession of major neuropathic disorders."[22] Whatever Freud's fondness for Zola, Janet's professional life brought him into much closer contact with the social reality which the novelist, with varying degrees of success, attempted to depict. Such experience did not make Janet any less the bourgeois, but it may have contributed to his genuine humility in regard to what psychology could accomplish in its present state and, hence, to the ultimate eclipse of his ideas by those of the more self-assured Freud.

Aside from the difference in subject matter, nothing of social significance can be wrung out of the comparison of the Freud's first publication, a study of a primitive fish, and Janet's first published effort, the brief *Fondement du droit de propriété*. It would be much more helpful to know more about the impressions made upon Freud by John Stuart Mill, for then it might be possible to compare his early socio-economic ideas with Janet's equally early musings upon such subjects. Describing Mill in 1883 as "the man of the century most capable of freeing himself from the usual prejudices," Freud went on to assure his fiancé, in a passage which has rightly roused the ire of feminists ever since the publication of a selected edition of his letters, that Mill "lacked the sense of the absurd, on several points, for instance in the emancipation of women and the question of women altogether."[23] But Freud had been stimulated enough to go beyond the feminist tract which he translated for Theodor Gomperez's edition of Mill's works, in which he "could not find a sentence or a phrase that would remain in one's memory," to "a philosophical work of his which was witty, epigrammatically apt, and lively."[24] Unfortunately, Freud did not identify the latter work, and we can only speculate about what it might have been and what he might have learned from it. While the mind boggles at any work of Mill's being described as "witty," it would be pleasant to discover that Freud acquired from Mill the convictions that property-holding had taken a variety of forms in the past, that it was still open to improvement in the present, and that it would be a long time, if ever, before its present form could be changed substantially.[25]

Such views would have brought Freud together with Janet intellectually even before the development of their common interest in hysteria and hypnotism. In any event, Janet's first published exercise remains banal enough for a mandarin-to-be and yet remarkable for a psychologist-to-be.

Janet's views on property parallelled those of enlightened bourgeois spread throughout the capitalist world at the time. Once evolved from that state of savagery where it did not exist, property had passed through a variety of configurations: the communism of the pastoral tribe; a completely agrarian form; a species, lingering in the Russian *mir* which allowed for periodic divisions into individual or familial plots; various sorts of feudal tenure and, thankfully, modern private property. Whatever the efforts undertaken to improve them, communist forms of property could never match private property in providing incentives to human industry and, hence, in increasing the wealth of society. Also viewed in the light of results, piece work showed itself superior to work done by the hour in modern society. But as a completely atomistic orientation of society would have been out of place in a nineteenth-century world of industry and railways, Janet argued that "true policy must make the egoism of each serve the utility of all." That did not imply justice for all. Janet did not mince words: seen in terms of the larger scheme of things, justice was but "a secondary question." Yet, given the claims for justice being advanced within his own society, he could not leave the matter there. From his perspective, one more often encountered within that society wealth produced by work rather than by luck. But seeking to avoid the full implications of a labour theory of value, he then had to acknowledge that "we have arrived at toleration, even while regretting them, of inequalities of condition: for fortunes acquired by the luck of lotteries, legacies, coincidences and windfalls and the solid fortunes acquired by merit and work are all placed on the same plane."[26]

Writing slightly more than a decade after the suppression of the Commune, Janet explained that toleration in terms of a recognition that "social wars do not destroy inequality by sometimes reversing the roles, but they surely produce misery for all." Unfortunately, "distaining reality" and "only conceiving of justice in the abstract," socialists threatened to turn society to the kind of class struggle which "had undermined" the early democracies of Greece and Rome. With the Third Republic apparently menaced in such a fashion, he hastened to assure his audience that "the social order founded in 1789" possessed strong bulwarks in the number of peasant proprietorships and other small holdings, its strength of intellect and science, and institutions like the insurance companies and the mutual aid societies of the workers. He could then bow condescendingly toward "certain collectivists, whose often impractical doctrines very much merit being admired for their high idea of justice." He argued now, however, that their case for an inheritance tax be used for "a social dowry," which would provide "the poorest children" with enough capital for a start in life had already been met in part by public schools, supported out of taxes, where "free instruction is in truth the beginning of the social dowry." Such considerations allowed him to conclude that private property, "created for interest and not morality," remained, first, not always "very equitable" and, second, "eminently perfectible." One could, after all, more and more "reconcile interest and justice in property...thanks to the work of each, to science, to the faith of the individual in himself and civilization, and by building upon the progress actually achieved in the past in order to claim still more from the future."[27] His audience, largely members of the Ligue de l'enseignement, must have applauded him, and his uncle must have been proud of him. Jule Ferry could hardly have recited the bourgeois republican litany more smoothly. Given his sentiments and his familial connections, it is likely that in his next teaching post, at Le Havre, the young man attracted the attention of the city's mayor, Jules Siegfried. Pierre Janet's youthful reflections fit very well into the more general atmosphere of the early Third Republic.[28]

Henceforth Janet steered away from this kind of an expression of his socio-political sentiments.[29] But the psychologist could not avoid sentiments having to do with social reality. Simply clearing the grounds for the claims of his discipline involved arguing that terms like "lunatic, mad, and insane" were popular rather than scientific and, indeed, "may even be said to smack of the police court." The definition of a lunatic did not depend upon "the sufferer's intrinsic character, or upon this or that change in his psycho-physiological functions, but upon an extrinsic character arising out of the situation of the patient." Janet had to insist:

> The danger to be apprehended from a patient depends far more upon his social surroundings than upon the nature of his psychological troubles. If he is rich, if he is surrounded by careful watchers, if he lives in the country, if his environment is uncomplicated, he may have a very serious mental disorder without being a danger to himself or any one else, and his doctor may euphemistically describe him as "neurasthenic."
> If he is poor, if he is a wage-earner, if he lives unguarded in a large town, if his position is one that presents delicate or complicated issues, the very same mental disorders, at the same level of intensity, will make him dangerous, and his doctor will have no choice but to have him certified as a lunatic and put under restraint.

Differences in social circumstances, in other words, led to "a practical distinction, a matter which concerns public order, but has no bearing on the outlooks of scientific medicine. The diagnosis is just the same in either case."[30] The medical scientist, however, could not escape social reality that easily, and, if Janet never drew together his social dicta, biases and insights in a sustained and internally coherent exposition, he could not avoid expressing them.

Recognizing that "human beings are continually acting upon one another," Janet argued that "social influences are among the most potent causes of health and disease."[31] Professional concerns, rather than great insight into the workings of society, led him to focus upon the latter factor: "The chief difficulties of life arise in connexion with social relationships, and it has long been felt that social activities are more exhausting than any other kind."[32] Believing "social functions" to be "the most important and also the most difficult and the most costly," Janet concluded that "neuropaths and those who are candidates for neurosis tend to get worn out in their everyday relationships with their associates."[33] Although it could not be avoided, social life profoundly threatened the psyche. Quantitatively in that "the acts that man must perform in society, in his relations with the persons who are in his immediate neighbourhood, make up the greater part of his life.[34] Qualitatively in that the acts having concluded early that "hystericals, above all, lose quickly social sentiments, altruistic emotions, perhaps because they are the most complex of all," Janet had gone on to establish a "hierarchical table of tendencies."[35] Viewed from such a perspective, "the social tendencies control the perceptive tendencies; the tendency to reflection checks and controls the tendency to immediate assent;" and so forth.[36] Prepared to consider "the tendencies of hierarchy, obedience and even servitude" as "the simplest social tendencies," he concluded that the higher the tendency, the greater its vulnerability to disturbance.[37] But aware of the inadequacies of such formulations, Janet also maintained that "we must gain more precise notions concerning the action exercised by human beings upon the other, concerning what [Gabriel] Tarde used to call 'inter-psychology' rather than 'social psychology,' which has never been adequately studied."[38] Janet's falling back on "inter-psychology" rather than "social psychology" may be as significant as his invoking Zola rather than Gistave Le Bon in analysing the miracles at Lourdes in light of crowd psychology.[39] Janet the psychologist paid no more attention than Durkheim the sociologist than to Le Bon. These academic pillars of a bourgeois republic recognized threats from the Right as well as the Left, and they never made Freud's mistake of coquetting with Le Bon's vicious ideas.[40]

Janet's more specific reflections on the links between the psychological and the social realms ranged from the banal to the acute. Class biases appeared in a passing reference to "instinctive respect for wealth, for power" and in his early definition of normality in terms of docility and obedience.[41] But he changed his mind in the latter regard and came to see normality as having to do with "the inclination to reflect."[42]

Normality, in any event, was less common than many believed: "We have to distinguish between persons of a psychasthenic temperament and persons in whom the typical symptoms of psychasthena have actually developed....Among our associates are a great many folk who have inherited a modest competence, who live in an uncomplicated environment, whose education has not been dangerous, has not been such as to arouse ambition.[43] Janet could not resist adding: "The ministries and government offices are often retreats for people who need a life ruled by superiors, without hard knocks and without responsibilities."[44] Given the benefits of the quiet life, it was hardly surprising that he had "seen hysterical patients cured by a comfortable legacy," though he had to admit that such a "remedy is not at every one's command."[45] He refused, moreover, to draw invidious class distinctions in connection with the workings of the psyche: "I cannot say that, like Bernheim, I have noticed any preponderant inclination to accept suggestions among the common people, among servants and soldiers and manual workers. It seems to me that excessive suggestibility is not peculiar to any particular class or occupation."[46] At the same time he took it for granted that "in the competition which is an inevitable feature of life, a normal human being endeavours to triumph by rising above his rival" and believed that "incidents in life which render a struggle necessary...have worked many cures."[47] Whatever the scientific worth of the latter judgment, Janet spoke more generally for the Third Republic when he affirmed that "nothing succeeds like success, and failure breeds failure."[48]

Product of and apologist for a bourgeois order which celebrated political equality [for males] and maintained social inequality, Janet emphasized that "psychasthenics are not fond of subbing shoulders with their equals. They seek their lovers and friends from among persons classed as their inferiors in fortune, station, or education....(W)hat the patient is looking for is an easy social situation; one in which unfailing consideration will be exhibited towards him."[49] He also argued that "jealousy makes psychoasthenics prone to associate by preference with persons who are beneath them in fortune and position. They are fond of the humble and poor; and...they have a special liking for their own employees and subordinates. Conversely, they have a natural detestation for their social superiors, and for persons who are wealthier than themselves; but their special animosity is reserved for those who rise in the social scale, and thus become superiors when they had been inferiors."[50] But Janet remained basically the psychologist. He did not go on to relate these observations to the bubbling *resentments* of the petit-bourgeoisie, the frustrations engendered by the coexistence of the ideal of "the career open to talent" and the real limits to social mobility, and the pseudo-paternalist traditions of French industry. To his credit, he did not make use of them to attack members of the bourgeoisie who had rallied to socialism. Neither sociologist nor ideological hack, he was at his psychological best in dealing with intra-group dynamics, including those of the family. But even here caution prevailed: "The pathology of groups and its relation to the pathology of individuals must be some day investigated. Here we are content with one point only, that social conduct often becomes ruinous for those of the members who have not sufficient resources."[51]

Explaining in part the speed with which his influence waned, caution also marked his more general approach to psychotherapy. Defining it briefly as "an application of psychological science to the treatment of disease," he constantly stressed its present limitations.[52] Psychology itself still remained "in its infancy," and, in regard to issues like therapeutic guidance, psychological knowledge can hardly be said as yet to exist."[53] Put bluntly, "our diagnosis of psychological troubles is rudimentary; our knowledge of essential psychological phenomena is minimal."[54] Judged in light of "practical success" as "the chief criterion of the worth of a science," psychology was at best "a science...detached from its object" which "has never been in a condition to guide either the diagnosis of the psychiatrists or the practive of the psychotherapeutists."[55] Janet even toyed with the idea that "in these circumstances it would be wise to draw the simple conclusion that an attempt to make use of of psychotherapeutics is premature, and to decide to reconsider the matter a century hence," but, unfortunately, "suffering humanity cannot wait."[56] Parallels with medicine at least offered some solace, for it too remained "for the most part in the stage of individual observations" where "a good description of a pathological type that has been well understood is worth more than a great many arbitrary theories and classifications."[57]

Several factors came together here. Janet's clinical practice had given him a profound sense of the "amazing variability and...disconcerting irregularity" of mental disorders.[58] Having already been exposed to the eclecticism of his uncle, the physician who had devoted the minor thesis required for his *Doctorat ès lettres* to a study of Francis Bacon's relations with the alchemists, Janet retained a healthy respect for empiricism. Indeed, in discussing alcoholism, Janet sounded a rare chauvinist note in proclaiming: "French psychiatry, which has unfortunately forgotten its traditions and is inclined to row in the wake of foreign metaphysics, would do well...to return to the observation of concrete facts."[59] Such sentiments involved more than strictly scientific considerations, for they allowed him to strike indirectly at his professional enemies, including the Freudians, by pointing to the "craze for systemisation in psychoasthenics." Eclecticism and empiricism neatly complemented more personal concerns when he argued that "the power of criticizing systems, the power of taking advantage of experience in order to confirm or to invalidate our hypotheses, the resignation and disinterestedness which enable us to abandon our systematized ideas when they conflict with observed facts—these are complicated and late acquisitions of our mental development. They are the first to disappear in all forms of mental degeneration....A systematized explanation of an inferior type of explanation, a primitive type."[60] More specifically, when it came to matters of mental health, he took comfort in the willingness of doctors "to turn a natural law to immediate practical use, even if it be a law which science itself has just begun to glimpse."[61] Making use of a wide variety of therapeutic techniques, Janet settled for contending that "a cure for at least a year in which there has been no relapse was a proof that a method of treatment was extremely valuable."[62]

Pragmatic methods occasionally produced results of worth, without necessarily leading to the ability to predict such results, and this had "occurred in exactly the same way in the evolution of every science."[63] In physics, for instance, "the study of electric currents could never have been made if scientists had refused to consider their effects or to make notes of their variations before knowing the nature of electrical forces."[64] But the example was not fortuitous. Like the other psychologists of his day, Janet had come of age in a century which began with the spreading of the steam engine and ended with the spreading of the dynamo, a century dominated by enormous manifestations of mechanical and human energy. The scientific thought of that century had been profoundly influenced by the work of G. Ampère (1775-1836), Michael Faraday (1791-1867), James Clerk Maxwell (1831-1879), and, with relevance to both physics and physiology, the great H.L.F. von Helmholtz (1821-1894) who in 1847 had outlined the principle of the conservation of energy. Consequently, Janet could distinguish between the "old psychological language" which seemed to imply "that the patient could be different if he wished" and the newer "physiological or pseudo-physiological language" which proclaimed that "the functions which preside over the formation of nervous force are altered; there is a decrease in the production of nervous impulses; the patient has a nervous weakness; he is an asthenic."[65] Disavowing any "philosophical speculation on vital forces," Janet defined "force" as "a possibility of action."[66] Concern with *"the mobilisation of forces"* led him back to William James, whose article "The Energies of Mankind" (1907) impressed him, and, more generally, to the whole question of energy.[67]

A generation of psychologists raised with the classics knew better than their successors that the notion of energy derived from the Greek "in work." They were less well aware that their own notions of work derived, in varying degrees, from its nature and conditions in their own capitalist societies. If Freud distinguished himself by taking work more seriously than his professional contemporaries, all had to confront it.[68] All could agree that the work of the psyche involved activity internal and external to the individual, but differences developed in regard to such matters as the sources of psychic energy and the weighing of internal and external factors in relation to each other. If Freud believed that "actions and consciously expressed opinions are as a rule enough for practical purposes in judging men's characters," he also stressed "the complexity of a human character driven hither and thither by dynamic forces" and did more than anybody else to define work, sometimes presented as metaphor and sometimes as actual force, as a central element in the internal dynamics of the mind.[69] Convinced that the "dynamic psychology of energy and tension" was "the most fruitful today in clinical psychiatry," Janet faced many of the same problems.[70] He was quite prepared to argue that "the circumstances that cause neuroses to develop often consist of excessive work or effort either physical or intellectual. It is true that many neuropathic disorders seem to be determined by emotion rather than by excessive work. But psychological analysis has demonstrated that in emotion there is likewise an excessive expenditure of force and that by many indications the phenomenon of emotion is only a variety of fatigue."[71] But in developing his impressive theories of psychic tendencies and levels of tension, he largely eschewed the notion of work and preferred to maintain that "the scientific study of psychology is only practicable if we look upon all phenomena of mind as actions, or grades of action."[72] Janet's thinking, his therapeutic concerns, along with his conviction that "psychological disorders are disorders of behaviour, and behaviour is simply a totality of the outward reactions of the living being," carried him much further than Freud in the external direction.[73]

While Janet believed that "persons who are suffering from...a loss of will power, a lack of power to believe, social abelias which occasion the many varieties of timidity, manias for being loved and for loving, and the countless forms of authoritarianism, are very numerous in present-day society," he concentrated his psycho-social analysis upon work.[74] Repeating the conventional imperialist wisdom of his day, he contended that "work is only performed by persons belonging to the higher races; it needs a peculiar collaboration of the whole mind; it gives rise to extremely complex ideas, such as those of production, aim, means and cause; it constitutes a highly specialised and exalted form of activity."[75] Allowing for some "very rare" cases to the contrary, he presented work as "the greatest manifestation of voluntary activity."[76] He had already concluded by then that, as an inability to work constituted the first sign of hysteria, "the will with hystericals must be at a very low ebb."[77] Far more sweepingly, he came to argued that "neuropaths have no liking for work of any kind."[78] Yet, if such a judgment hinted at the moral evaluations of the older psychology, Janet remained deeply aware that work itself could spawn psychic distress, a conviction derived from his clinical practice and amply confirmed by "the terrible overwork entailed by the war,"[79] Given such concerns, it was no more accidental that toward the end of his life he should turn his attention to "the application of psychology to industry" than that the American industrial psychologist, Elton Mayo, should have been one of the few to keep Janet's reputation alive in the years immediately after his death[80] Janet expressed a lively interest in the American psychology of the decades before World War I. His therapeutic concerns, along with his special interest in work, led him to pay close attention to the differences between S. Weir Mitchell's treatment by isolation, rest and over-feeding and the "work cures" advocated in somewhat different fashions by J.J. Putnam, Philip Coombes Knapp, Hugo Münsterberg and R.C. Cabot.[81] But his sense of the complexity of mental disorders, as well as the allied awareness that a therapy which worked in one case could harm in another, prevented him from deciding in favour of one or the other approach. Very typically, he preferred to inquire: "In the presence of a neuropath whose symptoms are quite diverse, should the physician order rest or work, the economy of strength or a speculative outlay?" While he held out the prospect that "a day will come when one prescription or the other will no longer be made at random, but will be the conclusion of serious psychological analysis," he believed that at the moment "we are still far from that ideal and shall long remain in the period of vague directions and groping."[82] But at least he had no doubts as to the benefits of activity, including work, in maintaining mental health.[83] Equally unmistakable is the note of fascination which appeared in his again ambivalent approach to movements like New Thought, with its gospel that "success and wealth are not reached by pure intelligence, but by the practical exercise of the will," and Mind Cure manuals which emphasized "the moral importance of 'actions which earn money.' "[84] Characterizing such notions as distinctly American, Janet also believed them to be to be exaggerated and "remarkably simple-minded." But he could not dismiss them, for their proponents possessed "a clear notion of the latent forces of which William James used to speak" and had contributed "very remarkable reflections concerning the balancing of the mental budget."[85] The carriers of Lears' "new faith in psychic abundance" had touched, indeed, upon some of Janet's vital concerns.

Once again the principles of the economy of energy central to physics and physiology lapped over into psychology and lent themselves a more strictly economic metaphorical interpretation. Janet proposed that psychology had "to take up the problem of the economic administration of the mind's forces." He went on to contend that "it is probable that we shall one day know how to establish the balance and budget of the mind as we establish that of a business firm. At that time the psychiatric physician will be able to make good use of slender resources by avoiding useless expense and by directing effort to just the necessary point: he will do better; he will teach his patients to increase their resources and enrich their minds." Janet hoped that his own work would "not have been entirely useless to those who will one day discover the rules of the good administration of psychic funds."[86] Such sentiments were not simply passing fancies. While he acknowledged on occasion that these were but analogies and comparisons, he still returned to them constantly.[87] Indeed, he structured the massive compendium devoted to "psychological healing" in such a fashion that Part III (pp. 371-708) dealt with "Psychological Economics" and Part IV (pp. 709-1205), with "Psychological Acquisitions." His condensed version devoted a chapter to "The Forms of Mental Economy" and another to "Psychic Income."

Placing the development of psychotherapeutic techniques in historical perspective, Janet moved from the vague ones in which "the healer was satisfied with exercising some sort of *moral action* upon the patient" to those which "acted by *utilisation of the patient's automatism*," to those concerned with "organising an *economy* of mind," and, finally, to those in which the therapist "aimed at supplementing the inadequate forces by happy speculations, by new *acquisitions*."[88] But he made use of economic imagery even before arriving at the latter two stages of development. Differentiating sleep from the hypnotic state, he compared the former to "a condition of minimal expenditure, in which economies are made to facilitate great expenditure in the waking state; just as people with a small income will sometimes live for six months of the year cheaply in a quiet country place that they may be able to spend freely in a town during the other half of the year."[89] He also argued that "we may compare human behaviour and the utilisation of the mental powers with pecuniary expenditure and the organisation of a budget. One who falls sick may be likened to one who is unable to balance his budget, so that bankruptcy is imminent; he has become incapable of meeting the cost of certain indispensable activities. The doctor is called in to liquidate the situation and reorganise the budget."[90]

Referring more specifically to the treatment by suggestion which "artificially induces, in the form of an impulse, the functioning of a tendency which the subject's personal will cannot activate," Janet maintained that it "does not modify the general tenor of the household, it does not provide the steward with new resources; it merely shows him that he possesses important resources which he has not been utilising, it opens drawers where precious rouleaux of gold pieces have been stored away and forgotten, and it puts these overlooked resources at the disposal of a poor wretch who had quite mistakenly fancied himself to be ruined." But if such a technique was to produce results, "the imminence of ruin must be more apparent than real, and the accountants who have been enquiring into it must have been so ill-informed as to cry bankruptcy when as yet there is nothing worse than disorder. As a rule, financiers know better." While it certainly opened the way for the therapist serving as financier, this method proved "inadequate, and…in most instances we have to search out other and more complicated ways for the reestablishment of fortunes that are seriously compromised."[91]

Janet then turned to the "methods of mental economy…which aim at reducing the work of the mind and promoting the storage of energies."[92] Here again he invoked a household budget which took into account "what articles are cheap and what are dear, what kinds of work are expensive and what kinds of work are inexpensive," and, thus, allowed one "to adapt expenditure to income." If the mental budget could not be balanced that easily because "our ideas of the price we shall have to pay for this or that kind of action are so exceedingly vague," this made scant difference to the healthy who "almost always have a superabundance of mental and moral energy to meet the expenditure they are called upon to make." But it was desperately important that the psychologically "impoverished…should know what they are spending."[93] Moving beyond the household economy in a much more distinctly capitalist direction, Janet entertained no doubts that "one who by hard work wins a fortune or learns a science does much to facilitate profitable behaviour in the future." But he also emphasized that "for the moment, expenditure is greatly increased." Pointing to the "buying of a costly machine, or…spending a large sum in the purchase of profitable shares," he stressed that, whatever the prospects of future returns, "some purses are so light that they are emptied before the necessary immediate expenditures can be met." So too some minds could not "sustain an action good in itself and likely to be beneficial in the future. The immediate expenditure cannot be met."[94] He also shrewdly observed that "nothing can be more costly than the perpetual mobilisations of capital with a view to purchases which are never made. The ineffective investor thus squanders his substance and will ruin himself in the end. The exhaustion from which the patient suffers is due, in most cases, to the perpetual recommencement of higher-grade operations which never reach their term."[95]

Believing that "the problem of psychological expenditure, the problem of the mental cost of activity, will be one of the cardinal problems of psychology and psychiatry," Janet lamented that "at the present time few people seem to suspect that such a problem exists." Convinced that "certain kinds of activity are, psychologically speaking, more expensive than other kinds, and have a more marked tendency to use up our energies," he still had to concede that it was "difficult to say precisely what are the costly types of activity, to specify the characteristics whereby these types of activity are distinguished from other and less dangerous types."[96] Such an admission further complicated the issue of therapy. Arguing that "most neuropaths...are suffering from exhaustion, and are on the verge of bankruptcy," Janet approved of limited amounts of rest: "The subject is not rich enough to bear the cost of the life he is leading. We need not trouble to enquire which items in his expenditure are excessive and ruinous; it will suffice if we simply prohibit every kind of expenditure."[97] And just as the exhausted should be "kept in bed for as short a time as possible," most of those confined to sanitariums and asylums should also be kept for limited periods. for they could be classified as "poor" rather than "positively destitute" and, hence, would benefit from "an environment which has more social reality than that of the ordinary asylum."[98] More generally, "neuropaths" had to be made to "understand...that they will avoid disastrous bankruptcy if they will only learn to husband their psychological resources day by day, and always to 'save the pennies.' "[99]

Scrutinizing the Freudian concern with traumatic memories, Janet acknowledged their existence. And once again he turned to the economic realm to buttress his analysis:

> Some of the patients appear to have adequate resources, and their ruin has resulted from a persistent expenditure over and above that required to meet the ordinary demands of life. It is the supplementary expenditure which has been disproportionate to the income. The reason for the supplementary expenditure has been the indefinite persistence of an unliquidated affair. The subject retains an interest in a concern which has got into difficulties, which demands very large and very and continuous expenditure, and will never return any profit. This is the way in which we have regarded traumatic memories and a great many fixed ideas.

As for therapy, "since the patient cannot achieve this unaided, we must help him to liquidate the concern which is ruining him. When we have done so, his income will suffice for current expenditure." Pursuing such parallels at greater length, he warned against "the exaggerations of Sigmund Freud."

As Janet perceived the matter, "excessive expenditure is not the only cause of financial ruin, and expenditure outside the domain of normal budgeting is not the sole cause of psychological depression...There are, alas, many other causes of poverty besides unthriftiness."[100]

Returning to mundane psychological considerations for the moment, Janet remarked that "even in cases in which the illness was occasioned by a particular happening, the symptoms may, after a while, become independent of the happening. The mind has been exhausted by a fruitless struggle; and even if in the end the struggle is abandoned, the exhaustion may persist." He went on to affirm that "in a great many instances the exhaustion from which the patient suffers is not due to any memory of a past happening; it is the outcome of actual events which recur from day to day. The patient, though a poor man, has an income which would suffice to meet moderate demands, but the circumstances compel him to keep up too costly an establishment." Such a situation again dictated that, "if bankruptcy and poverty are to be avoided, we shall have to curtail the ordinary expenditure of everyday life."[101] Yet Janet remained dissatisfied with this prescription. Viewed practically, it involved serious inconveniences for the patient and his relatives. Viewed in light of the comparison with economic life, it did not "promise anything more than a very slow increase in psychological capital. We know only too well that thrift, however rigid, will rarely suffice to lead to fortune."[102]

Janet, consequently, turned his attention to more risky, more speculative therapeutic techniques. But before considering them, he noted that the educational methods that aimed at securing "the correct and automatic reactions" associated with habits stood between "methods of pure economy, which make use of repose and isolation, and methods of pure acquisition, which make use of excitation." One did not seek in this middle ground "to increase our income by an economy of expenditure," but pursued instead "a prospective augmentation of income that will ensue upon an increase of capital."[103] Moving away from such automatic reactions, Janet proclaimed more generally that "a complete action, although for the time being, it involves expenditure, may subsequently lead to an increase in energy; it may be like a good investment which brings a large return in the way of dividends." Always willing to belabour such a point, he continued: "When the owners of a factory expend a large sum of money in buying new machinery or in providing a furnace, they are likely ere long, to win back more than they have spent. It is probable that an act well performed will thus be the starting-point for the acquisition of considerable profit in the long run."[104]

Such investments essentially involved, at least initially, capital acquired externally. But there could also be immobilized internal resources. Citing William James in support of his position, Janet argued that "in the activities of daily life, human beings do not expend all the energies they possess, for they keep a large amount of energy in reserve." Thus, "real activity" did "not depend upon the total energy of the individual, but upon his available energy, upon the amount which at a particular moment can be expended, can be put into circulation." Economics offered an explanatory parallel here too: "The work performed in an industrial enterprise does not depend only on its total capital, but also upon its circulating capital, upon the liquid cash. The enterprise may have large sums in the form of immobilised reserves in buildings. machinery, investments, outstanding credits which are not easy to collect, Yet, at a given moment, it may even, for considerable periods, find itself financially embarrassed, and be obliged to refrain from expenditure which might be most advantageous." Janet again invoked James in buttressing his contention that "neuropaths are often in a similar position." But carried out successfully, the mobilization of internal funds to meet a crisis could "do something more than repair the effects of the accident; it will lubricate the whole machinery of the undertaking, and may restore prosperity."[105]

More generally, "where there is a good deal of expenditure, there may occur favourable investments."[106] Such psychic speculation, of course, held its own dangers, Mental disorders, consequently, called for a delicate therapeutic balance in that the "good deal of work" required of the patient could not be allowed to "induce exhaustion." However, for Janet, that hardly constituted a novel situation: "Everyone who undertakes a commercial speculation has to encounter the same problem. The enterprise must be weighty enough to bring in a considerable profit, and yet it must not be so speculative that the investment in it will be likely to ruin the main enterprise. In a word, we have to do a good stroke of business." Janet went on to proclaim immediately in a profoundly revealing remark: "The problems of life are always the same." One can only wonder what patients from outside the ranks of the bourgeoisie would have made of such a sentiment. But then again none of the patients of the strongly interventionist Janet may have been allowed time for such reflections. From his perspective, yet another menace resided in permitting the patient "to act by himself," for then he would bankrupt himself through "foolish speculations." Ideally, in that best of worlds where psychology had finally become a true science, "it would provide the doctor with the means for putting his patient upon the track of a sound speculation without further ado." In the present, unfortunately, it could do no more "than furnish some useful hints.[107]

Such "useful hints," presented by Janet with a multitude of economic comparisons, might well lead a Freudian to perceive marked sings of "anility" and a psychological layman, whether historian or not, to settle for "obsession." But this matter cannot be left there. Janet simply carried to an extreme a way of thought which permeated the psychology of the turn-of-the-century. Ideas of energy central to physics and physiology had been carried over, for legitimate scientific reasons, into psychology. The difficulties arose when its practitioners reached out to social reality in order to express such ideas analogically and metaphorically. Energy lent itself to two related, but still distinct, usages. Its accumulation and expenditure could be conceived of in terms of either labour or capital. Nobody did more than Freud to internalize the imagery of work. While occasionally willing to argue in such a fashion, Janet preferred to concentrate upon the role of work in the external world. Having seized upon labour in that world, Janet then chose to conceptualize psychological energy in terms of capital. With the workings of the psyche perceived in such terms, serious psychic disorder could be, had to be, likened to bankruptcy, and, short of social revolution, bankruptcy constituted the greatest fear of the bourgeoisie of the age.

One might argue that whereas Freud, who had had to labour long and hard in the making of his career, was bound to focus upon work, Janet's fascination with investment reflected the mentality of a *renter* born into a family which undoubtedly possessed its railway shares and government bonds. One could also contend that Janet's concern with budgeting reflected the Third Republic's world of small producers and shopkeepers and that Freud's emphasis on labour mirrored the gap in Austria-Hungary between a hard-working bourgeoisie and a pleasure-loving, aesthetically sensitive aristocracy.[108] One might even find a reflection of the relative industrial weakness of France and Austria-Hungary *vis-à-vis* giants like Great Britain, Germany and the United States in the avoidance by both of them of much concern with "breakdown." But unless such interpretations could be refined through a more detailed investigation of the relevant documents, they would remain but crude hypotheses concerning the inter-play between particular personalities and specific societies.

At this point it would be safer to note that Freud and Janet were bourgeois who came of age as the nineteenth century waned. Neither entertained doubts about their class identity. With his view of the "mob" prefiguring his later depiction of the "id," the younger Freud believed that "it would be easy to demonstrate how 'the people' judge, think, hope, and work in a fashion wholly different from ours."[109] While Freud made some effort at a sympathetic understanding of those differences, Janet went out of his way to classify among the disturbed "those who detest a bourgeois existence."[110] Yet a greater openness to the problems and claims of the lower classes on the part of Freud cannot be used to explain the eclipse of Janet in intellectual and ideological importance. Not only is evidence of such sympathy on Freud's part scant, but Janet saw far more of the working class professionally and, if the presentation of his cases are any indication, treated them as humanely as his bourgeois patients. The explanations for the growth of Freud's reputation and the withering of Janet's must then be sought elsewhere. If their professional experiences differed greatly, so too did the conclusions they derived from them. Freud made no secret of his preference for theory over therapy, but he also made sweeping claims on behalf of his own version of the latter. Janet, on the contrary, accumulated an immense number of clinical observations, made use of a wide variety of therapeutic techniques, and severely limited the claims made for the psychology of his day. Despite its complexity, Freud's system could be more readily propagated, especially outside the realm of psychology, than Janet's fragmentary and disjointed general reflections which, in spite of all the economic imagery, remained much more narrowly restricted to psychological concerns.

The evolution of capitalism, moreover, entered into the picture. The emergence of its monopoly phase entailed a consumerism which discounted notions of scarcity. Freud certainly took external scarcity very seriously and hardly neglected problems of internal scarcity. But whatever the intellectual gymnastics required, his ideas lay more open to appropriation and trans-valuation by theorists of "polymorphous perversity" and the like than those of the more apparently plodding Janet. In the end the elements of romantic vitalism intertwined with his hard-headed positivism undercut the genuine, old-fashioned bourgeois integrity embodied in Freud's ideal, "Where id was, there shall ego be."[111] Janet lacked, along with the socio-political inclinations which carried Freud towards

Le Bon, those romantic vitalist tendencies which rendered Freud's system vulnerable to transformation. Whatever his hopes for investment and acquisition, hopes pointed toward a psychology of abundance, Janet remained closer to a psychology of scarcity. Rightly claiming to be one of the first to discover the subconscious, Janet entertained no more respect for it than Freud did for the id.[112]

Confronted with exaltations of the "peculiar energy of the inferior subliminal tendencies"—that is, "tendencies below the threshold of the individual consciousness"—Janet noted their "strange kinship with those philosophies of the day which despise the intelligence and would have us put out our eyes in order to see better—inasmuch as by suppressing the intelligence we shall give free rein to wonderful instinctive intuitions."[113] Quite as much as in his youthful musings on property, or as in his manias for comparisons between psychological and economic life, there spoke the true Pierre Janet, an academic mandarin of the Third Republic, the psychologist as captive and defender of a capitalist society, but a capitalist society which still possessed some values worthy of respect.

Notes

1. *Historical Reflections / Réflexions historiques*, l0, 2 (Winter, 1983), pp. 269-94.
2. Sigmund Freud, *Group Psychology and the Analysis of the Ego* (New York: W.W. Norton, 1959), p. 43.
3. Quinton Hoare and Geoffrey Nowell Smith, eds., *Selections from the Prison Notebooks of Antonio Gramsci* (New York: International Publishers, 1971), p. 423.
4. Quoted in Henri Ellenberger, *The Discovery of the Unconscious: The History and Evolution of Dynamic Psychiatry* (New York: Basic Books, 1970), p. 243. Ellenberger notes that "both the notion of the budget of nervous forces and the financial comparisons were to be found in a more systematic way in Janet's writings."
5. T.J. Jackson Lears, *No Place of Grace: Antimodernism and the Transformation of American Culture, 1880-1920* (New York: Pantheon Books, 1981), pp. 52-3.
6. Peter Gay, *Freud, Jews and Other Germans: Masters and Victims in Modernist Culture* (Oxford: Oxford University Press, 1978), p. 54. 7. Sigmund Freud, *Introductory Lectures on Psychoanalysis* (Harmondsworth: Penguin Books, 1973), pp. 353-54.
   While Freud's martial imagery has received a great deal of attention, I would suggest that his relationship to the classical economists deserves further study. The Malthusian influences are obvious. But Freud could also be viewed as a late Ricardian who at the time of the waning of the domestic *laissez-faire* market internalized its struggle within the individual just as others, who shared his penchant for martial imagery, externalized them through imperialist expansion. A Ricardian reading of Freud might also help to unravel a more minor problem. It has been noted that Herbert Marcuse, in dealing with "surplus repression" in *Eros and Civilization* (1955), "put on a spectacular performance...More particularly since Marx's name never appeared in his pages." H. Stuart Hughes, *The Sea Change: The Migration of Social Thought, 1930-1965* (New York: Harper and Row, 1975), p. 177. Ricardo's name also does not appear there. But if there is an implicit Ricardian strain buried within the Freudian system, then Marcuse's remarkable *tour de force* becomes more readily comprehensible as a trans-valuation of it.
8. Sigmund Freud, *The Interpretation of Dreams* (Harmondsworth: Penguin Books, 1976), p. 714. Throughout this article all emphases in quotations appear in the original.
9. Sigmund Freud, *Jokes and Their Relation to the Unconscious* (Harmondsworth: Penguin Books, 1976), pp. 210-11.
10. Emma Jung to Sigmund Freud, 6 November 1911, *The Freud / Jung Letters: The Correspondence Between Sigmund Freud and C.G. Jung*, ed. William McGuire (Princeton: Princeton Iniversity Press, 1974), pp. 455-57.
11. Sigmund Freud, *An Autobiographical Study* (New York: W.W. Norton, 1952), pp. 56-7; Piere Janet, *Principles of Psychotherapy* (London: George Allen and Unwin, 1926), pp. 41-6. The latter work is essentially a condensation of Janet's *Les Médiations psychologiques* (Paris: Alcan, 1919) which appeared in English in 1925 as *Psychologica Healing*. Its publication delayed by World War I, this massive worked reached back to lectures delivered at Boston's Lowell Institute in 1906.
12. I intend to deal with the philosopher, Paul Janet (1823-189), at greater length elsewhere. Perhaps a partial, and not especially selective, listing of his works will provide some indication of his ideological role: *Histoire de la philosophie morale et politique, dans l'antiquité et les temps modernes; La crise philosophique: MM. Taine, Renan, Littré, Vacherot; Les problèmes du XIXe siècle; Philosophie de la Révolution française; Saint-Simon et le Saint-simonisme;*

Philosophie du bonheur; Les origines du socialisme contemporain; Le matérialime contemporain; La famille, leçon de philosophie; Principles de métaphysique et psychologie.

Pierre Janet's mature reflections on his uncle and his teachings display some ambivalence. Rebutting the Swiss school of psychological moralism, he remarked: "We know this philosophy. There is a strain of Leibnitz in it, with a dash of Victor Cousin, and it has been admirably expounded by Paul Janet. It is the philosophy which presided over our childhood, which we passed on to others for years, and it still reigns suprme in manuals for students of moral philosophy. Far be it from me to decry it. I am convinced that in due time justice will be done to Paul Janet for his excellent presentation of it. But do all these medical philosophers really believe it to be the ultimate truth, or even the philosophical truth of our day?" Piere Janet, , *Psychological Healing: A Historical and Clinical Study* (New York: Macmillan, 1925), 1: 131-32. In his brief autobiography, Janet described his uncle as "an excellent man, industrious and intelligent, and today it seems to me that justice was not done to him. He was not only a spiritual metaphysician, the last representative of the eclectic school of Cousin, but he was a great spirit who was interested also in politics and the sciences." Perre Janet, "Pierre Janet," Carl Murchison, ed., *A History of Psychology in Autobiography* (Worcester: Clark University Press, 1930), 1: 123-33. Pierre Janet, an eclectic in his own manner, may well have been expressing fear about his own decline in influence in his concern for justice being done to his uncle. Yet he took a curious comfort in his position, one not uncharacteristic of the French bourgeoisie of the day: "It has been my tendency, my misfortune perhaps to have a fondness for moderation, and to dislike any absurd exaggerations of extremists…Moderation is the best aid to the discovery of the truth. If my book is ignored today, it will be read tomorrow, when there will have been a new turn of fashion's wheel, bringing back treatment by hypnotic suggestion just as it will bring back our grandmothers' hats." Janet,*Psychological Healing,* 1:151.

13. Ellenberger indicates that "five thousand or more patient files were burnt" after Janet's death. Ellenberger, *The Discovery of the Unconscious,* p. 352. Janet himself referred to 3,500 cases. Janet, *Psychological Healing,* 1:15. For Freud, see Benjamin Brody, "Freud's Case Load," Hendrik M. Ruitenbeek, ed., *Freud As We Knew Him* (Detroit: Wayne State University Press, 1973),pp. 495-503.

14. Janet, *Psychological Healing,* 1:421, 438.

15. *Ibid.,* pp. 423-24, 483.

16. Pierre Janet, *The Mental State of Hystericals* (Washington: University Publications of America, 1977), p. 402. Drawing upon his work for his medical degree, the French edition appeared in 1894. Janet, *Psychological Healing,* 2:1083.

17. *Ibid.,* 1:420.

18. *Ibid.,* 1:348, 459-60, 655; 2:1083.

19. Janet, *Mental State,* pp. 79, 312, 322, 331, 350, 457; Janet, *Psychological Healing,* 1:345, 399-400, 421, 423; 2:902, 1083, 1085.

20. Sigmund Freud, *The Psychopathology of Everyday Life* (Harmondsworth: Penguin Books, 1975), p. 228. Then again J net collected dried plants rather than ancient artifacts.

21. Freud, *Introductory Lectures,* p. 398.

22. Janet, *Psychological Healing,* 1:624-25.

23. Freud to Martha Bernays, 15 November 1883, Ernst L. Freud, ed., *The Letters of Sigmund Freud* (New York: Basic Books, 1965), pp. 74-76.

24. *Ibid.* There has been some confusion about which feminist work of Mill's Freud translated. Gertrude Himmelfarb has pointed out that it was the earlier "Enfranchisement of Women" and not, as often assumed, *The Subjugation of Women.* Gertrude Himmelfarb,*On Liberty and Liberalism: The Case of John Stuart Mill* (New York: Alfred A. Knopf, 1974), n. 29, pp. 220-21.

25. For a representative sampling of Mill's views on property, see John Stuart Mill, *Principles of Political Economy with Some of Their Applications to Social Philosophy,* Books 1-2, *Collected Works* (Toronto: University of Toronto Press, 1965), 2: 200-02, 208, 214; John Stuart Mill, "Chapters on Socialism," *Essays on Economics and Society, 1859-1879, Ibid.* (Toronto: University of Toronto Press, 1967), 5:703-53, 710-36, 750.

26. *Le Fondement du droit du propriété. Conference de M. Pierre Janet* (Châteauroux: Imprimerie Gallin, 1883), pp. 5-10, 12, 14, 17, 20.

27. *Ibid.,* pp. 21-27.

28. For the possible link with Siegfried, see Ellenberger, *Discovery of the Unconscious*, p. 337. For Ferry, Siegfried, the Ligue de l'enseignement, and the more general socio-political setting, see Sanford Elwitt's illuminating *The Making of Third Republic: Class and Politics in France, 1868-1884* (Baton Rouge: Louisiana State University Press, 1975).

29. But I have not seen the preface he contributed to W. Drobovich, *Fragilité de la liberté et séduction des dictatures; Essai de psychologie sociale* (Paris: Mercure de France, 1937).

30. Janet, *Psychological Healing*, 1:125; see also Janet, *Principles*, p 101.

31. Janet, *Psychological Healing*, 2:1157.

32. *Ibid.*, 1:484.

33. Janet, *Principles*, pp. 576. 583.

34. *Ibid.*, pp. 179-80.

35. Janet, *Mental State*, p. 208; Janet, *Psychological Healing*, 1:261.

36. *Ibid.*

37. *Ibid.*, 2:1153.

38. *Ibid.*, 1:496.

39. Janet, *Principles*, p. 119.

40. Freud, *Group Psychology*, pp. 4-9.

41. Janet, *Principles*, p. 119; Janet, *Mental State*, p. 270.

42. Janet, *Psychological Healing*, 1:274.

43. *Ibid.*, p. 472-73.

44. Janet, *Principles*, p. 168, see also Janet, *Psychological Healing*, 1:473.

45. *Ibid.*, 1:479.

46. *Ibid.*, 1:253.

47. *Ibid.*, 1:533; 2:884.

48. *Ibid.*, 2:936.

49. *Ibid.*, 2:965.

50. *Ibid.*, 1:530.

51. Janet, *Principles*, p. 188.

52. Janet, *Psychological Healing*, 2:1208.

53. *Ibid.*, 1:679; 2:1208.

54. *Ibid.*, 1:146.

55. *Ibid.*, 2:1209-10.

56. *Ibid.*, 2:1210.

57. *Ibid.*, 1:140.

58. *Ibid.*, 2:1210.

59. *Ibid.*, 2:1102.

60. *Ibid.*, 2:1180.

61. *Ibid.*, 2:1210.

62. *Ibid.*, 2:927-28.

63. Janet, *Principles*, p. 123.

64. *Ibid.*, pp. 150-51.

65. *Ibid.*, pp. 157-8. Even here the ever cautious Janet acknowledged that "all these pseudo-physiological expressions are only poorly made translations of psychological observations."

66. *Ibid*, p. 215. The disavowal, of course, is directed against Henri Bergson.

67. *Ibid.*, p. 226.

68. David Riesman dryly remarked that "just as Freud 'allowed' himself his book-collecting and other hobbies for their re-creative functions, so he 'allowed' mankind this apparent frivolity of foreplay for its procreative functions." David Riesman, "The Themes of Work and Play in the Structure of Freud's Thought." *Selected Essays from Individualism Reconsidered* (Garden City: Doubleday Anchor, 1955), pp. 175-205, p. 197. See also n. 6.

69. Freud, *Interpretation of Dreams*, pp. 782-83.

70. Janet, *Psychological Healing*, 1:686-87.

71. Janet, *Principles*, p. 86.

72. Janet, *Psychological Healing*, 1l:225.

73. *Ibid.*, 2:1031.

74. *Ibid.*, 1:569.

75. *Ibid.*, p. 452.

76. Janet, *Mental State*, p. 119.

77. *Ibid.*, pp. 118-19.

78. Janet, *Psychological Healing*, 1:497.

79. *Ibid.*, p. 400.

80. Janet, "Perspectives d'application de la psychologie à industrie," *Premier cycle d'étude de psychologie industrielle. Fascicule No. l, Psychologie et travail* (Paris: Cégpd. 1943), pp. 3-8, cited in Ellenberger, *Disacovery of the Uncosncious*, p. 412; Elton Mayo, *The Psychology of Perre Janet* (Cambrigde: Harvard Univerity Press, 1948).

81. Janet, *Psychological Healing*, 1:373-74, 385; 2:732, 872.

82. Janet, *Principles*, pp. 288-9.

83. Janet, *Psychological Healing*, 2:860.

84. *Ibid.*, 2:868, 985.

85. *Ibid.*, 2:871.

86. Janet, *Principles*, pp. 313-14.

87. Janet, *Psychological Healing*, 1:554, 682; 2:939.

88. *Ibid.*, 1:16-17.

89. *Ibid.*, 1:286.

90. *Ibid.*, 1:364-65.

91. *Ibid.*

92. *Ibid.*, 1:464.

93. *Ibid.*, 1:414-15.

94. *Ibid.*, 1:453-54.

95. *Ibid.*, 1:456.

96. *Ibid.*

97. *Ibid.*, 1:464.

98. *Ibid.*, 1:580-81.

99. *Ibid.*, 1:480.

100. *Ibid.*, 1:694-95.

101. *Ibid.*, 1:698.

102. *Ibid.*, 1:698.

103. *Ibid.*, 2:737.

104. *Ibid.*

105. *Ibid.*, pp. 339-42.

106. *Ibid.*, p. 942.

107. *Ibid.*, p. 976.

108. Here Carl E. Schorske's *Fin-de-Siècle Vienna: Politics and Culture* (New York: Alfred A. Knoft, 1980) is suggestive.

109. Freud to Martha Bernays, 29 August 1883, Freud, ed., *Letters*, pp. 50-52.

110. Janet, *Psychological Healing*, 2:905. To be fair to Janet, he might well have had in mind bourgeois bohemians rather than militant workers and/or socialists. Given their own enormous capacities for hard work, neither Freud nor Janet had much use for the first social type.

111. Sigmund Freud, *New Introductory Lectures on Psychoanalysis* (New York: W.W. Norton, 1965), p. 71.

112. Janet, *Psychological Healing*, 1:672.

113. *Ibid.*, 1:256, 258.

10

SOCIAL PSYCHOLOGY AS POLITICAL IDEOLOGY: THE CASES OF WILFRED TROTTER AND WILLIAM MCDOUGALL[1]

In *Massenpsychologie und Ich-Analyse* (1921), Sigmund Freud drew upon and criticized the views of three early social psychologists: Gustave Le Bon (1842-1931), Wilfred Trotter (1872-1939), and William McDougall (1871-1938). There, as elsewhere, Freud made use of the works of others to clarify his own ideas. However necessary that process may have been to him, accuracy sometimes fell victim to it.[2] But his occasional misreading of his sources seldom prevented him from grasping the essence of the perspectives of others. Freud recognized clearly, for instance, that, whereas McDougall had focused his attention upon "stable associations," Trotter had "chosen as the center of his interest" the Aristotelian "political animal."[3] That insight, however, can be phrased in more historically specific terms.[4] It will be argued here that McDougall and Trotter pursued a quarrel which in England reached back at least as far as the confrontation between Tom Paine and Edmund Burke at the time of the French Revolution. Despite sweeping social and intellectual changes, the argument between Liberals, Radicals and Conservatives continued to reverberate throughout the nineteenth century, and Trotter and McDougall, draping it in post-Darwinian scientistic garb, carried it forward into the twentieth century. In brief, their divergent social psychologies constituted adaptations of political ideology to transformed social conditions and altered forms of intellectual discourse. The changed circumstances, however, tended to favor one position at the expense of the other, and McDougall's idiosyncratic Conservatism proved in the end more resilient than Trotter's individualistic Radicalism.

Reba Soffer presents Trotter as "the most perceptive of the (English) social psychologists before 1914, distinguished surgeon and Fellow of the Royal Society, a skeptic who had overcome his sense of obligation."[5] Such a view oversimplifies matters. There can be no doubt, of course, of Trotter's professional eminence. Born the son of a Gloucestershire merchant, he entered University College, London, in 1891 and five years later received his medical degree. Having already become a Hartley Street consultant, he assumed in 1906 the post of staff surgeon at University College Hospital, a position he retained until 1937. Gifted with a remarkable openness of mind, he not only made important contributions to the study of cutaneous sensation, but also noted the new psychological ideas which emanated from Vienna. Indeed, Trotter first called the young Ernest Jones' attention to Freud's work and in 1908 accompanied Jones, by then his brother-in-law, to the Salzburg Congress of the International Psycho-Analytical Association. If Trotter did not become a Freudian, he never allowed his reservations about Freud's system to stand in the way of his respect for him. In 1936 he made use of his position on the Council of the Royal Society to help in obtaining the Corresponding Membership which Freud especially cherished, and two years later he drew upon his Royal Society connections to aid in securing the entry permits which allowed Freud and his daughter to leave Nazi-Occupied Vienna for England. He provided his last service to his brother-in-law's master when called into consultation for the dying Freud. By then Trotter had become England's greatest surgical specialist on cancer and had long since ceased to voice, at least publically, any views in regard to social psychology.

Trotter had traveled a long way from the pre-World War I days when he had frequented the meetings of the meetings of the Sociological Society where he had clashed with H.G. Wells and read the two papers which, after being published in the *Sociological Review* in 1908 and 1909, served as the introductory chapters of *Instincts of the Herd in Peace and War*. As that work only appeared in 1916, it is difficult to see why Soffer so firmly fixed in 1914 his drift from social responsibility to skepticism. But after the war his willingness to concern himself publically with social issues dwindled away, and his earlier iconoclasm might well have mellowed into skepticism. The sheer burden of his medical practice could account for such changes. But another interpretation is also possible, for the postscript added to the 1919 edition of his book reveals a bleak view of post-war conditions. It had not been unusual for nineteenth-century Radicals, disillusioned by events beyond their control, to retreat to the skilled practice of their crafts, often enough book-binding, shoe-making and the like, and Trotter's craft may simply have differed from theirs. Such withdrawals from the public forum did not necessarily imply the jettisoning of all social and political convictions. Surely, a knighthood would not have been out of the question for a master of his particular craft, and yet Trotter steadfastly refused "all public honors."[6]

Perhaps a residual Radicalism lingered in the eminent surgeon who had once proclaimed: "We tend to get at the summit of our professions only those real geniuses who combine real specialist capacity with the arts of the bagman."[7] Be that as it may, such a view neatly complemented the larger perspectives offered in *Instincts of the Herd in Peace and War*.

Trotter began that work by reducing sociology to "another name for psychology in its widest sense." He then moved on to the different kinds of psychology. He dismissed the introspective type, for, in his view, it lacked the objective standards which would allow for predicting or influencing conduct. Finding the newer "human" psychology to be more promising in these respects, he did not hesitate to proclaim that "the most remarkable attack upon the problems of psychology from the purely human standpoint is that in which the rich genius of Sigmund Freud was and still is the pioneer."[8] Trotter accepted Freud's distinction between the conscious and the unconscious, his emphasis upon the importance of childhood experience, and his focus on mental conflict. But he was by no means uncritical, and his objections to the Freudian system reveal at least as much about his own concerns as they do about Freud's.

Trotter thought that class differences had more to do with the sexual experiences of children that the Freudians allowed. Concerning sex in more universal terms, he argued that Freud had paid insufficient attention to the repressive forces which "take the immensely powerful instinct of sex and mold and deform its prodigious mental energy." However unfair to Freud, that objection sprang from Trotter's emphasis upon a biologically determined "strong and persistent jealousy between adult and child." He related this, in turn, to one of his central concerns: "Herd instinct inevitably siding with the majority and the ruling powers, has added its influence to the side of age and given a very distinctly perceptible bias to history, proverbial wisdom, and folklore against youth and confidence and enterprise and in favour of age and caution, the immemorial wisdom of the past, and even the mumbling of senile decay."[9] The suspicion of the majority may recalled John Stuart Mill more readily than Tom Paine, but even Paine had sided with the Girondins rather than the Jacobins in the French Revolution. Trotter's sentiments, in any event, had nothing to do with Conservatism.

The Englishmen proved to be one of the first to raise the kind of objection which later became standard in Leftist criticism of the Freudian system. Noting that the Freudians had been concerned primarily with "the treatment of abnormal states," he questioned "the value of the 'normal' to which the patient has been restored." Equating the "normal" with the "healthy" led to the acceptance of existing conditions. In fact, normality was scientifically "no more than a statistical expression implying the condition of the average man," and, in Trotter's view, this "normal type is far from being psychologically healthy, is far from rendering available the full capacity of the mind for foresight and progress, and being in exclusive command of directing power in the world, is a danger to civilization." When measured against Trotter's concern for "foresight and progress," Freudianism turned out to be "mainly descriptive and systematic rather than dynamic" and "more notably a psychology of knowledge than a psychology of power."[10]

Misunderstandings intrude here. Given his own intense commitment to the comparative or biological school of psychology, Trotter underestimated the strength of Freud's biological concerns. Indeed, that "biologist of the mind" would eventually praise "a valuable remark of Trotter's to the effect that the tendency towards the formation of groups is biologically a continuation of the multicellular character of all the higher organisms." At the same time he also objected to Trotter's positing a basic "herd instinct (gregariousness)" which, in Freud's view, could not be "primary in the same sense as the instinct of self-preservation and the sexual instinct."[11] But Trotter never made such a claim. Having defined self-preservation, nutrition, and sex as the "primitive instincts," he added to them the gregarious or herd instinct which differed from the others in that it exercised "a controlling power upon the individual from the outside." He never equated its strength with the powers of the self-preservative and sexual instincts, but he both lauded and feared its potency. The herd instinct protected humans from "the immediate workings of natural selection" and, indeed, made possible "the multifarious activities of man and...his stupendous success as a species." But much like Freud's later notion of civilization, it did so at a high price, for it functioned as a mechanism through which "the sanctions of instinct are conferred upon acts" which the individual did not necessarily find "pleasurable or even acceptable."[12]

Given the resistance to change nurtured by the herd instinct, the contradictory efforts of Nature to nudge humans in the direction of altruism had "never gained more than a grudging and reluctant notice from the common man, and from those intensified forms of the common man, his pastors and masters."

At best, in Trotter's view, the gregarious instinct entailed "inevitable and serious disadvantages as well as enormously greater potential advantages." The challenge resided in taming "the tyrannous power of the social instinct" in such a fashion as to allow for the promotion of "the personal and social effectiveness of the individual to the maximum extent."[13] If he was none too clear in regard to how to achieve that goal, he did lend a biological twist to a problem faced by individualistic Radicals throughout the nineteenth century when he insisted that, unless humans made intelligent use of the opportunities still open to them, Nature might give up on them as a botched job.

Trotter came close to implying on occasion that only biological psychologists like himself could prevent such a calamity. But he never said that explicitly. And his treatment of the crowd reveals nothing of the elitism characteristic of others who addressed themselves to that phenomenon. Rather than returning to the French Revolution to illustrate the horrors of mob action, he simply pointed out in regard to it that equality had buttressed national unity and that, in turn, had bolstered moral and military power. Far more strikingly, unlike Le Bon, McDougall and Freud, Trotter never equated the members of the crowd with children or savages. Equally democratic proclivities were reflected in his scorn for the eugenicists whose notion of breeding "for reason" seemed a "fit companion for the device of breeding against 'degeneracy.' " Still, he accepted the mental instability of the so-called "degenerates" and acknowledged that the "steady increase, relative and absolute, of the mentally unstable" constituted a "danger to the State." But Trotter presented the mentally stable as equally, if not more, dangerous: "the persistence of a mental type which may have been adequate in a simpler past, into a world where environments are daily becoming more complex—it is this survival, so to say, of the wagoner upon the footplate of the express engine, which has made the modern history of nations a series of hair-breath escapes."[14] In short, Trotter posited the fundamental conflict within society as one between two mental types: the stable. who tended to be resistant to the changing teachings of experience, highly motivated, and remarkably persistent in pursuit of their goals, and the unstable who showed themselves to be adaptable to experience, inclined to flit from position to position, vaguely skeptical, and lacking in energy and will power.

Having found these types at all levels of society, Trotter might have made use of this distinction to discount the significance of social cleavages. Refusing to do so, he argued instead that the mentally stable constituted the "directing class" of all "the first-class powers" in the pre-war world. Neither then nor later did he display any special affection for the English ruling class. While at the height of the war he granted its members certain virtues, he still insisted that "they are in no way redeemed in social value by them." This "parasitic" class had "drawn from the common stock...wealth and prestige...immensely larger than what they had contributed of a useful activity in return."[15] But an even more important issue was involved here, and Freud somewhat misconstrued the matter when he charged that Trotter took "too little account of the leader's part in the group."[16] True, the Englishman paid scant attention to the relations between leaders and led. He preferred instead to challenge leadership itself. In Trotter's view, whatever its past utility, it was no more adequate to the challenges of the present than the mental stability and primitive herd instinct hitherto associated with it. Should society continue to rely upon such leadership, he thought it highly probable that "civilization will continue to rise and fall in a dreadful sameness of alternating aspiration and despair until perhaps some lucky accident of confusion finds for humanity in extinction the rest it could never win in life itself." Only "a continuously progressive co-ordination which will enable it to attract and absorb the energy and activity of its individual members" offered the species the chance to escape from such a prospect.[17]

Whereas a nineteenth-century Radical would have been more likely to speak of "cooperation," the newer "coordination" pointed toward some degree of control from above. If Trotter once again flirted with the notion that biologically-oriented psychologists would be best qualified to undertake such "coordination," his democratic convictions continued to check his elitist inclinations. But stripped of its biological dimension, this dilemma would have been all too familiar to John Stuart Mill. Post-Darwinian progressive Liberals also have had to encounter it, and, indeed, it can be seen as a central problem within the tradition of democratic Liberalism. In any event, convinced that sweeping biological change offered the way to escape, Trotter insisted that only the tapping of a "new resource of Nature" could give rise to the sorely needed "conscious direction of society by man, the refusal by him to submit indefinitely to the dissipation of his energies and the disappointment of his ideals in uncoordination and confusion." Believing such "a step of evolution...could have consequences as momentous as the as the first appearance of the multicellular or of the gregarious animal," Trotter defined the "new and intrusive factor" as the human intellect with its "capacity for purpose."[18]

Perceived in these terms, the war assumed extraordinary evolutionary importance for Trotter. He took the view, unpopular in scientific circles at the time but treated with increasing respect today, that "the process of organic evolution has not been and is not always infinitely slow and gradual." He argued that "perhaps as a result of a slowly accumulated tendency or perhaps as a result of a sudden variation of structure or capacity there have been periods of rapid change which might have been perceptible to direct observation." In other words, there might have been, and might yet still be, periods in which the tempos of biological and historical change coincided. Trotter thought that "the present juncture in human affairs probably forms one of these rare modes of circumstances in which the making of an epoch in history corresponds with a perceptible change in the secular progress of biological evolution." Consequently, he saw in the war "one of Nature's august experiments."[19]

With the very size of the nation providing the measure of the unique status of humans among the gregarious animals, Trotter argued that the realization of "a true moral unity of the nation" would constitute "something different, not only in degree but also in quality" from anything yet encountered in human affairs. Whatever the horrors, the war offered the opportunity to achieve such unity. And although singularly free from the crude racism of so many of his contemporaries, he still managed to present that struggle as "a war not so much of contending nations as of contending species." He did so by postulating three kinds of gregariousness: "the aggressive, the protective, and the socialized which are exemplified in Nature by the wolf, the sheep and the bee respectively." Trotter had by no means abandoned his distaste for the existing English society, "irregular, disorganized, un-coordinate, split into classes at war with one another, weighted at one end with poverty, squalor, ignorance and disease, weighted at the other end by ignorance, prejudice, and corpulent self-satisfaction."[20] He especially excoriated the failure of the upper classes to make adequate concessions to the workers who, consequently, had not developed a sufficient sense of national unity. But when all was said and done, he still thought that the English had embarked upon the more socialized, the more advanced, the more civilized path of the bee.[21] He contrasted his nation, with its potential for becoming the society of the hive, with Imperial Germany which had more fully realized its character as a lupine society. While the degree of coordination achieved by the Germans fascinated him, Trotter did not doubt that their atavism doomed them to defeat.

The eventual defeat of the Germans found Trotter in a sober frame of mind. There is little in the postscript of 1919 which recalls his previous championing of youth, instability, and openness to new experiences. Fear and sorrow had usurped the place of the hope and anger which had hitherto underlaid his musings. The dream of hive had been smashed: with "the few conventional restraints upon the extremity of class feeling...before the war...greatly weakened," class identification now asserted itself at the expense of national reconciliation. Lamenting that "change has become familiar, violence has been glorified in theory and shown to be effective in practice, the prestige of age has been undermined, and the sanctity of established things defiled," he also worried about the "relative moral instability" which marked the return of peace. Viewing the matter in larger terms, the disheartened Trotter perceived society as "setting out upon what is generally regarded as a new era of hope without the defect that made the war possible having in any degree been corrected." The fundamental fault lay in the continuing monopoly of power by the mentally stable who had waged the war with "a mere modicum of help from the human intellect." Put in other terms, either the streams of biological and historical development had failed to coincide or, if they had, the opportunities central to such a coincidence had not been seized upon. Hardly one to embrace Bolshevism, Trotter now settled for an evolutionary gradualism:

> If the effective intrusion of the intellect into social affairs does happily occur, it will come from no organ of society now recognizable, but through a slow elevation of the general standard of consciousness up to the level at which will be possible a kind of freemasonry and syndicalism of the intellect.[22]

Yet this kind of gradualism still differed substantially from the Conservatism espoused by the far more prolific William McDougall.

McDougall's family background possesses its own fascination.[23] His paternal great-grandfather, a Scots cobbler, eloped into Lancashire with an heiress. One of their sons founded a boarding school for boys, studied and hobnobbed with scientists like John Dalton, Angus smith and Sir James Simpson, argued that the teachings of science and Christianity did not conflict, and, perhaps most important, founded a chemical factory. McDougall's father eventually took over the major responsibility for that concern. He also established an iron-foundry and a pulp-mill, both of which he made use of in trying out his own inventions. If McDougall felt dubious about the latter activities, he still presented an engaging portrait of a father who, having been "successively a member of most of the leading Christian sects...in later life adhered to none."[24] The older McDougall's political convictions seem to have been firmer than his religious ones, for, suspecting Cambridge and Oxford as bastions of Toryism, the staunchly Liberal manufacturer sent his son off, first, to a *Realgymnasium* in Germany and, then, to the University of Manchester where he earned a first-class honors degree. Eventually, when the young McDougall had fulfilled the condition of earning a scholarship, the father allowed him to embark on earning a second degree at Cambridge.

This is the very stuff, not only of Victorian social history, but also of the Victorian novel.[25] But McDougall preferred to emphasize another dimension of his family life, the fusion of his parents' racial types. As he viewed the matter, while such a blending had provided the basis for the historical development of the English people, he happened to be "of the first generation of crossbreeds" and, hence, "never felt altogether and typically English or altogether at home in the English social atmosphere."

More generally, he believed that his genetic inheritance explained why he "never fitted neatly into any social group," why he had never been "at one with any party, or system," why he "always stood outside, critical and ill-content." He also confessed to a native arrogance. Whatever may be thought of the genetic basis of such a quality, it can hardly be denied to a somebody who claimed in 1931 that "perhaps no man living...has had a more intensive and varied training in the natural sciences."[26]

To put the matter more accurately, McDougall received an excellent scientific training which he made use of in a variety of areas. He received his medical degree at Cambridge where he became a Fellow of St. John's College. He then accompanied an anthropological expedition to the Torres Straits, off the coast of New Guinea, and lingered for a time in Borneo. Having considered and rejected the idea of a career as an anthropologist, he became in 1900 Reader in Experimental Psychology at University College, London, where he worked with, among others, the eugenicists, Francis Galton and Karl Pearson. He had already begun the experiments, many of them concerned with the psycho-physiology of vision, which in 1912 would bring election to the Royal Society. In 1904 McDougall moved to Oxford where he became Wilde Reader in Mental Philosophy and soon encountered trouble. He would later explain his difficulties in terms of being "neither fish, flesh, nor fowl... The scientists suspected me of being a metaphysician, and the philosophers regarded me as representing an impossible and non-existent branch of science."[27] In brief, psychology had not yet achieved the status of a institutionalized discipline at Oxford—it would not do so fully until after World War II—and McDougall found himself trapped in the ill-defined borderlands of several areas of inquiry.

His problems, however, were also more specific. The founder of the readership, a successful businessman devoted to Lockean empiricism and associationist psychology, objected strongly to McDougall's teachings. So too, from an entirely different perspective, did the Oxford Idealists. Two of McDougall's concerns, psychical research and hypnosis, especially roused the ire of his opponents. While committed to the exposure of fraudulent mediums and even once involved in "the corporal punishment" of one of them, he took psychical phenomena quite as seriously as did William James, whom he would one day succeed as a president of the Society for Psychical Research.[28] McDougall carried his other concern into the classroom with displays of hypnotism. His students, some of them women, may have been instructed and/or entertained. But Oxford dons were not amused. It seems that it was only through the intervention of Sir William Ostler, then Regius Professor of Medicine, and at the price of removing hypnotism from the classroom, that McDougall retained his position.

After service in World War I, first in the ranks of the French army and then as a psychiatrist with the British forces, McDougall returned only briefly to Oxford before accepting, in 1920, the chair of Psychology at Harvard. Still pursuing his experiments, he began there the lengthy series of exercises designed to test the Lamarckian view of evolution, with its emphasis upon acquired characteristics, to which he, like Freud, clung stubbornly. But Harvard proved less of a respite from battle than the combative McDougall had expected. He soon clashed bitterly with the American behaviorists who challenged the purposive elements central to his psychology. While at the end of his life he dismissed behaviorism as a passing "bad dream," there can be little doubt who won that particular battle.[29] But McDougall also blamed his troubles on a press angered by the Lowell Lectures which he published as *Is America Safe for Democracy?* (1921). The tide in this area was, in fact, actually with him, for while journalists like Walter Lippmann did attack the eugenicist arguments presented by McDougall and others, they could not prevent the enshrining of such thinking in the Immigration Law of 1924 and the Supreme Court decision of 1927 which upheld Virginia's sterilization law. In the later years the aggrieved McDougall left Harvard for the chairmanship of the Duke University Psychology Department where he backed strongly J.B. Rhine's parapsychological work. While no university could have provided the ideal setting for this self-proclaimed outsider, it may well be that the Duke University of that era best suited a man who, having announced that he had "two hobbies—Psychical Research and Eugenics," went on to argue that their "convergence may in the end prevent the utter collapse which now threatens."30

The danger of decay had already appeared in his *Social Psychology*.[31] There he lamented in Burkean terms that "custom, the great conservative force of society, the great controller of the individual impulses being weakened, the deep-seated instincts, especially the gregarious instinct, have found their opportunity to determine the choices of men." Pointing to the growth of great cities, he grieved that "the excessive indulgence of this impulse is one of the great demoralizing factors of the present time in this country, just as it was in Rome in the days of her declining power and glory." Contemporary intellectual developments also prompted unease. While he acknowledged that "at the present time it may seem that in one small quarter of the world, namely Western Europe, society has achieved an organization so intrinsically stable that it may with impunity tolerate the flourishing of the spirit of inquiry and give free rein to the impulse of curiosity," he cautioned that "the flourishing of skepticism has been too often the forerunner of social decay, as in ancient Greece and Rome." A problem which would continue to haunt McDougall then made its appearance: "This change of belief. the withdrawal of supernatural power from immediate intervention in the life of mankind, inevitably and greatly diminishes the social efficacy of the supernatural sanctions. Whether our societies will prove capable of long surviving this process is the most momentous of the problems confronting Western civilization."[32]

McDougall believed that social psychology could contribute decisively to the elucidation and resolution of that and other problems. Challenging the claims advanced for sociology by Comte and Durkheim, he announced that social psychology constituted "the essential foundation on which all the social sciences...must be built up." If the Darwinian emphasis upon "the continuity of human with animal evolution" opened the way to a psychology which could serve that purpose, it also posed a vital question: how could men, "moved by a variety of impulses whose nature has been determined through long ages of evolutionary process...ever come to act as they ought, or morally and reasonably?" Dismissing the answers of the utilitarians, the intuitionist and the champions of moral faculties, McDougall reserved his sharpest words for Liberals who had exaggerated the role of reason in human affairs: utilitarian ethics were "degrading"; classical political economists had overestimated the role of "enlightened self-interest" in the marketplace and the "cosmopolitanism of the Manchester school, with it confident prophecy of the universal brotherhood of man" had been shown to be fallacious by the "great outburst of national spirit which has played the chief part in shaping European history during the last half-century."[33]

Morality interested McDougall more than reason.[34] In his view, "the fundamental problem of social psychology" was "the moralization of the individual by the society into which he is born as a creature in which the non-moral and purely egoistic tendencies are so much stronger than the altruistic tendencies."

Refusing to recognize the intrusion of special faculties like conscience, he tried to show "the continuity of the development of the highest types of human will and character from the primary instinctive dispositions that we have in common with the animals." After isolating a multiplicity of basic instincts, he explained how the emotions associated with them became transformed into sentiments more open to "volitional control." Following James and Bergson in emphasizing the "will" and the "*élan vital*," McDougall defined volition in a fashion which embraced far more than "clear foresight of the end desired."

As "moral conduct consists in the regulation and control of the immediate prompting of impulse in conformity with some prescribed conduct of conduct," society played a major role in the shaping of the human will.[35]

McDougall argued that "the social genesis of the idea of the self lies at the root of morality." To be more specific, there took place "an improvement or refinement of the 'gallery' before which we display ourselves...and this refinement may be continued until the 'gallery' becomes an ideal spectator or group of spectators or, in the last resort, one's own critical self standing as representative of such spectators." If relatively few managed to reach this last level, the social process of moralization still carried "the great mass of men" beyond "mere law abiding" to a stage where "the praise or blame of our fellows, especially as expressed by the voice of public opinion, are the principal and most effective sanctions of moral conduct."

Presumably one of the favored few who had reached the final level, the highly independent McDougall recognized the nefarious pressures which could be exercised by public opinion. But he again struck the Conservative note when he extolled "the higher kind of morality of the man who, while accepting in the main the prescribed social code, attempts by his example and precept to improve it in certain respects." It could hardly be otherwise with a man who believed that "all that constitutes culture and civilization...is...summed up in the word 'tradition.' "[36]

McDougall confronted the undermining of tradition at greater length in *Body and Mind: A History and Defence of Animism* (1911), a stout volume wholly neglected by Soffer. Defining the underlying notion of all forms of animism as the belief that "all or some of those manifestations of life and mind which distinguish the living man from the corpse and from inorganic bodies are due to the operation within him of something which is quite different from that of the body, an animating principle generally, but necessarily or always conceived as an immaterial and individual being or soul," McDougall sought to defend such thinking against a variety of attacks which ranged from "the crudest materialism...to the grossest subjective idealism." Undoubtedly willing to group some Oxford colleagues under the latter rubric, he still took the materialist challenge more seriously. Indeed, in his view, one had to choose "between Animism and Materialism."[37]

McDougall was remarkably fair in presenting the arguments for "the mechanistic dogma" which he perceived as central to materialism. He took into account, in his own field, the localization of brain functions, the non-volitional nature of reflex actions, the workings of the unconscious, and the older notion of the association of ideas and, more generally, the conservation of energy and the operation of natural selection as presented by Weisman and his neo-Darwinian followers. McDougall then sought to refute the materialistic and mechanistic conclusions derived from these discoveries and hypotheses, not all of which he fully accepted, by basing his arguments upon "the methods and aims of empirical science."[38] This stance, then and later, allowed him to invoke his impressive credentials as an experientialist when pursuing his parapsychological interests. By no means wholly a matter of personal eccentricity, those interests possessed distinctly ideological features.

The consequences of a decline in the appeal of animist notions of life after death especially worried McDougall. Disavowing any great personal interest in immortality, he still doubted whether "whole nations could rise to the level of an austere morality, or even maintain a decent standard of conduct after losing these beliefs." He thought that proof of some sort of immortality, perhaps to be provided by psychical research, "must add dignity, seriousness, and significance to our lives, and must throw a great weight into the scale against the dangers which threaten every advanced civilization." In his view, "the passing away of this would be calamitous for our civilization. For every vigorous nation seems to have possess this belief, and the loss of it has accompanied the decay of national vigor in many instances."[39] Animism, in brief, possessed social utility. And that, in an age of imperialism, had to be equated with national utility. But neither had anything to do with the utilitarianism of the Philosophical Radicals whose individualism, psychological associationism, and hedonist calculus continued to rouse his scorn. No more than the materialism which he associated with it could such Liberal thinking meet the larger needs of society.

In his *Psychology: The Study of Behavior* (1912), a concise work as notable for its subtitle as for its long life as an introduction to the subject, McDougall allowed magnanimously that utilitarianism had "exercised great and beneficent influence throughout the civilized world and has done much to shape our laws and institutions." But once again he insisted that the pleasure-pain calculus central to it could not constitute an adequate theory of human motivation. He offered his own solution to the problem in a theory of purposive, teleological behaviour which stressed the importance of the will or connotation. Having defined the operations of the will in terms which went far beyond those of the mere intellect, McDougall detected a correspondence between his ideas and those of the Freudians. Admiring their therapeutic successes, he also noted approvingly that "they are heading to a great extension of the psychological attitude toward mental disease of all kinds; and they are opening great extensions of our knowledge of the workings of the normal mind; especially they are revealing a realm of subconscious mental activity, the existence of which has been vaguely conjectured, but which had remained unexplored and altogether problematical."[40] But however sympathetic his presentation, he still skirted the central place of sexuality in Freud's system. McDougall, the biologist and physician, had already recognized earlier that the reproductive instinct, "more than any other, is apt in mankind to lend the immense energy of its impulse to the sentiments and complex impulses into which it enters, while its specific character remains submerged and unconscious." But McDougall, the Scots-English gentleman, had also announced that "it is unnecessary to dwell on this feature since it has been dealt with exhaustively in many thousands of novels."[41] Not surprisingly, he refused in 1913 an invitation to join the British Branch of the International Psycho-Analytic Association.

The *Psychology* ended with a chapter devoted to social psychology. Having defined mind as "an organized system of mental or purposive forces," he argued that "every highly organized human society may properly be said to possess a collective mind." The collective mind, like the social actions it dictated, was more than a mere sum of its parts, for "the thinking and acting of each man, in so far as he acts as a member of society, is very different from his thinking and acting as an isolated individual." The question then arose as to whether collective thinking involved a "degradation" of the individual's moral and mental life. While McDougall recognized instances like panic in which was indeed the case, he also argued that "it is only by sharing in the collective life of the organized societies that the mass of men is raised above a very low level of almost purely selfish behavior; and it is through such sharing that great numbers of men are raised to the level of a consistently public-spirited conduct and even to the heights of heroic self-sacrifice." No friend of social spontaneity, McDougall stressed throughout the importance of organized groups in the forging of moral conduct. While such groups could be as diverse as "the savage tribe, the secret society, the political party, or the trade union," McDougall believed that the study of such units paled in significance when compared to arriving at "some understanding of the most complex, interesting, and important form of the collective mind; namely, the mind of a modern nation state."[42]

According to McDougall, social psychology would have to draw upon "the comparative psychology of races and classes, before it can hope to accomplish its proper share in the interpretation of history and in accounting for the peculiarities of the collective life of each nation." Only on the bases of these psychologies would it be possible to arrive at a clear distinction between "the innate and acquired mental structure." McDougall already had his own ideas along these lines. Discussing child psychology earlier in the same work, he had declared that "though education may do much, heredity is all-important." Leaving open the question of the transmission of acquired characteristics, he insisted that "so long as we have no answer...there can be no progress made with many of the major problems of biology and sociology, and a wise decision on some of the most far-reaching legislative and administrative problems is wholly impossible." This eugenicist allowed that "if acquired characteristics are transmitted, even in a very slight degree only, we may reasonably hope that, after the Negro race shall have been subjected for the better influence of civilization for a number of generations, it will be raised to a higher level of innate intellectual and moral capacity." He was also prepared to consider the converse of the proposition: "If...acquired characters are not in any degree transmitted, as the majority of biologists assert, then there is no hope that the civilization and education of the Negro peoples, no matter how wisely and beneficially the work may be directed, will of themselves raise them to a higher level of innate capacity." Whatever his uncertainties in that area, he was convinced that "if a tenth, or even a hundredth, part of the money which is diverted to research in the physical sciences, in order to add to our material comforts and conveniences, could be diverted to promote the study of animal behavior, this problem could be rapidly solved."[43]

Properly erected upon a biological foundation, class psychology promised to answer equally vital questions. McDougall wanted to know "whether any differences of innate mental quality obtain between the various sections and social strata of our great complex national societies." More specifically, he wished:

> ...to know what changes, if any, are being brought about in the innate mental constitution of these populations under their present conditions, whether, as some assert, various forms of social selection are making strongly for deterioration; or whether, as is commonly believed, the civilized stocks continue to evolve a higher type of mental structure; or lastly whether the principal change being effected is not a greater differentiation, resulting in the production of a comparatively low-grade mass of population at one end of the scale, and of a number of stocks of exceptional ability and moral stamina at the other.

Arguing that "all these are questions which must be answered in detail before we can build up a true science of society, a science that will point the way to such a political and social organization as will offer some guarantee of stability and some prospect of the continued progress of the human mind and culture," McDougall concluded this book by insisting "all these problems fall within the province of psychology, and can be solved only through the progress of that science."[44]

McDougall presented his fully developed social psychology in *The Group Mind* (1920), a work largely completed before the outbreak of World War I.[45] The global struggle, however, did deepen some of the ambiguities buried within it. Convinced that "a society not only enjoys a collective mental life, but also a collective mind or...a collective soul," he argued that a long-lived and highly organized society possessed "a life of its own, tendencies of its own, a power of molding all its component individuals, and a power of perpetuating itself as a self-identical system, subject only to slow and gradual change." But such sentiments now had to be distinguished from German notions of social organicism and collective consciousness. In McDougall's view, "the analogy between the organization of the national collective mind and that of the individual mind...is so much closer and illuminating than that between a society and an organism." Implicitly abandoning the idea of a whole greater than the sum of its parts, he now seemed to settle for arguing that the group mind, like the individual mind, should simply be seen as "an organized system of interacting mental or psychical forces." Yet this collective mind remained all-important. While it would have been easy enough to confuse this position with those of some of the Germans, McDougall not only denied any such convergence of ideas, but used the occasion to settle some scores closer to home: "the political philosophy of German 'idealism,' which derives in the main from Hegel, which has been so ably represented in this country by Dr. Bosanquet, which has exerted so great an influence at Oxford...is as detrimental to honest and clear thinking as it has proved to be destructive of political morality in its native country." He went on to insist that "in order to further guard myself against the implications attached by German 'idealism' to the notion of a collective mind, I wish to state that politically my sympathies are with individualism and internationalism."[46]

If he defined and accepted those positions in highly idiosyncratic terms, McDougall now at least acknowledged that political concerns played some role in shaping this work: "If this book affords any justification for any normative doctrine or ideal, it is one which would aim at the synthesis of the principles of individualism and communism, of aristocracy and democracy, of self-realization and service to the community." Expecting that "many...will reproach me with giving countenance to communistic and ultra-democratic ideas," he thought that others, "whose sympathies are with Collectivism, Syndicalism, or Socialism will detect in this book the cloven foot of individualism and leanings toward the aristocratic principle." The latter group of critics were, in fact, the more likely to be correct, McDougall, at his most democratic, had arrived at a notion of the social contract as "the constitutive principle of the ideal State towards which progressive nations are tending."[47] But in analyzing one of his own dreams three years later he threw more light upon his basic position: "The figure of Lord T. is a composite figure, an illustration of the principle of condensation pointed out by Freud as frequently operative in dreams. It stands for or symbolizes both aristocracy and democracy. I had recently written in the preface to my Group Mind that my political theory required a synthesis of the aristocratic with the democratic principle. In the dream I was to be the spokesman of a figure which represented in one person both these principles. But I failed to reach my public; my defense of aristocracy will not go down with the public, which, in the dream passes away to the left-side of radicalism and ultra-democracy."[48]

McDougall abhorred "two of the extreme forms of political doctrine or ideal, current at the present day; first, the idea of the brotherhood of man in a nation-less world; secondly, the extreme form of democratic individualism which assumed the good of society is best promoted by the freest possible pursuit by individuals of their private ends, which believes that each man must have an equal voice in the government of his country." He opposed to such tendencies "the political conservatism of such a thinker as Edmund Burke, who is keenly aware of the organic unity of society and looks constantly to the good of the whole, deriving from that consideration its leading motives and principles, and which trusts principally to the growth of the group spirit for the holding of the balance between conflicting interests and for the promotion of the public welfare." Nothing could be more Burkean than McDougall's view of public opinion as "not the sum of individual opinions upon any particular question...[but] the expression of that tone or attitude of mind which prevails throughout the nation and owes its quality far more to the influence of the dead than the living, being the expression of the moral sentiments that are firmly and traditionally established in the mind of the people, and established more effectively and in more refined forms in the minds of the leaders of public opinion than in the average citizen." Yet McDougall could not simply proclaim himself to be a Burkean Conservative, for despite his continuing concern with morality, he remained very much the positivist in arguing that the development of the "human sciences" had been "confused with and hampered by the effort to show what ought to be." His lauding of the situation where "the positive element" now "tended to be preponderant over and completely supplants the normative view" possessed its own advantages: not only did it permit him to bludgeon once again Adam Smith, Bentham and the Mills, but it also allowed him to equate his own ideological obsessions with truth.[49]

While McDougall rejected the crude racism of Gobineau and Chamberlain, he also scorned the "popular humanitarianism," espoused by J.S. Mill, Buckle and Durkheim, which "would regard all men and races as alike and equal in respect of native endowment." While he acknowledged that "all existing stocks (with a few exceptions) are the products of race-blending," he still detected substantial differences among the races. Buttressing his contention with Le Bon's measurements of cranial capacity, he found a purported black inability "to form a nation" to be rooted in a more fundamental inability to produce "individuals of really high mental and moral endowments." Closer to home, if the English possessed "greater self-reliance and capacity for individual initiative," the French, along with "greater sociability," displayed "greater violence of collective mental processes, those of mobs, assemblies, factions and groups of all kinds."[50]

McDougall acknowledge, however, that the French held no monopoly rights over the collective thinking and acting of the crowd, the relatively simple group marked most strongly by an "exaltation or intensification of emotion." Believing this to be "for most men an intensely pleasurable experience," he thought that "the repeated enjoyment of effects of this kind tends to generate a craving for them, and also a facility in the spread and intoxication of emotion" which, in turn, was "probably the principal cause of the greater excitability of urban populations as compared with dwellers in the country, and of the well-known violence and fickleness of the mobs of great cities." While he admitted that "a crowd is more likely to be swayed by the more generous of the coarse emotions, impulses, and sentiments than by those of a meaner, universally reprobated kind," he also invoked all the usual images in his portrayal of "the psychological character" of the unorganized or simple crowd:

> ...excessively emotional, impulsive, violent, fickle, inconsistent, irresolute and extreme in action, displaying the coarser emotions, and the less refined sentiments; extremely suggestible, careless in judgment, incapable of all but the simpler and imperfect forms of reasoning; easily swayed and led, lacking self-consciousness, devoid of self-respect and without a sense of responsibility, and apt to be carried away by the consciousness of its own force, so that it tends to produce all the manifestations...of any irresponsible and absolute power.

Finding "all these characteristics of the crowd...exemplified on a grand scale in Paris at the time of the great Revolution," he compared the worst cases of crowd behaviour to "that of a wild beast rather than...human beings." Proposing as one condition which could "raise the behavior of a temporary and unorganized crowd to a higher pane...the presence of a clearly defined common purpose in the minds of all its members," he placed the lynch mob in the American South upon that plane."[51] Perhaps that geographical area already struck McDougall as somewhat more congenial than the historical heritage of the French Revolution.

However threatening crowd action might continue to be, McDougall had to confront the dangers embodied in more modern forms of collective endeavor. Exalting the role of the guilds within medieval society, this manufacture's offspring lamented that "the violent changes of industrial life, the development of the capitalist system and industrialism, distorted and largely destroyed these occupational groups to the great detriment of social well-being." Occupational groups, however, had reasserted themselves. But modern corporations held scant appeal for McDougall: "In these the group spirit commonly remains at the lowest level, for the dominant motive is individual financial gain and the common bond among the shareholders is their interest in the management of the company as it affects the private and individual end of each one." Trade unionism, however, constituted "the climate of this tendency for occupation to replace and overshadow all other forms of self-conscious grouping." Unfortunately, "lacking the guidance and conservative power of old traditions, and depending for their strength largely upon the identification of the material interests of each member with those of the group," the trade unions displayed a narrowness of outlook, a lack of stability and internal cohesion, and a tendency to ignore the place and function of the group in the whole community." But McDougall still hoped that "these groups which at present seem to some observers to threaten to destroy our society and to replace the rivalry of nations with an even more dangerous rivalry of vast occupational groups may become organized within the structure of the whole and play a part of the greatest value in the national life."[52]

The "rivalry of vast occupational groups" served as a euphemism for class struggle. If only to belittle its importance, McDougall confronted the issue more directly:

It is sometimes contended that the realization of principles of equality and justice for all men has been secured only by the strife of social classes, by the success of the lower classes in forcing a series of concessions from the ruling classes. This is a very imperfect and partial view of the process. If the ruling class had consistently sought to maintain their power and exclusive privileges, and to maintain all the rest of society in a state of servitude and serfdom, there is do doubt that they could have done so.

Pointing to the series of reforms undertaken in Great Britain in the nineteenth century, he argued that they had been brought about by the ruling class as a result of "the extension of their sympathies," a process which still "in respect to our relations to the lower classes...holds good." Although he worried greatly about some of its effects, McDougall held that "the progressive extension of the sphere of imaginative sympathy, has broken down all the social barriers that confined the energies of men and has set free their various faculties in that competition of ever increasing severity which is the principal cause underlying the progress of modern nations."[53]

Seen from this perspective, Socialism could only threaten "the continued welfare of the whole and its perpetuation as an evolving and progressing organism." McDougall admitted it to be "highly probable that, if any great nation should unanimously and wholeheartedly embark upon a through-going scheme of state-socialism, the miseries of the vast majority of individuals would be greatly promoted; they would be enabled to live more prosperously and comfortably, with greater leisure and opportunity for the higher forms of activity." He did not doubt that "the adoption of socialism...by almost any modern nation would increase the well-being and happiness of its members most decidedly on the whole for the present generation and possibly for some generations to come." But he thought it equally certain "the higher interest of the nation would be gravely endangered, that it would enter upon a period of increasing stagnation and diminishing vitality and, after a few generations had passed away, would have slipped far down the slope which has led all great societies in the past to destruction."[54]

The nation emerged once again as McDougall's central concern: "The nation alone is a self-contained and complete organism; other groups within it do not minister to the life of the whole; their value is relative to the whole; the continuance of results obtained on their behalf is dependent on the continued welfare of the whole (for example, the welfare of any class or profession—a fact too easily overlooked by those in whom the class spirit grows strong)." Historians had not defined the nation to McDougall's satisfaction, for they, like political philosophers, had failed to understand that "political problems" were "psychological through and through." As "nationhood" was "essentially a psychological conception," only social psychology with its grasp of "the group mind," could resolve this "riddle."

McDougall did not hesitate to claim that "to investigate the nature of the national mind and character and to examine the conditions that render possible the formation of the national mind and tend to consolidate national character...are the crowning tasks of psychology." To perform these tasks properly, psychologists would have to scrutinize closely the factors which "determine the evolution of national character": first, the "innate moral disposition" and "innate intellectual capacities" or, in other words, the "racial qualities"; second, the moral and intellectual traditions which constituted "national civilization"; and, third, "social organization."[55]

While McDougall warned that care had to be taken "to assign to each of these its due importance and its proper place in the whole complex development," he himself remained the captive of his eugenicist convictions. The factors which interfered with the proper workings of biology constituted the fundamental danger to civilization. With their productive powers enormously increased by the triumphs of science, "the civilized populations" had multiplied their numbers enormously in the eighteenth and nineteenth centuries, but that phase of demographic growth had been "succeeded by a new period characterized by three features which threaten to exert a most deleterious effect upon the mental qualities of the peoples." First, increasing economic competition, as well as a tendency to regard previous luxuries as present necessities, made it difficult to maintain "a family in the upper strata of society" and, hece, led to the limiting of births. Second, there had taken place "a great development of humanitarian sentiment, one result of which has been the breaking down of class barriers and the perfecting of social ladders." Humanitarianism had "produced such changes in our laws and institutions as tend in ever increasing degree to lighten the economic burden of the poor and to consummate by social organization the abolition of natural selection; that is to say, these changes are putting a stop to the repression by natural laws of the least fit, those least well endowed morally and physically." Third came the threat which he had struggled against in *Body and Mind* and, more generally, in his psychical investigations: "The influence of religion and custom has men weakened, and men are more disposed to adopt the naturalistic point of view." This concern did not signal a departure from his biological emphasis, for he argued that "the acquirement by any class of leisure, culture, the habit of reflection (the malady of thought) partially emancipates that class from the empire of instinct, custom and the religious sanctions of morality," the very forces which "have been acquired for the good of the race or of the society considered as an organism."[56]

These forces had encouraged biological reproduction at all levels of society. But as their powers waned, such reproduction declined. Equating class status with innate qualities, McDougall proclaimed that "it is shown statistically that this falling off of fertility, chiefly affects the classes above the level of ability, the upper and middle classes and also the superior part of the artisan class." But he did not neglect those beelow these groups, for, in his view, "the social ladder, becoming more perfect, perpetually drains the mass of the people of its best members, enabling them to rise to the upper strata, where they tend to become infertile." He also worried about the impact upon heredity of "the so-called emancipation of women," for he believed that "the most able women are more and more attracted into independent careers." All in all, he detected "a tendency for the population to be renewed in each generation preponderantly from the mentally inferior elements." On the verge of abandoning his country for the United States, this proponent of the primacy of the nation announced lugubriously that "in England, where the operation of the social ladder has been more effective and of longer duration than in any other country," the stage of "national decay" might already have been reached.[57]

Yet McDougall did not despair. Committed to securing the victory of altruism over egoism, he projected a future in which, "while the common end of collective action is willed by all, the choice of means is left to those best qualified and in the best position for deliberation and choice." Despite all his continuing concern for morality, he presented intelligence as the fundamental qualification for such a role. Conditions, rather than McDougall, appeared to have reversed themselves: "The free play of the spirit of inquiry, which in all earlier ages has been highly dangerous for the stability of nations and which, while it has been the sole cause of progress, nevertheless destroyed many of the nations whom it impelled upon that path, will make for a greatly accelerated progress; and, at the same time, it will enable us to secure, by deliberate voluntary control, the bases of society, which in all previous ages have rested solely upon customs, instinct, and religious sanctions." To be more precise, eugenics held out the promise of social salvation: "The modern nations...may even hope to progress not only in respect of the intellectual and moral tradition, but also in respect of racial qualities; for a better knowledge of the factors at work and the laws of heredity will enable them to put an end to the influences now making for race deterioration and to replace them by others of the opposite tendency." If he had by no means abandoned his respect for tradition, his scientistic proclivities had come to outweigh that veneration. At best a precarious bridge between the two positions lay in McDougall's self-centered claim that "the interval...between the modern man of scientific culture and the average citizen of our modern states is far greater than between the latter and the savage."[58]

Wilfred Trotter also flirted with such positivist elitism. Even at the height of his post-war discouragement, he did not rule out the possibility of a "scientific statecraft" which might halt "the dreary oscillation between progress and relapse which have been so ominous a feature in human history."[59] As competent a scientist as McDougall, he too endeavored to base his social psychology upon biological foundations. Intellectual elitists prepared to advance sweeping claims for what could be accomplished through the development of this new branch of inquiry, both wrestled with the instincts in their efforts to outline the conditions in which the victory of altruism could be secured within society. Both confronted difficulties associated with behavior and purpose. Both entertained on occasion apocalyptic and millenarian visions of the human future. Yet their views differed profoundly. Wedded to scientific parsimony, Trotter avoided McDougall's multiplication of the instincts. Suspicion of the domination of the "mentally stable" in all areas of life, along with a more specific scorn for the eugenicists, served to check Trotter's inclinations toward positivist elitism. If McDougall found purpose at work from the beginning throughout the organic world, Trotter perceived it as an element yet to be introduced into human affairs through a recognition of the claims of the intellect. McDougall venerated tradition as an instrument of social control, feared its decay in the present, and looked to psychical research and eugenics to provide the moral and intellectual regeneration of the future. With the war providing the watershed, Trotter's views changed over time. But in general he dismissed the stifling traditions of the past, located opportunities for progressive change in the present, grieved when they appeared to have been missed, and, in the aftermath of the war, abandoned the notion of a coincidence of biological and historical times in favor of an evolutionary gradualism.

Behind such differences lay fundamentally different visions of the good society. Although reformulated in post-Darwinian terms, these visions remained rooted in older forms of political ideology. Eschewing any move in the direction of the newer Socialism, Trotter and McDougall remained locked a conflict between Radical Liberals and Conservatives which had done so much to shape English political thought throughout the nineteenth century. For all the apiary imagery spawned by the impact of World War I, Trotter never lost sight of the ideal of society as the setting in which the full capacities of the individual could be realized. Whatever the denials engendered by German thinking alone the same lines, McDougall never abandoned his concern with and commitment to social organicism. But in one respect the Conservative proved more "radical" than the Radical, for McDougall embarked upon the intellectually risky, as well as more socially dangerous, path. However conservative its orientation since the days of Auguste Comte, scientistic positivism at best coexists poorly with Burkean Conservatism. Scientistic eugenics further sharpened the contradiction. While it might be used in the short run to bolster Burkean values, it led to a starkly reactionary trans-valuation of those values. Whatever his Burkean veneration for tradition, McDougall took the step which threatened to destroy the values he claimed to cherish. Trotter faced another sort of problem. More firmly rooted in the nineteenth century and, hence, simultaneously more progressive and more old-fashioned than McDougall, he found himself with no place to go politically after the war, and, like other weary Radicals before him, fell back upon the skilled practice of his craft. The victory, in this instance, lay with the focus upon "the stable associations" rather than with the "political animal." Perhaps the great apolitical Liberal of Vienna would not have been surprised unduly by such an outcome.

If only by using them as stalking horses for his own ideas in regard to social psychology, Freud did as much as anybody to preserve the names of Trotter and McDougall. They were, after all, but marginal figures in the intellectual world of their day. Yet the differences between their positions possessed significance in that day. So too did the outcome, however limited, of the conflict between those positions. And the matters in dispute have not wholly lost their significance. Although it might be possible to present a convoluted argument to the effect that Trotter's concern with and respect for the mentally unstable came to delayed fruition in the work R.D. Laing, it is much more likely that his ideas died along with the individualistic Radicalism of the nineteenth century which had done so much to shape them. Less fortunately, some of McDougall's ideas thrive to the extent that it is all too easy to construct an intellectual genealogy which runs from Francis Galton, to Karl Pearson, to William McDougall, to Cyril Burt, to Arthur Jenson and Richard Herrnstein.

Notes

1. *Historical Reflections / Réflexions historiques*, 12, 3 (Fall, 1985), pp. 375-401.

2. For instance, believing him to be influenced excessively by the examples of the crowds of the French Revolution, Freud wrongly charged Le Bon with being concerned solely with "groups of short-lived character." Sigmund Freud, *Group Psychology and the Analsis of the Ego* (New York: W.W. Norton, 1959), 1959), p. l5.For other such examples, see below.

3. *Ibid.*, p. 51.

4. For one effort in this direction, see Reba Soffer, *Ethics and Society in England: The Revolution in the Social Scineces, 1870-1914* (Berkeley: University of California Press, 1978). While this not the place to pursue the matter, I believe that it can be shown that Soffer's analytical framework is flawed seriously.

5. *Ibid.*, p. 249.

6. F.M.R. Walsche, "Wilfred Trotter (1872-1939)," *Dictionary of National Biography*, Compact Edition, II (Oxford: Oxford University Press, 1975), p. 2934.

7. W. Trotter, *Instincts of the Herd in Peace and War* (London: Ernest Benn, 1919), p. 136.

8. *Ibid.*, pp. 11, 70.

9. *Ibid.*, pp. 80, 84, 86.

10. *Ibid.*, pp. 89, 90, 91.

11. Freud, *Group Psychology*, pp. 19, 50, 51. For Freud's biological orientation, see Frank J. Sulloway, *Freud, Biologist of the Mind: Beyond the Psychoanalytic Legend* (New York: Basic Books, 1979).

12. Trotter, *Instincts*, pp. 47, 48; 103; 48.

13. *Ibid.*, pp. 124, 135, 252.

14. *Ibid.*, pp. 63; 55.

15 *Ibid.*, pp. 54; 161; 153.

16. Freud, *Group Psychology*, p. 51. Freud went on: "Let us venture, then, to correct Trotter's pronouncement that man is a herd animal and assert that he is rather a horde animal, an individual creature in a horde led by a chief." *Ibid.*, p. 53.

17. Trotter, *Instincts*, pp. 247-48, 158.

18. *Ibid.*, pp. 139, 255-56.

19. *Ibid.*, pp. 101, 156, 174.

20. *Ibid.*, pp. 151-52; l74; 171; 238.

21. Spanning at a minimum the period between Bernard de Mandeville's *Fable of the Bees* (1714) and the contemporary sociobiological currents, the use of insect analogies and models in regard to the structuring of human societies deserves further attention. More specifically, the image of the bee-hive cut in two very different directions in nineteenth-century England. Whereas George Cruikshank provided in 1867 an etching of a human hive which stressed the harmony of existing British society in answer to demands for an extension of the suffrage, the working-class journal *Bee-Hive* simultaneously struck a much more radical notes.

22. *Ibid.*, pp. 238; 237; 240; 239; 259.

23. Much of the following biographical material is derived from William McDougall, "Autobiography," Carl Murchison, ed., *A History of Psychology in Autobiography*, I (New York: Russell and Russell, 1961), pp. 191-223. That work first appeared in 1931. See also Sir Cyril Burt's introduction to the 1952 reprinting of McDougall's *Psychology: The Study of Behaviour*. Burt, the first knighted psychologist, had been McDougall's student. Having now been proven to have invented and distorted data, he might be taken as an extreme illustration of Trotter's remark on the combination of "real specialist capacity with the arts of the bagman." See "The Real Error of Cyril Burt: Factor Analysis and the Reification of Intelligence," Stephen Jay Gould, *The Mis-measure of Man* (New York: W.W. Norton, 1981), pp. 234-320.

24. McDougall, "Autobiography," p. 191.

25. The material also admits of other readings. Denying that any "father-complex" drove him to rebellion, McDougall used his relations with his father in an effort to discredit the universalistic claims of the Freudian system. But the sweeping nature of his rejection of his father's political beliefs poses problems in that area. *Ibid.*, p. 194.

26. *Ibid.*, pp. 191, 198. McDougall still remained more modest than Le Bon who claimed to have arrived at the theory of relativity before Einstein.

27. *Ibid.*, p. 207.

28. William McDougall, "Fraudulent Mediums Exposed," *Two Worlds*, 28 July 1899, in Raymond Van Over and Laura Oteri, eds., in collaboration with Professor Angus McDougall, *William McDougall: Explorer of the Mind; Studies in Psychical Research* (New York: Helix, 1967), pp. 210-12.

29. William McDougall, *Psychology: The Study of Behavior* (London: Oxford University Press, 1939), p. xxviii. 30. William McDougall, "The Need for Psychical Research," *American Society for Psychical Research*, 12 (1923), 4-14, Van Over and Oteri, *William McDougall*, pp. 42-50, p. 47.

31. The title would later be changed to *An Introduction to Social Psychology*.

32. William McDougall, *An Introduction to Social Psychology* (Boston: John W. Luce, 1923), pp. 304, 305; 327; 326; 327. Note that McDougall classified "gregariousness" as a primitive instinct and found it reprehensible. Later he would castigate Trotter's "famous little book" for its purported confusion of "gregariousness" with "suggestion." William McDougall, *Outline of Abnormal Psychology* (New York: Charles Scribner's Sons, 1926), fn.1, p. 117.

33. McDougall, *Introduction*, pp. 1, 5, 10, 11-12.

34. Although McDougall gave no sign of being aware of it, much of what follows in this and the next paragraph echoes the views of the moralists of the Scots Enlightenment. For all his hatred of the economic ideas of Adam Smith, McDougall's views of the role played by society in the forging of morality are none too distant from those expressed in Smith's *The Theory of Moral Sentiments* (1759). At a time when McDougall's reputation stood higher

than today, Gladys Bryson noted correspondences between his views and those of the Scots theorists. Glays Bryson, *Man and Society: The Scottish Inquiry of the Eighteenth Century* (Princeton: Princeton University Press, 1945), p. 141. More generally, the Scots moralists, perhaps especially Adam Ferguson, had no difficult in admitting the existence of a "gregarious" or "herd" instinct.

35. McDougall, *Introduction*, pp. 18, 270; 165; 248; 368; 363.

36. *Ibid.*, pp. 185-86, 263; 194; 320, 335.

37. William McDougall, *Body and Mind, A History and Defense of Animism* (London: Methuen, 1920), pp. viii; 126; ix.

38. *Ibid.*, pp. xi; xiv.

39. *Ibid.*, pp. xiv; xiii.

40. McDougall, *Psychology*, pp. 98; 142.

41. McDougall, *Introduction*, p. 85. The shifts in McDougall's appraisals of the Freudian system deserve further study. So too do the similarities and differences in their views. Here only two examples of the kinds of problems encountered can be indicated. McDougall's dream of "Lord Trafford de Redcliffe" contains an explicitly recognized political content somewhat comparable to that which Carl Schorske has detected in some of Freud's dreams. A comparison of the differing uses to which McDougall and Freud put James Atkinson and ANdrew Lang's *Primal Law* (1903) is also revealing. McDougall, *Abnormal Psychology*, pp. 147-49; "Politics and Patricide in Freud's *Interpretation of Dreams*," Carl E. Schorske, *Fin-de-siècle Vienna: Politics and Culture* (New York: Knopf, 1980), pp. 181-207; McDougall, *Introduction*, pp. 291-92; Sigmund Freud, *Totem and Taboo* (1912-1913).

42. McDougall, *Psychology*, pp. 155-56, 164-65. 167.

43. *Ibid.*, pp. 168, 169; 118; 119.

44. *Ibid.*, p. 119.

45. Accepting the argument that it had ben completed in large part before the war, Soffer makes far more use of this volume than Trotter's complete *The Instinct of the Herd in Peace and War*.

46. William McDougall, *The Group Mind: A Sketch of the Principles of Collective Psychology with Some Attempt to Apply Them to the Interpretation of National Life and Character* (New York: G.P. Putnam's Sons, 1920), pp. 10, 12; 201-02; 66; xii; xv.

47. *Ibid.*, p. 240.

48. McDougall, *Abnormal Psychology*, p. 148.

49. McDougall, *Group Mind*, pp. 248, 249; 271-72; 5.

50. *Ibid.*, pp. xv; 331; 188; 187; 315; 306-07.

51. *Ibid.*, pp. 35. 56, 64, 67.

52. *Ibid.*, pp. 131; 125; 107; 131.

53. *Ibid.*, pp. 403-04.

54. *Ibid.*, pp. 237; 21; 237; 21.

55. *Ibid.*, pp. 274; 139; 141; 283.

56. *Ibid.*, pp. 283, 351-52, 353, 355.

57. *Ibid.*, pp. 353, 354; 357; 356; 353.

58. *Ibid.*, pp. 73; 412; 413; 106.

59. Trotter, *Instincts*, p. 252.

BLACK
ROSE
BOOKS

also by John Laffey

CIVILIZATION AND ITS DISCONTENTED

Nominated for the 1993 QSPELL Award

Civilization and Its Discontented investigates various beliefs about civilization, from the appearance of the 'word' in the late 18th century, to its varying definitions, and its transformation in the 19th century.

The book also identifies those people relegated to civilization's margins: the "savages" abroad or on the frontiers; the "savages" at home, that is, the working class, criminals and the insane, and women of all conditions. Laffey pays special attention to the way in which all groups were equated with each other, with the ultimate equation to be found in depictions of the crowd as savage, criminal, mad and woman-like in its hysteria and openness to seduction.

The concluding chapter is devoted to Sigmund Freud's ambivalent relation to the idea of civilization and argues that he too very much participated in the discourse of marginalization and equation.

The craft of the historian is to study the past and analyze it for present and future generations. Laffey certainly does this. The academic community will recognize the merits of the work in its scholarship and research materials.

The Montréal Gazette

Extremely detailed and well-researched look at what civilization actually is and the role which discontented individuals within civilization play and represent.

Humanist in Canada

180 pages, index
Paperback ISBN: 1-895431-70-0 $16.99
Hardcover ISBN: 1-895431-71-9 $45.99
1993

also of interest

HOW THE FIRST WORLD WAR BEGAN

The Triple Entente And The Coming Of The Great War Of 1914—1918

Edward E. McCullough

By reviewing the events of the pre-1914 period, this book attempts to understand the real causes of the Great War and to dissociate propaganda from historical fact; the responsibility of Germany for the outbreak of the war is reconsidered.

It begins with a short account of the situation after the Franco-Prussian War, when France was isolated and Germany secure in the friendship of all the other Great Powers, and proceeds to describe how France created an anti-German coalition. The account of the estrangement of England from Germany attempts to correct the usual pro-British prejudice and to explain the real causes of this development. The centrepiece of the work is the creation of the Triple Entente.

For 32 years, Edward E. McCullough has taught as a university teacher in Montreal and he is currently Professor Emeritus at Concordia University.

Historian Edward McCullough pulls no punches in this controversial book. He offers new insights into the Great War.
St. Catherine Standard

256 pages, bibliography, index
Paperback ISBN: 1-55164-140-2 $28.99
Hardcover ISBN: 1-55164-141-0 $57.99
January 1999